Reaching for the Stars

REACHING FOR THE STARS
A New History of Bomber Command in World War II

MARK CONNELLY

I.B.Tauris *Publishers*

LONDON • NEW YORK

Published in 2001 by I.B.Tauris & Co Ltd
6 Salem Road, London W2 4BU
175 Fifth Avenue, New York NY 10010
www.ibtauris.com

In the United States and Canada distributed by St. Martin's Press
175 Fifth Avenue, New York NY 10010

ISBN 1-86064-591-7

A full CIP record for this book is available from the British Library
A full CIP record for this book is available from the Library of Congress

Library of Congress catalog card: available

Typeset in Garamond by The Midlands Book Typesetting Co, Loughborough
Printed and bound in Great Britain by MPG Books Ltd, Bodmin

Contents

7897

Illustrations

Acknowledgements

Many people and institutions have helped me with the research and writing of this book. Firstly I would like to thank the British Academy for providing funds for a research fellowship, which allowed the project to get started. The book was inspired by the work of Martin Middlebrook and Len Deighton. Their fascinating investigations of Bomber Command led me to the subject and Len Deighton was kind enough to answer some of my queries about his work. Don Shaw replied to a list of questions about his play *Harris* and so I extend my gratitude to him. The staff of I.B.Tauris provided some excellent advice and many helpful suggestions. Professor Jeffrey Richards proved once again how generous he is with his knowledge and time. I would also like to thank all my friends who listened to my monologues on the RAF, Harris and a dozen other related subjects with great patience.

The staff of the British Library and British Newspaper Library, the Public Records Office, the University of London Library, the BBC Written Archives Centre, the Imperial War Museum, the Royal Air Force Museum and the British Film Institute all provided valuable assistance and material. I owe them all man thanks.

I would also like to take the opportunity of expressing my deepest gratitude and love to my family, who made all this possible. They are always enthusiastic about my work and in being so take many other responsibilities from my shoulders. This book is for them.

Introduction

Bomber Command's role of honour stands at 55,000 dead. 55,000 dead, and a great number of them were just the sorts of men the new Britain of 1945 so desperately needed. In the Great War 38,000 British officers were killed. If the Western Front stripped Britain of some of its most promising young poets, composers and artists, then the Second World War bomber offensive denied the nation thousands of highly trained technicians – wireless operators, engineers, navigators, pilots. Men that had so much to offer their nation in peacetime. But those dead men were also sons, brothers, husbands, fathers, lovers. Men like Flight Sergeant Ron Thomas of Cornwell.[1] On the night of March 30/31 1944 he set out with his Lancaster and six comrades, their task was to bomb Nuremberg. They were a brand new crew flying their first mission. It was their last too. On of its way home Lancaster LL622 was shot down by a fighter. The bomber crashed on the edge of the battlefield of Waterloo. Thomas and all his crew were killed. They had spent over a year training, costing the tax payers many thousands of pounds. The aircraft they flew that night cost considerably more. Ron Thomas had flown half way across Europe and his mates then managed to drop a few bombs some-where near Nuremberg. That ended their contribution to the British war effort. It also ended the dreams and hopes of seven families. On that same night Bomber Command lost over 90 other aircraft and over 500 crew members.

One of my mother's earliest memories is of being hurried into a brick tunnel at the start of an air raid, close to the railway viaduct at Bad Oeynhausen. She says she remembers mutters and prayers and the crash of bombs. Looking up Bad Oeynhausen in the index of Martin Middlebrook's and Chris Everitt's *Bomber Command War Diaries*, I found that the town was attacked only once, on March 23 1945. Eleven Lancasters of 1 and 5 Groups attacked the railway bridge in the town of her birth. Ironically the people of Bad Oeynhausen had sought shelter directly underneath the target. Presumably if the RAF had scattered their bombs (perhaps they were using the new Barnes Wallis tallboys designed to wreck things like railway viaducts) more widely my mother might not have made it to adulthood.

When the Bomber Command Association unveiled a statue to their most important wartime leader, Sir Arthur Harris, in May 1992, a large crowd gathered to witness the event. The Queen Mother had been given the honour of pulling the cord on the Union Jack draping the impressive statue. Time and again the Queen Mother was interrupted as she tried to make a speech paying tribute to the man and his crews. Many in the crowd jeered and hurled insults. The police had to deal with many scuffles. Why was this? Why had so many gathered to protest at a statue aimed not only at commemorating Harris but his men as well, men like Ron Thomas?

The morning of February 14 1945 was cold. The freezing winter was showing no signs of abating. During December and January bitter winds and snow had kept the allied air forces grounded for many days and nights. On the days and nights when they could fly it wasn't much better. But anyone near Dresden on that morning would not have felt the icy blast of a northerly wind, but the heat of the fires still burning in the heart of that great baroque city. In the gutted ruins of its buildings, in the rubble that was the glorious Fraukirche church, over 30,000 people were dead. Some say 100,000 people. On the night of 13/14 Bomber Command had sent out 805 aircraft carrying 1,478 tons of high explosive bombs and 1,182 tons of incendiary bombs. The first wave of bombers was not particularly successful, cloud cover making it hard for the Pathfinder marking aircraft. But three hours later the second wave arrived over a target denuded of cloud. 529 Lancasters dropped 1,800 tons of bombs. A raging whirlwind tore through the city, sucking people in, throwing them into the sky, burning everything in its path. For many of the pilots and crew looking on the armageddon the Nazi regime had threatened against others, and in some places carried out, had rebounded.

By the end of the war Bomber Command had killed over half a million German civilians, destroyed 3.37 million houses, had ripped the guts out of the German railway system and ruined millions of square feet of industrial plant. But it had cost 55,000 British, Commonwealth and allied lives and it had taken invading armies from the east and west to finally end the conflict.

Ever since the Second World War ended – since before it ended in fact – Britain has struggled to come to terms with what Bomber Command did in its name. For years the veterans of Bomber Command have had to endure the torture of accusations of murder. Of being told that their contribution played no role in ending the war; of being shunned for doing what their nation wanted during the dark days of the war, and then wanted to forget later.

I was curious as to how and why this had happened. Most books on the British role in the Second World War refer to the tremendous efforts the nation put into the bombing war, how it swallowed millions of manhours and millions of pounds. So how did something the nation had supported so vigorously come to be regarded so dubiously? The answer often put before the reader of Bomber Command histories is that Dresden finally opened people's eyes as to what area bombing meant and they turned their backs on the men who had carried it out. Frankly I doubted whether one raid could have that effect and set out to uncover what the British people knew about the campaign, what they expected from it at the time, and how it has been remembered since.

Another element which sparked my curiosity is the fact that Bomber Command is often labelled as a publicity conscious organisation, an organisation which dominated wartime propaganda. But, of the many books written about Bomber Command and on British propaganda in the Second World War, none has directly tackled the question of how the British bombing war was presented. When Sir Arthur Harris died in 1984, two biographies of him appeared in quick succession, the *Spectator*'s review noted that a key omission in the works was that: 'Neither address themselves to... [an] important question: what the people of Britain and allied countries were told, while it was going on, of the nature of the campaign.'[2] This book seeks to answer the question of what the British people were told at the time, and what they have found out and come to believe since.

The modern popular memory of Bomber Command was partly forged during the war when the government could not quite decide what to tell the people and Bomber Command itself could not quite decide how best to prosecute the war (at least during the early days). Another element important in shaping the modern memory, and one which few people still seem to realise, is what a crude instrument a bombing plane was in 1939. Few realise that the night area bombing campaign was the only way to fight the war given the difficulty of operating in daylight over Germany and the general difficulty of navigating in any sort of condition. This book was begun in the spring and summer of 1999 when the NATO bombing campaign was raging against Serbia and targets inside the province of Kosovo. Despite the brilliance of modern technology, NATO aircraft found that they hit the wrong buildings, that bombs fell in the wrong place, that the weather played havoc with the campaign. And yet still it is assumed that 'Bomber' Harris pursued a campaign of wanton destruction out of sheer malice, as if he had a range of other options available to him. It is also assumed that Bomber Command somehow managed to operate outside government control. The entire policy is therefore laid at Harris's door, with few realising that he was carrying out an agreed strategy. On the other hand, the defenders of Bomber Command, and many of its veterans, often overstate the innocence of the campaign. Make no mistake about it, the British bombing of Germany was hideous because it was designed to be. In part this book seeks to show why.

What this book also seeks to uncover is how the modern memory of Bomber Command was formed. The history of the campaign presented here is both narrative and historiographical, and is then examined against the knowledge the British people had of each stage of the campaign at the time.

Finally, I must declare a bias. I have tried very hard to show that modern opinions on the morality of the British strategic bombing campaign and on the clamour of the time are somehow a little too glib. While examining all the evidence put in front of the British people I became more and more aware of how intense was the feeling of the struggle for national survival, of how vicious a people can become when they feel that their backs are collectively pushed up against the wall.

My bias was therefore to expose such a feeling and, yes, it has to be said, perhaps even elicit some sympathy for it, which might then explain how and why the British bombing campaign was allowed to run the course that it did. Too often historians seem to have missed out on this angle. Reading of the collapse of Singapore and the escape of the German warships the *Scharnhorst, Gneisenau* and the *Prinz Eugen* from underneath the noses of the British in February 1942 I was left with the impression that the nation, in its very deep depression, believed its enemies were capable of anything. At just this moment an instrument of hope appeared, Bomber Command. As a half German, whose mother was made fatherless two days before her birth thanks to the titanic struggle unfolding at Kursk, I would like to believe that I am not insensitive to the horrors the German people had to face. But I felt the conditions which led to the area bombing offensive, and its general acceptance, needed to be stressed more forcefully and understood in their proper context.

The Machine Gun Corps memorial at Hyde Park Corner in London carries on it an inscription from the First Book of Samuel. It also seems a fitting epitaph on Bomber Command and its struggle against the Germans: 'Saul hath slain his thousands, and David his tens of thousands.' In the following pages I intend to show the British people's knowledge of, and intentions, in using the unsheathed sword of David.

. . . .

CHAPTER ONE

Hoping the Bomber will always get through

Berchtesgaden is a small town high in the mountains of southern Germany. It looks across to the Obersaltzburg and one can see well into Austria on a clear day. Here, in the clear air, with the brooding mountains in the background and the fresh alpine flowers and shrubs flourishing in the fields Hitler chose to build his country retreat. The Berghof was a home fit for a great statesman who liked to pretend he was a humble German as well. A flight of steps led up to a neat, white house with a chalet roof. The main drawing room had a huge picture window providing a stunning view across the valley. Here Hitler entertained his guests. Lloyd George, the British prime minister during the Great War, came here to converse with the man who had rejuvenated Germany. Lloyd George found him a most charming, courteous and sincere man. Here Hitler planned his war, his war designed to ensure the survival of the German race and bring it to its inheritance.

It was over Berchtesgaden on a freezing April day in 1945 that 375 aircraft of Bomber Command carried out the last major raid of the war. It was the last raid in an extremely long campaign. Night after night Bomber Command had been out in pursuit of victory. Nearly 400,000 sorties had been flown and nearly 500,000 tons of bombs dropped. 55,000 men had lost their lives and hundreds of aircraft had been lost.

By April 1945 Hitler's Germany was in ruins, much of it had been flattened by Bomber Command's operations. Perhaps it was fitting that this last major operation of the war should have been against the lair of the architect of it all. In the event the usual problem hindered the airmen – weather. Despite advances in navigation the weather could still make a hash of everything. The ground was still covered in snow and a mist clung to the hills making it very hard to identify the targets on that morning of April 25. But, in the true spirit of Bomber Command, the crews pressed on and bombed the target. Some crews reported accurate bombing, others like Larry Melling reckoned the effort a waste of time. Melling turned his Pathfinder Force Lancaster towards home having flown his last sortie of the war.[1] He could be fairly confident of a quiet flight for the allied air forces had achieved total air superiority. This allowed the bomber forces to strike, in broad daylight, at will. Bomber Command had come a long way since 1940 when daylight bombing had been abandoned in the light of startling losses. Bomber Command had transformed itself from a spluttering force at the start of the war to a weapon of awesome power.

At the moment the bugles sounded out the ceasefire on the Western Front on November 11 1918 three Handley Page V/1500 aircraft, each carrying two 3,300lb bombs, capable of flying 1,200 miles, stood ready to attack Berlin. A truly strategic bomber had arrived just too late to make an impact. But its shadow was already well defined and had cast its impression across many minds.

These bombers were a tiny part of the world's largest air force. At the Armistice the Royal Air Force consisted of 188 operational and 194 training squadrons. Britain had created a bomber force partly as a reaction to the shock of being bombed itself. In January 1915 *Zeppelins* raided Norfolk, killing two people and wounding thirteen others. London was bombed for the first time in May that year, when over a ton of bombs were dropped killing seven and wounding thirty-five. The most powerful raid came in September 1915, when £500,000 of damage was done in London. The fear of the *Zeppelin* rose and occasionally panic set in. However the *Zeppelin* was hardly an effective bombing platform. Large, cumbersome and vulnerable to aircraft armed with incendiary bullets, they never posed a significant threat. By late 1916 a combination of anti-aircraft guns, searchlights and fighter aircraft, combined with the weaknesses of the airships themselves, had defeated the *Zeppelin*.

Rather than abandon their bombing campaign, the Germans turned to the heavy bomber. In 1917 air raids became more frequent and more dangerous. A significant technological leap was made in the twin-engined Gotha. On May 25 1917 the first Gothas appeared over Folkestone, where they killed 95 people and injured nearly double that in ten minutes. A few weeks later came the raid which really struck terror. Fourteen Gothas flew in a diamond formation over London on June 13. Bombs fell in the City and on a Poplar school, killing 16 children. It was indiscriminate and awful. It was a portent of what could be achieved by a bigger and better force. A ferocious anti-German backlash took place and angry citizens demanded the government do more to protect them.

But the great size of the force created to defend British air space and take the war to the enemy was no guarantee of its survival. Formed only a few months before the Armistice, on April 1, the Royal Air Force faced an immediate withering barrage from the army and navy. Both the Admiralty and War Office doubted whether Britain needed an independent air force. The established forces saw aircraft as useful tools best kept under firm control. They feared that ambitious air men might attempt to divert resources from the older services. By 1921 nine-tenths of Britain's Air Force had been broken up. It had fallen victim to the hostility of its rival services, both of which saw no reason for the continuation of an independent air force. An added problem was the lack of finance. Huge cuts were made in military budgets and spending was kept at a minimum level. Ironically, it was the sharp deterioration of the Franco-British alliance that saved the Air Force. In 1923, when Britain openly disagreed with Franco-Belgian policy over the enforcement of the Versailles treaty, the French air threat became all too apparent. In an extremely odd turn of events Britain found itself distrustful of its former ally. The British government feared France was seeking to dominate the continent, which led to unfavourable comparisons with the Germany of 1914. Trouble exploded when the Secretary of State for Air announced that the RAF had only 16 serviceable machines and the service was grounded in India for want of spares. Something had to be done, Ten Year Rule or no Ten Year Rule. The British had imposed this system soon after the end of the war. It was assumed there would be no major conflict for at least ten years and therefore all defence spending could be cut. The problem lay in the fact that it was renewed each year and never allowed to count down. A Home Defence Force was to be built consisting of fifty-two front line squadrons, two-thirds bombers to one-third fighters. No sooner was this scheme passed than Anglo-French, and indeed European relations generally, thawed considerably with the signing of the Locarno treaty.[2] Everything in the garden looked rosy so there was no need to rush through the rebuilding programme. The Home Defence Force was allowed to languish. It languished still further when financial collapse hit Britain in 1931. By 1933 it was still ten squadrons short of its target, but the situation was changing rapidly.

The rise of Hitler, the greater ambitions of Mussolini, and the fragility of European and world peace demanded that more money be spent on the armed forces. Even Baldwin, a man wedded to the principle of the balanced budget and fine statements about peace and disarmament, knew that something needed to be done. The pace quickened considerably. Air defence was deemed to be a priority. Since 1908, the year in which H.G. Wells' published his novel *The War in the Air*, the fear of bombing had found its way into the national psyche. The Great War had increased that fear enormously. The government could not ignore the international situation or the nightmares of the population.

The British were a people obsessed by the air during the twenties and thirties. The pilots of the Great War, such as Albert Ball and 'Micky' Mannock, were still household names. There was also the great fictional character, Captain James Biggleworth, created by W.E. Johns and based upon his own wartime experiences. Biggles inspired boys across the empire. Air was seen as the way of linking that empire and by the thirties regular airline services brought mails and passengers from places such as Auckland to London and on again to Halifax, Nova Scotia. The aeroplane was glamorous and modern. T.E. Lawrence had disappeared into the RAF as a way of escaping his fame as 'the uncrowned King of Arabia'. His work on the early days of the RAF, *The Mint*, was not published until after the Second World War thanks to its warts and all approach, but it did capture something of the romance of the service felt by millions of young men: 'We had enlisted in hope that our improving hands might aid those who strove against the air.'[3] It was a romance seen in Alexander Korda's 1936 (though not released until 1940) movie, *The Conquest of the Air*. The film consisted of a series of tableaux in which key moments in the history of aviation were mounted, starting with Icarus, through the Montgolfier brothers with their balloons, to the achievements of Supermarine Aviation for Britain in the Schneider air trophy.

But the romance was always balanced against the horror. Alexander Korda's London Films at Denham managed to make the ultimate expression in this field too. In 1935 his adaptation of H.G. Wells' *The Shape of Things to Come* (retitled *Things to Come* for the film) was released. It is a chilling vision of a world dominated by war from the air.

Society is bombed into a state of chaos and anarchy, civilisation breaks down to be replaced by a tribal world of warlords. Salvation ultimately comes from the air in the form of scientist-aviators. But this was not really the vision which stuck in the minds of the thirties audience, it was the one of indiscriminate bombing. The seemingly limitless ability of air power was promoted most effectively by cinema in the form of feature films and newsreels. By the late 1930s cinema's ability to influence the hearts and minds of people was well known. The combatants of the Great War had harnessed the propaganda value of film for their war efforts. In 1939 the vast power of cinema to shape minds, entertain and inform was incorporated into the British government's armoury via the Films Division of the newly established Ministry of Information.

In May 1935 it was planned to increase the Home Defence Force to 112 squadrons by March 1937 instead of March 1939. Scheme F was to be implemented; this was designed to give the RAF more depth because, as Air Marshal Sir Arthur Harris was to later write, the RAF suffered from the fact that 'everything we had – and that was little – was in the shopwindow, with nothing behind it.'[4] In other words the situation was largely based on bluff. It was the image of a large force but there was no real ability to maintain it or replace losses in any sort of genuine emergency.

Bombers were given top priority in 1936 with the Air Ministry scheduling the design and production of a new breed of bombers. Out of these decisions would come the future four-engined Stirling, Halifax and the Manchester, immediate predecessor of the Lancaster. However these were very much medium term projects. With this sudden stepping up of the tempo something needed to be done about building capacity. British governments were reluctant to interfere in industry, requisition supplies, or direct workers or production and yet it was hard to see how the existing aircraft industry could cope with the new demand. Fortunately Lord Swinton was a dynamic Secretary of State for Air. In 1936 he directed the car-manufacturing firms of Austin, Morris and Rootes to build aircraft factories under the guidance of aviation firms, at government expense. Unlike many other aspects of British preparation and execution in the late thirties and early days of the war, this was a success. By 1940 British aircraft production had overtaken that of Germany.

Sir Hugh Trenchard was undoubtedly the greatest influence over the Royal Air Force during its formative years. Commander of the Royal Flying Corps, when it was a part of the army, he became the first Commander of the independent force, fighting fiercely for it in the lean years after the war.

Trenchard was fascinated by the power of the bomber. He developed a theory of aerial bombardment, similar to those of Douhet and Mitchell but independent of them.[5] Along with the government he had been much impressed by the disruption the German raids caused. Some 300,000 Londoners nightly sought shelter in Underground stations in the second half of 1917 regardless of whether there was a raid or not. For Trenchard the air had created a whole new paradigm of war. The air was, according to this theory, a vast, indefensible frontier. Bombers could therefore carry the war to the strategic heart of the enemy without a preliminary battle. Unlike armies or navies the bomber, it was thought, could avoid defenders and arrive in force, intact, ready to wipe out the vitals of the enemy. Contrary to popular opinion, however, Trenchard did not say that the bomber alone would win the war. Instead, he argued that it would reduce the enemy's powers of resistance so much that the army and navy would be reduced to sweeping up the last vestiges of resistance. Trenchard's conception of this revolution in the rules of war made the fighter redundant. In his opinion there simply was no defence against the bomber, so he encouraged all energies to the creation of a strategic bombing force. It was a situation neatly summed up by Stanley Baldwin, when he told the Commons on the eve of Armistice Day 1932, that 'the bomber will always get through'. Having studied the 1919 British bombing survey of Germany Trenchard realised how little damage had been done to industry. However he did note the stress laid on the effect on morale. A key element had been identified, for, according to Trenchard, 'the moral effect of bombing stands to the material effect in proportion of 20 to 1.'[6] Clearly, long before the outbreak of war, the RAF was very aware of the fact that a general attack on an enemy people, especially their working classes (thought to be more susceptible to demoralisation and panic), might bring dramatic results.

Problematically the RAF managed to create a schizophrenia complex for itself as regards bombing policy. For running alongside the 'Trenchard concept' was an idea of precision bombing, taking out vital enemy targets. This theory also argued that the bomber would be able to defend itself to, from, and over the target, using daylight to negate the problems of navigation and target identification. When he retired in 1929 Trenchard was given much respect for his establishment of a Staff College and a Cadet School and keeping the RAF going on an average annual budget of £16 million. However it was also a force lacking a clear understanding of its function.

Bomber Command was formed on July 14 1936 at a time of growing international tension. Nazi Germany was becoming a more aggressive and de-stabilising force in Europe, the Spanish Civil War exploded and Italians launched an invasion of Abyssinia. The new Command and the Air Ministry were forced to consider their roles. A new generation of bombers was planned and Germany was identified as the primary potential target. That October the Air Ministry produced its Western Air Plans, finally committing Bomber Command to a definite course of action in the event of hostilities breaking out:

The Western Air Plans, 1937.

Group I.

W[estern].1	Plans for attack on the German Air Striking Force, and its maintenance organisation.
W.2	Plans for reconnaissance in co-operation with the Navy in Home Waters and the Eastern Atlantic.
W.3	Plans for close co-operation with the Navy in convoy protection in Home Waters and the Eastern Atlantic.

W.4   Plans for attacking the concentration areas of the German Army, and the interruption of its communications in the event of an advance into Belgium, Holland and France.

W.5   Plans for attacking the enemy's manufacturing resources in the Ruhr, Rhineland and Saar.

Group II.

W.6   Plans for attacking the enemy's air manufacturing resources in Germany.

W.7   Plans for counter-offensive action in defence of seaborne trade in co-operation with the Navy.

Group III.

W.8   Plans for attacking especially important depots or accumulations of warlike stores other than those relating to air forces, in an enemy country.

W.9   Plans for putting the Kiel Canal out of action.

W.10   Plans for the destruction of enemy shipping and facilities in German mercantile ports – precedence to be given to the Baltic.

Group IV.

W.11   Plans for attacking the enemy's manufacturing resources other than in the Ruhr, Rhineland and Saar.

W.12   Plans for an aerial attack on the German Fleet or section thereof either in harbour or at sea by air in concert with the Navy.

W.13   Plans for an attack on enemy's headquarter and administrative offices in Berlin and elsewhere.

Any reference to an attack on the housing districts or morale of an enemy people was completely absent from these plans. Instead the new directives implied that the bombing force should be used surgically, to hit targets with precision, to ensure that the enemy's ability to wage war was neutralised by striking both at his armed forces and his industries.

Bomber Command now had a clear battle plan but could it carry it out? Just before the publication of these plans, Air Chief Marshal Sir Edgar Ludlow-Hewitt was made Commander-in-Chief Bomber Command. Ludlow-Hewitt immediately made a tour of inspection, taking very careful notes as to what he saw. When he reported to the Air Ministry he did not mince his words. He stated that he expected to see some confusion, he knew it was inevitable in a force expanding so rapidly. He found the training of the RAF Flying School produced excellent pilots and that everyone was in high spirits. However he was worried by the fact that Bomber Command was 'entirely unprepared for war, unable to operate except in fair weather, and extremely vulnerable both in the air and on the ground'.[7] Further he criticised navigational aids, safety devices and safety arrangements. With great insight he declared that:

a fair weather force is relatively useless and is certainly not worth the vast expenditure now being poured out on the air arm of this country. And yet today our Bombing Force is, judged from a war standard, practically useless and cannot take advantage of the excellent characteristics of its new and expensive aircraft.[8]

He compared the dire record in night flying and lack of modern navigational aids with the situation in civil aviation. Most importantly the RAF complacently believed in the idea that bombers could defend themselves and so were capable of taking part in daylight operations. Ludlow-Hewitt urged the Air Ministry to revise training methods in the vital area of welding together crews (effective bombing was impossible without it), gunnery and navigation. But as late as August 1939 he still had to contend with the fact that over forty per cent of his force was unable to find a friendly city in daylight.

On the outbreak of war Bomber Command was therefore in an ironic position. Trenchard's doctrines were still present but the Western Air Plans seemed to commit the force to a different concept. A force, which Trenchard knew could be used as a bludgeon, was suddenly given the idea of being sabre sharp, slashing open the enemy. A force that was once thought to be able to avoid battle was now taking comfort in the idea that it could defend itself. A force that had been committed to a set of plans had a commander with serious doubts as to its ability to find its own airfields let alone the enemy.

Thanks to the organisational skills of Trenchard the RAF had an excellent administrative framework on which to base its expansion. As well as a Staff College and Cadet College, the RAF boasted research establishments and Apprentices' Schools. To ensure a flow of trained pilots the Auxiliary Air Force was set up along with the University Air Squadrons (by 1939 over 700 pilots were available from the Oxford University Air Squadron alone) and the great innovation of short-service commissions of five years followed by four in the reserve. In 1937 the Force made a deliberate attempt to appeal to young boys with a grammar school background, exactly the sort bred on exciting boys' own tales of the air, with the introduction of the Royal Air Force Volunteer Reserve providing weekend flying lessons and training. Designed to produce 800 additional pilots a year, the response was overwhelming; in three years the scheme turned out over 5000 pilots. Overwhelmingly lower middle class, the pilots fitted the social profile the scheme was aimed at. They were boys with a solid standard of education and highly stimulated imaginations desperate to avoid the grind of the 8.15 to London Bridge and a clerking job in Mincing Lane. There was also a female service. The Women's Auxiliary Air Force (WAAF) was separated from the Auxiliary Territorial Service in 1939. Without the work of the WAAFs the operational existence of any station would soon have dwindled to nothing. Of huge significance was the fact that soon after the outbreak of war the Empire Air Training Scheme came to life. Using the vast, unthreatened spaces of Canada, South Africa and Rhodesia the British and Dominion governments sent their young men for training, which provided the vital flow of aircrews once the war gathered pace.

The young men of Bomber Command were nearly all great romantics, having been brought up on a diet of aviation, often military aviation, stories, telling of Red Barons, gallant Camel pilots and Flying Circuses. Larry Donnelly recalled being fascinated by aeroplanes as a child in the early thirties and was an ardent Biggles fan.[9] In 1936 he followed his enthusiasm by applying to the RAF. Wilfred Lewis, a young Canadian, was inspired by *Flight* magazine and *Aeroplane*.[10] He hung round his local bookstore waiting for the new issues. Then he saw an Air Ministry notice advertising short service commissions. Having spent two years in an army reserve regiment Lewis felt a life in the RAF was far likelier to suit him and so he applied. Many volunteers for the RAF noted that they had no desire to be in the army. Too many images of the trenches and the muck of the Western Front had been past their eyes for it to seem attractive. Flying was glamorous, exciting and clean.

Everyone wanted to fly. That was the glamorous job. But the pre-war RAF was very much a class-ridden club despite its appeals to those who wanted to climb the ladder. Flying jobs seemed reserved for the right accent from the right school. Harry Jones was on the receiving end of this snobbery. He qualified as an air gunner in the mid-thirties, but at his aircrew interview it was pointed out to him that most flying jobs were beyond his grasp.[11] It wasn't until about 1937 when the impending emergency made the first in-roads into such stuffiness that fitters and riggers were allowed their chance to qualify as aircrew.

It was so different by 1942. The service continued to maintain its class prejudices but it had to bow to the inevitable. In the massively expanded service grocers' sons became sergeant pilots and were placed in charge of thousands of pounds worth of equipment. But despite this, as sergeants they were not allowed into the officer's mess and were still not regarded as quite the right sort. The People's War did not annihilate class prejudice, it only managed to force it back a little.

The pre-war RAF bombers' names reflected the real psyche of the service. They are names reminiscent of favourite fox hounds, the hunt or the sort of place where a dowager aunt might have lived – Hind, Hart, Gordon, Heyford, Harrow. By 1942 it was the names of industrial and northern Britain that came to dominate, names full of dour resolution – Halifax, Manchester, Lancaster, Stirling.

Life in the pre-war service could be casual and easy-going. Larry Donnelly's earliest posting was to RAF Dishforth in Yorkshire.[12] After the strict discipline of his training at Cranwell he was agreeably surprised to find life on base was not one of endless, mindless routines. For others it could be a shock. Hamish Mahaddie, who was later to become one of Bomber Command's most celebrated pilots, returned to the service in 1935.[13] He was horrified to find the man detailed to deliver the squadron post was hardly wearing a piece of his uniform and what he was wearing looked appalling. When questioned about his attire and the reason for having a patch over one eye he replied that it was because it was full of bullshit and walked on.

As the service expanded new stations had to be built. With Germany the obvious enemy ease of access to the North Sea was important and so the vast majority of bomber stations ran up the east coast of England, arcing out into East Anglia and then up through Lincolnshire and into Yorkshire. Drainage was one of the most important matters in selecting a site. Bumpy land could be levelled, but not easily drained land would cause problems for heavy aircraft. Each station centred on the huge tarmac cross runway. Running round the edge was a circular road dotted with circular pans, parks for each aircraft. High ceiling hangars provided shelter for the aircraft and their maintenance crews. Corrugated iron Nissen huts provided stores and sometimes accommodation. Proper barrack blocks were usually built in a T shape, often over-looking the parade ground. There would also be the Control Tower and administration offices. The most remote set of buildings were those containing the bomb stores. These were insulated by tons of soil to prevent any accidental blast causing too much damage. With hundreds of men and women living and working on station each was almost a mini-village in itself. A station might have a library and a cinema. It certainly had to have room for all the services vital and ancillary to maintaining a highly complex weapons system. Getting around was a problem and so bicycles were issued. These could be seen propped up against buildings and railings all round the airfield.

In 1939 Bomber Command consisted of 23 squadrons, amounting to only 280 aircraft and trained crews. They were divided into four groups scattered across East Anglia and into Yorkshire. Other aircraft and crews had been siphoned off to form a reserve. Bomber Command headquarters was at Richings Park, Langley, Buckingham-shire but in March 1940 it made the short move to a new location at High Wycombe. 1 Group was not part of the formal structure of Bomber Command for it was despatched to France to form the Advanced Air Striking Force with its ten squadrons of Fairey Battle light bombers and two Blenheim squadrons. 2 Group consisted of six Bristol Blenheim squadrons based close to the Norfolk and Suffolk coast due to the shorter range of these aircraft. Group headquarters were at Wyton in Suffolk under the command of Air Vice-Marshal C.T. Maclean. Mildenhall, Suffolk, was the headquarters of Air Vice-Marshal J.E.A Baldwin, commander of 3 Group, made up of six Vickers Wellington squadrons. Air Vice-Marshal A. Coningham commanded the five Armstrong-Whitworth Whitley squadrons of 4 Group from his headquarters at Linton on Ouse, Yorkshire; this was the only Group within the Command trained in night bombing. Lastly, 5 Group under Air Commodore W.B. Callaway, but to change to Air Vice-Marshal A.T. Harris within a fortnight of the declaration of war, with its head-quarters at Grantham in Lincolnshire and its six squadrons of Handley Page Hamp-dens.

None of these aircraft had any major design or building faults. But they were to suffer from a catalogue of minor problems, all of which were destined to make the life of Bomber Command extremely tough. Perhaps the single greatest problem was the lack of speed, especially for a force about to launch a daylight bombing campaign based upon a concept of close formation flying providing mutual support. The fastest British bomber, the latest mark of Blenheim, was capable of 266 mph, but the Messerschmitt fighters flew at 350 mph. All of the aircraft were extremely cold, a condition made even worse when flying either at night or towards the maximum ceiling. They were also all too lightweight in their arsenals. The .303 machine gun was no match for the 20-30mm cannons of the German fighters either in terms of range or weight. The bombs themselves were a further problem. Stocks of bombs were tiny and of a small calibre, forty pounds or 250 pounds, being a standard size of the Great War. Most vulnerable by far were the Fairey Battles of the Advanced Air Striking Force. The story of the Battle is pathetic in the extreme. Hailed as a technological marvel when it first appeared in 1936 and yet by 1940 it was utterly outclassed by Messerschmitt fighters. Any survivor of those early days in France recalls the name of the Battle with a shudder.

To an extent this was the problem of the entire Command – nothing wrong with the design but things had moved on. Timing was actually one of the biggest problems. Bomber Command's machines had all appeared wonderful when they started to come on-line from 1936, but by the time 1939 came around technology and design had jumped on again making the aircraft vulnerable to the newest generation of German fighters. The Command needed its new models planned in 1936 ready for 1939 but they were still a couple of years off. An interesting comparison can be made between the Wellington and the Halifax, one of the new breeds of the 1936 planning round, which made its debut in action in 1941. The Vickers Wellington made its prototype flight in 1936, and was delivered to the service in 1938. This excellent bomber designed by Barnes Wallis, could carry 4,500 pounds of bombs a distance of 1,200 miles at a speed of 235 mph. The Handley Page Halifax, on the other hand, was capable of carrying 6,000 pounds of bombs over 2,000 miles at a height of 22,000 feet at 265 mph.

Most of the heavy bombers had a crew of five. There were two pilots with the first pilot acting as skipper regardless of whether he was an officer or not. In 1942 the second pilot was dropped in favour of a flight engineer. The pilot relied absolutely upon the navigator. Navigators got the reputation of being a clannish lot constantly chatting with one another about the rigours of their job. Prior to 1942 the navigator also had the job of bomb-aimer and would take the 'bombing photo' if the aircraft was fitted with a camera. The wireless operator was also given instruction as an air gunner. This did not make for too imposing a strain for the vast majority of missions were carried out in strict radio silence. The most important job a wireless operator might carry out was the 'fix signal' in the event of a ditching over the sea. Without a correctly broadcast fix the crew stood little chance of rescue. The gunners could often spend very long, very boring hours staring out into space. But they had to remain alert and vigilant constantly looking for enemy fighters. Constricted in their tiny turrets their joints stiffened and their bottoms became absolutely numb. After long flights they would pummel their muscles in order to bring back movement to stiff limbs. These crews would have to rely on one another. Success was dependent upon mutual concentration and skill. In the early days the class divisions of the service often stifled camaraderie but the war melted distinctions. In the black night skies over Germany with a fighter spitting flaming cannon shells there were no officers, N.C.O.s or other ranks, just brave young men struggling to help one another survive.

By 1939 Britain had an obsession with the bomber. The British people were presented with two images. On the one hand a future in which enemy planes would smash their way across Britain bringing untold destruction. On the other a British force capable of doing exactly the same to an enemy. Whether this was the reality of the situation was questioned by very few and was to lead to some of the early disasters of the British bombing campaign. In the spring of 1937 the Luftwaffe had aided Franco by bombing Guernica and the vision of *Things to Come* seemed to have come true. The Munich Crisis in the autumn of 1938 led to the digging of trenches in British cities and the issue of gas masks. The British government prepared for a grim bombing war in which troops might have to shoot rioters and looters. But this was not going to be a war in which the British lay back. Bomber Command was preparing for a war of the offensive. Ironically, given the terror inspired by the idea of bombing, Bomber Command felt ready to launch a precision campaign in which collateral damage would be minimised with bombing used as skilfully and effectively as a surgeon's scalpel. Already, therefore, there was confusion in the public mind, and in that of Bomber Command. Was bombing a cudgel or a sabre? It was a confusion that was to grow.

Bomber Command in 1939 was ready for war, but not ready. It had machines and men of quality and yet it was unclear as to whether they were really up to the job. The Commander-in-Chief was impressed by some of the skills but had massive doubts about others. It might be read as a metaphor for the nation itself in 1939. However, with the army hardly ready to take on the offensive, and the French Army on its right hardly bothered about launching a strike into Germany either, the only way the war could actually be carried to the enemy was by Bomber Command. Within a day of the declaration of war this capability was put to the test.

CHAPTER TWO

The Lion Tries His Wings,
September 1939–February 1941

On September 5 1939 the *Daily Express* front page headlines announced, with the sensationalism it had become famous for under its flamboyant owner Lord Beaver-brook, that: 'RAF Bomb Two Battleships/ Several Direct Hits on Kiel Canal/ Mid-Air Battle: Some Casualties.'[1] The story under the headlines was quoted verbatim from an Air Ministry communiqué. It told of how the German fleet was attacked in the ports of Wilhelmshaven and Brunsbüttel by British aircraft. Several hits were reported which had resulted in some damage. In return the RAF aircraft had encountered attacks from the German air force and from anti-aircraft fire that had resulted in 'some casualties'.

So with the war just a few days old the British public woke up to the exciting news that the RAF had drawn blood in the war against Nazi Germany. Further, the raid had shown Britain's newest weapons, the aircraft of the 21 year old RAF, attacking examples of Britain's most traditional nightmare, enemy battleships. But when the story is examined a little more closely barely a fact can be deduced from it. Did Bomber Command actually manage to sink any ships? Were any explosions seen? What exactly does 'some casualties' mean?

On September 3, the day war was declared, a reconnaissance Blenheim took off for Germany and became the first British aircraft of the war to cross the German coast. Flying Officer McPherson and his crew, including a naval liaison officer, spotted German warships north of Wilhelmshaven. When this news was reported units of Bomber Command were ordered to prepare themselves for an attack. This was in accordance with the pre-war Western Air Plans. Plans W9, W10 and W12 were aimed at attacking the Kiel Canal and destroying the German navy. These plans appealed to the Chamberlain government as they would attack a particular British nemesis, enemy warships. They would also show the Germans that the British were ready to fight, but not prepared to bomb innocent civilians or 'up the tempo' too much. A gesture could be made towards the alliance with Poland, British safety could be advanced and the 'Phoney War' could be announced by an attack that was not to drop bombs on German soil under any circumstances.

Therefore on September 4, 15 Blenheims of 2 Group and 14 Wellingtons of 3 Group set off to raid targets at Wilhelmshaven and Brunsbüttel. Five planes from each force completely failed to locate the target in the low cloud. This was an immediate blow at much of the planning and thinking of Bomber Command. Since the thirties it had rested on the strategy of hitting targets with precision in daylight. The remaining Blenheims pressed home their attacks on the cruiser *Emden* and the pocket battleship *Admiral Scheer.* Some bombs hit both ships but they failed to explode and caused only minor damage. The attack of the Wellingtons was even more of a failure. Of the six that managed to find the target only one attacked, unsuccessfully. One of the Wellingtons, obviously hopelessly lost, dropped bombs on the Danish town of Esbjerg killing two civilians. Esbjerg is over 110 miles from Wilhelmshaven.

But this was not the end of the story for five Blenheims were lost in the attack. Tragically all five came from one squadron, 107. It must have been a devastating blow to one compact unit. One day into the war its guts were ripped out. Two Wellingtons were also lost, both falling victim to fighters. The balance sheet did not make good reading. Some German warships had received dents and chipped paintwork in exchange for the loss of seven aircraft, or a shocking 23.3 per cent of aircraft despatched. This was the reality behind the headlines, but no one in Britain was going to be allowed to know it.

The raid had been presented as a success. This 'fact' was buttressed a few weeks later when Alexander Korda's film *The Lion Has Wings* reached the cinema screens. It was the first film to be made in Britain after the outbreak of war. A large portion of the film was dedicated to the planning and execution of the raid, using both genuine footage and reconstructed scenes. The film was made at Korda's London Films complex at Denham in incredibly quick time. In the last few days of peace Korda was already contemplating making some sort of propagandist war film. He gained the co-operation of the Air Ministry – the liaison officer was the splendidly named H.M.S. Wright – and so became an official part of the government's propaganda machine while making a film entirely within the commercial system. Production took no longer than six weeks. A trade show was given on October 17 and it went on general release on November 3. The film is actually little more than a documentary interspersed with some fictional scenes and reconstructions. Its theme was the advanced state of British preparations for an air war. Newsreel footage of RAF air shows sought to reassure the British public that enemy fighters and bombers would face a hot reception if they tried to violate British air space.

Running alongside the theme of home defence was the message that Britain would be able to dish it out as well. Bomber Command was presented as the weapon for the job. The film stressed that in both its fighter and bomber force Britain's hardware was the best. Shots of the Vickers Armstrong Weybridge assembly line were shown with the frames of the Wellington bomber clearly visible. E.V.H. Emmett, the distinguished Gaumont British newsreel commentator spoke, and provided most of his dialogue. He reassured the public that Britain's engineering proficiency had already been put to good use. He told his audience the Wellington was based on the geodetic principle of construction. Of the great weight the bombers were capable of carrying; of the Wellington's endurance and speed and the great expectations the British people had of such a weapon.

When it came to the Kiel raid section itself the technical precision of all involved in a bombing raid was stressed:

> Inexhaustible supplies of petrol, the life-blood of modern war… Next to go in is the complicated apparatus for bomb aiming, for bombing now is exact and mathematical. Speed of flight, strength of wind, altitude, a hundred factors must be taken into account before the pressure of a thumb lets loose these tons of roaring chaos. With the utmost care and precision they load up their cargo of destruction.

But an older national stereotype came through too for it was also mentioned that British equipment was made by 'craftsmen' and that 'we learned early in history to study our weapons, as well as our men. Crecy and Agincourt were won partly because the English archers were the best in the world, but partly also because they carried the best bows.' Craftsmenship has an air of gentility about it and was therefore more in tune with the English love of the artist and artisan rather than the manual worker. The commentary fully reflected the early atmosphere of the war, before the paradigm and semantic shift of 'art of war' to 'science of war' had made its real leap.

Running alongside the proficiency of the aircraft and all its ancillary equipment the film also stressed that Britain had thought out its plans for attacking Germany. Emmett stated that: 'we *were* ready. Behind each bushy hedgerow a battleship of the sky stood ready: massive, forbidding, deadly, the symbol of modern Power, waiting for the word to go.' Here was a reference to the industrial might of Britain, balancing slightly the reliance on craft skills. So like Boy Scouts RAF Bomber Command was prepared. Prepared to launch a precision bombing campaign on German warships within a day of hostilities breaking out.

Michael Powell, the respected film director, had travelled to RAF Mildenhall where he had obtained footage of the actual Wellington crews coming back from the raid. The commentary, set against these shots of the bomber station preparing for action, left the viewer in no doubt that the RAF knew its business. Soon after the film was released John Ware, chief publicist for London Films, wrote a book to accompany the film, also entitled *The Lion Has Wings*. He too stressed that the RAF was ready to fight a highly accurate, precise bombing war: 'Bombs are not dropped haphazard over a target today. Bombing is now a mathematical science and the intricate apparatus for sighting, aiming and releasing is fitted to the plane at the last minute before take-off.'[2]

Bomber Command was also shown to be backed-up by an excellent intelligence service, briefing the crews as to what they might expect. The crews were seen gathered round a table of charts, photos and documents. An intelligence officer addressed them and gave them detailed instructions as to the best way of attacking the ships.

But once again traditional national traits of the island race came through even when war had become more mathematical. Unlike the more dour and realistic responses seen on camera later during the war, Emmett here told the audience that: 'they're heading east on a great adventure'. Ware's book does mentioned the dangers but he too pulled through on what now seems a rather glib line: 'even on a job that carries a fifty-fifty chance of death the boys of the Royal Air Force start out with a joke.'[3] Coming out in early 1940 this book unwittingly reflected the fact that the bombing war had already shown up some remarkable deficiencies in British planning and execution leading to a high attrition rate. Attrition was an apt word, with its echoes of the Western Front for this was exactly the point Ware made: 'Grim, you would think, and worried. But no, the spirit that saw the British troops through the horrors of Flanders 20 odd years ago is the same today.'[4] This is another sentiment that died off rapidly. The Great War became taboo for it was felt to have been fought the wrong way and about the wrong things. When the Germans overran France in 1940 people became more sensitive about the nature of the war: no one wanted a repetition of the Somme and Passchendaele. As more and more people were dragged into the struggle, either in the services or in industry, a desire arose for a people's peace to crown victory in the people's war. It was a demand partly motivated by the broken promises of 1919 when the people of Britain did not gain a land fit for heroes. Thus by 1941 it became unthinkable to make comparisons with the Great War.

The raid was successfully carried out because the RAF is shown to be a force capable of attacking legitimate targets with ease. The British public was told that the RAF had not resorted to indiscriminate bombing. The commentary stated that: 'They had dropped their bombs, not upon unfortified towns, but upon a heavily protected naval base; a legitimate target of modern warfare, an objective bristling with anti-aircraft guns and guarded with fighters.' Further the British people were absolved from all blame. The war was something imposed upon them and so all consciences were clean: 'Yes – whether we liked it or not, it was war… [the bombers are] Messengers of havoc, yet it had not been our will that sent them forth.' It was pointed out that the raid had avenged the sinking of the British passenger liner, *Athenia*. It was a blow that fell on the first day of the war shocking the nation. Ware also reminded his readers the RAF had stolen something thought to be the prerogative of the Germans – low-level bombing.

These skills, combined with the spirit of adventure, were probably the reason why the bomber crews did not seem unduly worried by the resistance of the enemy. In fact the Wellingtons coped rather easily with the flak and Messerschmitt fighters. This entire sequence was re-staged after the raid for the benefit of the cameras. Only the briefest of mentions was made of the casualties of the raid: 'but not all came back.' The gap between filmed reality and the actual historical record itself was vast.

The critics and public generally liked the film. In the first few days of war with the government policy on information and propaganda not yet fully formed any reportage of the war was bound to receive public interest. The bombing scenes were picked out for praise. The high-minded *News Chronicle* liked them best of all noting that it showed a 'matter of combining an expert and resourceful reconstruction of the feat with actual pictures of some of the heroes as they leave their planes in their home aerodrome.'[5] Across the Atlantic it got a warm welcome in America, after some wrangles about whether it was overt propaganda and therefore in contravention of US neutrality. The *Motion Picture Herald* also found the bombing raid the best sequence: 'the reconstruction of the epic Wilhelmshaven exploit... of nonchalant lads piloting the heavy Wellingtons to enemy objectives, is engrossing screen entertainment.[6] It was also a roaring success in the Dominions chalking-up record runs and attendances in Australia and New Zealand.

The accuracy and value of *The Lion Has Wings* is easy to doubt and, given the distance in time from its original showing, easy to ridicule. However it is accurate in one respect. The film reflected the genuine feelings of the RAF at the time. Bomber Command did have confidence in the ability of its bombers to navigate successfully, find targets, bomb them accurately and defend themselves from attack. Only time and bitter experience would prove this totally wrong.

The campaign against the German navy continued throughout the autumn and winter of 1939. Bomber Command continued its searches for German warships and submarines, none of which were particularly successful. Pilot Wilfred Lewis recalled that: 'after war broke out we were placed on standby to attack German naval units if they ventured out into the North Sea and that's as far as we could go. We could not drop bombs on land. Most times we didn't find anything at all.'[7] When such operations were not boring they were very alarming. For instance, on September 29, 18 out of 24 Hampdens despatched to search the Heligoland area were lost, including the commander of 144 Squadron, Wing Commander J.C. Cunningham. This initial phase of the bombing war came to a head in December when two disastrous raids forced Bomber Command to think seriously about its planning and expectations.

On December 14 a typical North Sea shipping search made up of 23 Hampdens, 12 Wellingtons and 7 Whitleys got under way. When the bombers set off the most important point was its significance as the largest operation of the war so far. However it was to be remembered for other reasons. None of the bombers could find a favourable bombing position. This led the Wellingtons to remain in the area for half an hour while they vainly searched for an opportunity to release their bombs. Flying at a low level in order to counteract low cloud and poor visibility the Wellingtons were susceptible to attack and it duly came in the form of heavy flak and fighters. Five Wellingtons were shot down, nearly half the Wellington force despatched. Four days later the lesson was repeated. Twenty-four Wellingtons were despatched to Wilhelmshaven and ordered to attack at less than 10,000 feet in order to avoid the worst flak. The perfect conditions allowed 22 aircraft to make it to the area and bomb shipping in the approaches to the port. However, the Germans had tracked the raid on their radar station on the nearby island of Wangerooge and directed a swarm of fighters onto the bombers. The Wellingtons lost their tight formation, which was thought to be the key to the self-protecting force, and fell easy victim. In an appalling 'turkey shoot' German fighters destroyed exactly half the force, 12 bombers going down.

The problem lay only partly in the aircraft themselves. The Hampden was a strange machine. Wilfred Lewis remembered it as a 'beautiful plane to fly, terrible to fly in'.[8] The pilot was wedged in, unable to move and yet he had an array of tasks to perform aside from flying the aircraft because most of the instruments were gathered around him. But Lewis liked the Hampden because of its reliable engines. This was vital because in other respects it did not show much ability to stand up to punishment. The Whitley on the other hand was like the Wellington, it rode punches well and persevered. Whitley crew members like Larry Donnelly had a great deal of affection for the aircraft.[9] But it was slow and made lugubrious progress accentuated by its strange nose-down attitude in flight. The war artist Paul Nash thought they looked like prehistoric sea monsters at play. Wellingtons moved gracefully and never let its crews down. As a consequence it was the last of the original bombers to be phased out of operational use. It was in terms of speed and maximum ceiling that all three bombers were vulnerable and it was precisely these vulnerabilities unescorted daylight raiding were so cruelly exposing.

Bomber Command was profoundly shocked by the experience of December 18. Ludlow-Hewitt flew from his headquarters to 3 Group in Norfolk in order to hear first hand accounts from the survivors. Austere and somewhat ethereal looking, as though he were a great conductor or concert violinist rather than a warrior, Ludlow-Hewitt was an immensely sensitive man. A devout Christian Scientist and a teetotaller, he cared deeply for his men and felt their losses personally. He often rang squadron leaders to pass on his condolences. Though reserved and mild mannered he had a sharp mind and had pointed out the problems of the Command when other men might have thought it expedient not to. On this day he heard confirmation of the Wellingtons' lack of speed and how this had made them easy targets for the German Messerschmitt 110s. They were also out-gunned having neither heavy enough ammunition nor waist guns. The Wellingtons were shockingly susceptible to beam (waist) attack, an eventuality that does not seem to have been seriously considered. Lastly, in this catalogue of disasters, the lack of self-sealing fuel tanks was shown to be an awful oversight. Wellingtons were seen to go down with flaming wings caused by aviation fuel spilling out of ruptured tanks.

Ironically, given the stinging rebuke the Germans had inflicted on British strategy, Bomber Command clung to its belief that the self-defending bomber force was a viable concept. Air Vice-Marshal Baldwin drew up a report for Ludlow-Hewitt that blamed poor leadership and poor formation flying for the disasters, rather than the strategy or tactics in themselves. 3 Group's summary of the lessons learned stated: 'There is every reason to believe that a very close formation of six Wellington aircraft will emerge from a long and heavy attack by enemy fighters with very few, if any, casualties to its own aircraft.'[10] Baldwin also downplayed the significance of the waist attacks on the Wellingtons, conceding only that a gun should be mounted in the top astro hatch. His best recommendation was the need for self-sealing tanks. This at least revealed a slightly better understanding of the realities. After considering the matter Ludlow-Hewitt expressed a desire that all flight commanders must be told of 'the vital importance of good formation flying'.[11] The weight, consistency and accuracy of mutually supporting fire were felt to be the solution. It was the fighter, not flak, which was proving the main enemy. This lesson could no longer be avoided and closer formation flying was considered the best solution.

As Bomber Command mulled over the actions of December, the public was told a particular version of events. The Bomber Command Daily Bulletin of December 8, just before the two disasters, stressed that in recent operations 'the fact that our aircraft held off and bombed the German warships supports the view that our well-armed bombers are a match for any day fighter opponent.'[12] On December 19 the tone was slightly different. The losses could not be denied, but the report, printed in most papers, managed to soften the blow by not referring to the total losses. Instead they were mentioned in groups, deflecting attention from the cumulative total, and covered by an up-beat opening statement:

> At least 18 Messerschmitts are claimed to have been shot down in the action over Heligoland Bight on December 18... In such a fierce action it was inevitable that we should suffer some losses ourselves. Four were seen to be shot down, and another three, with petrol pouring from punctured tanks, were seen heading towards Holland [raising the possibility of safe-landing in a neutral country]. A further three are also missing. On their way home two other bombers were forced to come down in the sea, some 80 miles off the English coast. The crew of one of these was, after some considerable time, picked up in the rubber dinghy by a passing trawler.[13]

The *Daily Express* took up the official line and played up the positive sides. In fact it was difficult to deny the success of the operation according to these reports. On December 19 the *Express* claimed British losses were a fiction invented by the Nazis in order to deflect German opinion from the loss of the *Graf Spee*. The pocket battleship had been scuttled by its crew in the estuary of the River Plate outside Montevideo in Uruguay a few days earlier. The headlines proclaimed: 'Biggest Air Battle/ Nazis Lose 12 and We Lose 7/ Berlin Claims 'Victory' as Spee Tonic.'[14] The *Express* blithely told its readers the RAF had outwitted the German air force, with the bombers easily able to protect themselves against German attacks. Further, it was claimed that this revealed yet another deficiency in the German force because German bombers had been shot down easily by British fighters. It was reported as the biggest air battle of the war so far and, of course, as a British victory. The British public was fed a manipulated version of the bombing war – the seeds of later confusions, controversies and conflicts were being sown.

Peter Grant, a veteran of the December 18 raid, was sent to a Bomber Command gunnery school to pass-on the wisdom of his experiences.[15] He spared no detail. This did not win him any praise, instead he was reprimanded for having given 'an unpatriotic talk likely to cause dismay and demoralisation'. Whatever shine was put on the fact for the public and new recruits, Bomber Command went into a period of reflection. Ludlow-Hewitt was still deep in thought, despite the report and recommendations prepared for him by Baldwin. He was not going through a conversion in his thinking, rather it was no more than the resurgence and confirmation of his earlier doubts about the capabilities of Bomber Command and the viability of the Western Air Plans. Just a few weeks after seeming to confirm the cosy theory that close formation flying and mutual fire-support would protect bombers he was making different remarks to the Air

Staff. Ludlow-Hewitt took the results of the December raids as evidence of the implausibility of Plan W11. This was the 'Ruhr Plan', operations designed to attack the vital German war industries in this district in broad daylight. If Bomber Command's groups could not achieve much success flying over the sea and the coast what possible chance did they have flying over German territory proper? The shift towards night bombing was starting.

Night flying was not something Bomber Command was used to. Almost all thinking, theorising and planning in pre-war years had concentrated on the idea of precision bombing by daylight. Prior to the war two years of night flying practices by the Command had resulted in 487 forced landings thanks to crews losing their way at night. And this was over the British Isles, a Britain burning bright at night thanks to the millions of street lights and uncurtained windows in its tightly packed towns and cities. Could this force really be expected to navigate over a blacked-out, unknown country? Ironically one of the most maligned and ridiculed aspects of the air war in this early, relatively non-aggressive period was to help overcome some features of this problem.

The government believed that a leafletting campaign of Germany might persuade the German people to see the error of their ways, become disaffected with their government, overthrow it and want to come to a peaceful settlement with the French and British empires. A fanciful prospect, but one that held much attraction for Chamberlain and similarly minded ministers. Bomber Command therefore began its nightly task of dropping millions of leaflets over Germany. Harris wrote in his war memoirs the only thing this achieved was 'to supply the Continent's requirements of toilet paper for the five long years of war'.[16] Though this is a typically forthright and memorable comment from Harris it is not to be taken entirely at face value. The leaflets themselves might have been toilet paper, but the means of delivering them taught lessons cheaply. Between the start of the war and the invasion of Norway Bomber Command flew 366 leafleting sorties ('Nickel' sorties in Bomber Command operational code). The crews that delivered them gained much experience in night flying and navigation.

Navigation was the key difficulty. At this stage of the war a navigator was absolutely reliant on gaining pinpoints from the ground below. On very clear nights it was possible to use the sextant and fix the position from the stars. But to achieve this a navigator would probably have to lie flat on his back to ensure a steady hand and the pilot would have to fly straight and level, which was not a good idea when enemy aircraft might be about. The wireless operator might try to get a fix from a ground station using his trailing loop aerial, but the Germans often jammed the signals and they could easily be misread. Planes were pushed miles off course by inaccurate wind predictions that were never properly corrected once a mission got underway. Moonlit nights helped the crews, but cloud cover could then negate the advantage and over enemy territory the solution of diving below the cover was not that appealing. If no sort of fix was gained a crew could fall back on the device of bombing on estimated time of arrival, but this often resulted in almost surrealistically inaccurate bombing as explosions occurred in fields hundreds of miles away from the actual target. The list of 'buts' in each sentence above shows just how imprecise a science night navigation was in 1939.

After navigational problems, cold was the greatest difficulty aircrew had to face. Night temperatures over Europe and the North Sea froze airmen to the marrow. Aircraft design had made little provision for heat, an oversight for which airmen suffered. The interiors of the bombers iced up causing ungloved hands to incur ice burns and stick to the metal struts. Fingers that should have been able to feel the triggers of machine guns were numbed. Crews put on layer after layer of clothing to try to combat the problem. It often made little difference. Greg Gregson, a Wireless Operator/Air Gunner (WOP/AG), wore silk stockings, then put on woollen socks and then his fur-lined flying boots. On top of his shirts and jumpers came a 'teddy bear' lined inner coat with a canvas covering, then a fur-lined leather flying coat and then three pairs of gloves – a silk pair, followed by wool, then leather gauntlets.[17] The exterior of the aircraft also suffered from the cold. John Gee worried about ice getting into the carburettors of the engines and noticed how the weight of ice actually deformed the shape of the wings during flight.[18] On the night of October 27/28 1939 with the outside temperature -38°c Larry Donnelly recalls seeing huge lumps of ice fly from the propeller of a nearby aircraft which crashed against the fuselage with shocking thumps.[19] Turrets and guns froze solid making the aircraft indefensible in an attack. The cold, when combined with an inadequate oxygen supply, caused men to react sluggishly or even pass out. On a leafletting raid Donnelly joined one of his colleagues at the flare chute down which the bundles of leaflets were thrust. Each bundle was held together by a rubber band which was removed by the slipstream when the bundle had left the aircraft. The leaflets would then cascade down to earth. Occasionally a bundle would lose its band in the chute and become clogged causing the leaflets to blow back into the aircraft. The two men had to be careful because there was only one oxygen point available in this part of the aircraft and so would swop places whenever the other looked like fainting. Mental alertness was therefore very hard to maintain and it was hard to keep reactions sharp.

'Nickelling' raids taught Bomber Command that something more had to be done about crew comfort, and navigational aids were a necessity. But for the crews involved the compensation of learning these lessons did not make up for the frustration at making no genuine contribution to the war effort. One Squadron Leader recalled such missions:

> The fuselage forward of the door was crammed with large parcels of leaflets wrapped in coarse brown paper tied with thick twine. Access, normally difficult enough because of the retracted ventrical turret, was now extremely difficult through the narrow alley between the parcels on either side both fore and aft of the turret. At the evening briefing we were acquainted with the purpose of the mission and the reader will understand our feelings at not being called upon to deliver anything more damaging than a good supply of paper and stout rubber bands on Germany's industrial heartland.[20]

The newspapers did not report on these aspects, because, of course, it seemed there was little about Bomber Command that needed improving. Besides nickelling made far from great reading, while fighting off Messerschmitts did, and bombing German battleships did. Dropping leaflets about the state of the Nazi economy certainly did not (and besides the material contained in the leaflets was, for some bizarre reason, classified).

Churchill defended leaflet raids in the Commons, as *The Times* reported in January 1940. He drew a thick line between the policy of the British and that of the Germans:

> The question then arises ought we, instead of demonstrating the power of our Air Force by dropping leaflets all over Germany, to have dropped bombs? Then I am quite clear that our policy has been right. In this peaceful country governed by public opinion, democracy, and Parliament, we were not as thoroughly prepared at the outbreak of war as was a dictator state whose whole thought was bent on the preparation for war. We know from what they did in Poland that there is no brutality or bestial massacre of civilians by air bombing which they would not readily commit if they thought it were for their advantage.[21]

But what would he say if British bombs ever did happen to fall on civilians whether by accident or design?

Many of the questions, doubts, worries and thoughts about the role and ability of Bomber Command that had been growing since the start of the war came to a head with the Nazi invasions of Norway and then the Low Countries and France. But they were questions to be answered by some new faces. On April 3 1940 Sir Edgar Ludlow-Hewitt moved on to the post of Inspector General of the RAF, to be replaced by Air Marshal Sir Charles Portal. Ludlow-Hewitt has been subjected to some criticism of his command, most of which solely relies on the fact that his spell in charge coincided with a period in which the Command hardly covered itself with glory. However both contemporaries and historians have defended him from these charges. Ludlow-Hewitt was trying to make the best of a bad job, and his great intelligence and ability to learn served the Command well. He helped the Command immeasurably by insisting upon proper Operational Training Units. His sharp eye for technical details and improvements led to numerous small, but effective, changes in production and design. These qualities were taken into his new post of Inspector-General of the Service. Sir Arthur Harris, his contemporary and eventual successor, called him 'the most brilliant officer' he had ever met; he added: 'We reaped where he had sown and no man deserved better from his country than he did.' Harris was also convinced that Ludlow-Hewitt's clear vision of the limitations of the Command and its need to conserve its strength led to his removal. According to Harris Ludlow-Hewitt had revealed 'the sins of omissions of… [previous] politicians' and refused to 'provide a smokescreen to hide the shortcomings of those who are really responsible for the country's unpreparedness.'[22]

Just before Ludlow-Hewitt moved on there was a flurry of interest in what seemed like an important escalation of the war. On March 17 the Luftwaffe had attacked Scapa Flow naval base in the Orkney Islands and killed two civilians. The government ordered a reprisal raid on one of the German seaplane bases, but only where there was no nearby civilian settlement. Fifty bombers were despatched to Sylt to bomb the base at Hornum on the night of March 19. It was both the biggest raid of the war so far and the first on German soil. The press loved it. The British people could glory in the fact that the RAF was capable of hitting back and hitting back harder. Once again the *Daily Express* treated the news to their full-blooded treatment: 'MPs Cheer as Prime Minister Tells Them "We Are Now Bombing Sylt"/ Five Hour Reprisal Raid on Nazi Air Base/ First RAF Bombs on Land – to Avenge Scapa' ran the headlines the next morning.[23] They told the dramatic story of how Sir Kingsley Wood, Secretary of State for Air, had slipped the Prime Minister a piece of paper during the evening sitting in the Commons. Chamberlain then announced that: 'at this moment our planes are bombing Sylt', which brought forth cheers. Analysing the raid the aviation correspondent of the *Express* noted the fact that: 'in choosing Sylt as the first land target for bombing, the RAF gave no opportunity for the Germans to make serious allegations of civilian casualties.' Clearly the government and the nation was sensitive to the issue of what was and was not a legitimate target. But the other side of the coin was seen in Lord Stragboli's statement on the German raids in the Lords. He said that the British people would 'look for instant and successful *reprisals* for Scapa' (emphasis added), which presumably they now had.

For some of the crews involved it was the taste of real action at last, a welcome change from the nickel runs. Larry Donnelly was certainly excited by the prospect, a feeling he shared with the other crews at the briefing.[24] Real bombs for a real target instead of those 'bloody leaflets'. The flight over the North Sea was uneventful but they all became excited when the island was spotted. The bomb-aimer went to his position and the pilot dropped the Whitley to 4,000 feet for the bomb-run. Everyone felt a rush of adrenalin when the target was identified and the message 'bomb doors open' was announced. As the Whitley came in the flak hammered away and searchlights bobbed. As the bombs fell away from the aircraft it lurched gracelessly upwards relieved at shedding its load. Donnelly gave the searchlights a spraying with his machine guns as the flak got closer. The Whitley rose away from the island. Donnelly had completed his first genuine bombing sortie. Even though the bomb-run itself had only been a few minutes it had felt much longer. During the coming years thousands of crews were to feel the same sensation, no matter how experienced they were.

A day later the *Express*'s 'Opinion' column declared itself in favour of a more bellicose policy: 'That is the way the public wants to see Britain fight the war. For every crack they give us we pay it back double.'[25] It concluded on an extremely sanguine note: 'Our defence lies in the proof that we can strike back with more than we are given, and in the fact that the Ruhr is far more vulnerable than the Thames.' Within six months the Luftwaffe would be making a mockery of this statement and the crews of Bomber Command would be flabbergasted by it. Myths and legends started to cover the bombing war from its earliest days.

Hitler's ambitions exploded again on April 9 with the invasion of Denmark and Norway. Such a development caught Britain completely unaware. Bomber Command certainly did not have a prepared answer, the invasion was utterly beyond the scope of the Western Air Plans. To make matters even worse the Germans managed to establish the Luftwaffe in Norway almost immediately. Bomber Command was therefore operating at extreme distance against locally based aircraft. It was not an appealing prospect. Mike Lewis was ordered to attack a German cruiser and destroyers in Kristiansund.[26] Twelve aircraft were despatched. They flew straight into a pack of fighters from the *Richthofen* squadron. In a cloudless sky the fighters fell on the under-armed Hampdens. It was clear to Lewis that the Germans had studied the Hampden and knew where to attack it. Five Hampdens were lost. If the German aircraft had had a better fuel consumption they would probably have destroyed all the attackers. For Lewis it was a terrifying experience.

Ditching into the freezing waters of the North Sea was another experience not forgotten in a hurry. During the fight for Norway Raymond Chance's Whitley was crippled by a Messerschmitt. Everything was thrown out to gain as much height as possible but it had little effect.[27] He realised the Whitley was finished and asked how many of the crew could swim. Two were non-swimmers, so he told them to stick close by when the aircraft hit the sea. As the aircraft started losing height he broke down the rear hatch with the fire axe. Chance then ordered everyone to get into the ditching position braced against the bulkhead. The Whitley refused to level out when close to the sea and splashed down with a terrible crunch. There was an explosion and Chance found himself catapulted into the wreckage of the nose section. He started to hallucinate. He thought he drifted for hours, but it could only a have been a couple of minutes at most because he was brought back to reality by the smell of fire. The aircraft was still afloat, but one of the wings was on fire. Hauling himself along the fuselage he saw no sign of the crew, but did see the dinghy pack which he pounced on. On reaching the hatch he flung the pack out and jumped after it. His Mae West lifejacket shot him to the surface and he pulled the cord on the dinghy allowing it to inflate. At this point he was joined by the two men who could not swim. He presumed they had been holding onto the tail. The bomb-aimer then came across. Unable to haul himself in Chance stayed in the water clasping the rat-line round the dinghy. The great weakness Chance was feeling was due to his crushed ankle, broken leg and hair-line fracture of the skull. It was probably a blessing that he did not realise the seriousness of his injuries.

For fifteen minutes he stayed in the water, summoning up the mental and physical energy to clamber into the inflatable. Once he managed it he flopped down and was saved from drowning in the small pool of water at the bottom by one of the crew wedging his boot under his chin. Their agonies increased when they heard the cries of Pilot Officer Hall, who was still in the water. He was only about 50 yards away, but they were so shocked and weakened by wounds that they did not have the strength to row towards him. They suffered the anguish of listening to him slowly drown.

Just before dawn a British destroyer searching for a u-boat caught them in its searchlight. A boat was dropped to bring them in. When they were brought alongside the ship they had to put every last ounce of energy into climbing the rope ladder. Not having a doctor onboard the ship's crew did their best. Chance's blackened foot was wrapped in cotton wool and a bottle of Scotch and cigarettes were left beside him.

Chance spent a long time in hospital, but he recovered in time to see action in the Battle of France and was serving in the Far East when the war ended. After the conflict he became a barrister.

Over the years many bomber crews were forced to ditch in the North Sea. Sometimes the impact with the sea snapped the bomber like a toy and killed everyone. Sometimes they survived only to drift on the tides suffering slow, agonising deaths. Sometimes they were rescued. The sea could be as cruel to airmen as it was to sailors.

The first great lesson the Norwegian campaign rammed home was one the Command had been reluctantly coming to accept for some time – daylight raids were impossible. Eighty-three bombers were despatched to Stavanger on April 12, nine Wellingtons and Hampdens were lost. Bomber Command conceded defeat. Wellingtons and Hampdens were withdrawn from major daylight operations. Such losses were proving a disastrous drain on the pool of available aircraft and were decimating crew numbers, not to mention the hammering of crew morale. Only the light Blenheim bombers were to continue in daylight.

Changing the Wellingtons and Hampdens to night operations did not make much difference. The Norwegian campaign, which only lasted a month, proved extremely frustrating for Bomber Command. Though the survival rate improved with the switch bombing accuracy certainly did not. In addition, the Command made no appreciable impact on the campaign. However this was just the beginning for the main battle in the West was about to unfold.

Unlike the campaign in Norway the German invasion of the Low Countries and France had been expected and Bomber Command had made plans. At the outbreak of war 1 Group had crossed to France with its ten squadrons of light Fairey Battle bombers and two Blenheim squadrons. This became the Advanced Air Striking Force under Air Marshal Sir Arthur Barratt. Later additional squadrons of Blenheims from 2 Group were added to this Force, as were some squadrons of 4 Group's Whitleys.

With extreme force the storm in the west broke on May 10 1940. The allies were on the backfoot from the start. The Advanced Air Striking Force Fairey Battles and Blenheims did not stand much chance of playing a useful role when left to fend for themselves against the much faster and more manoeuvrable German fighters. As the Germans streamed forward the slow British light bombers did their best to create bottlenecks by attacking bridges and lines of communication, often with suicidal bravery. It was also a shock to see what the Luftwaffe was capable of doing to its enemies. Wilf Burnett flew over Rotterdam a day after it had been subjected to German bombing:

> By that time the fire services had extinguished a number of fires, but they were still dotted around the whole city. This was the first time I'd ever seen devastation by fires on this scale. We went right over the southern outskirts of Rotterdam at about 6,000 or 7,000 feet, and you could actually smell the smoke from the fires burning on the ground.[28] I was shocked to see a city in flames like that. Devastation on a scale I had never experienced.

The prohibition of attacking Germany was finally abandoned. Back home the public never really got a chance to understand just how outclassed the British machines were, and how little damage Bomber Command actually could do to the German war machine. Once again the *Express* was the yardstick of popular knowledge. On May 13 its headlines read: 'RAF Destroy Bridges. Cut German Lines.'[29] On May 15 'RAF Bombers Smash Up Tanks as Fighters Clear Air.'[30] The report continued: 'British bombers are giving Hitler a lesson in blitzkrieg war today. They flew all twenty-four hours of the day, blowing Hitler's own blitzkrieg troops off the roads.'

In the middle of this period of extremely naive reporting the strategic air offensive against Germany started. The night of May 15/16 saw 90 aircraft attack industrial targets in the Ruhr. This activated one of the Western Air Plans, but it was a long way from the initial assumptions made about such operations. Despite this, wildly optimistic ideas about cutting off German artificial oil supplies were made at this time. Portal wrote that it was possible for Bomber Command to do 'immense damage' to German oil production with his current force. On June 4 it was predicted that German oil supplies might be reduced by up to half a million tons within the next two-three months. In fact German production was reduced by 150,000 tons over the next three and a half years of war! The *Daily Telegraph* carried an article by Oskar Tokayer, 'An Expert on World Petrol Supplies', in which he argued the 'RAF onslaught is crippling Nazi oil reserves'.[31] In September the leader writer of the *Telegraph* estimated that somewhere in the region of 80 per cent of Germany's refineries had been hit and 90 per cent of its synthetic oil production destroyed.[32] The newspapers were hardly likely to be realistic when Bomber Command itself was also living in dreamland.

Back in France, the situation was becoming increasingly grave. The Blenheim crews were pressing home their attacks with a manic desperation, a desperation barely perceptible in the press. The divergence between reality and propaganda was fully illustrated by the raid on Gembloux on May 17. Twelve Blenheims attacked German troop concentrations in the area, losing 11 in the process. The Air Ministry's communiqué, quoted in most papers, was a beauty of understatement: 'They encountered a large formation of enemy fighters and intense AA fire. In spite of great gallantry and determination 11 of our aircraft failed to return.'[33] The *Daily Mirror* ignored the communiqué and, unbelievably, stated that no aircraft were lost.[34] Far more mileage could be got out of the raids on Germany itself. After a raid on Cologne, Hamburg and Bremen the *Daily Express*'s aviation correspondent wrote: 'I can but imagine the dismay of the German people supporting the Nazi rupture of world peace when the homes of those close enough to the military targets attacked trembled to the shattering explosions.[35] This was something their Fuehrer had not promised them in his wild urgings to war.' The *Daily Mail* commented on the heroic efforts of the RAF to support the armies.[36] It stressed the courage and inspiration of the RAF, commenting on the fact that operations were continuing day and night in an effort to help the armies. It was pointed out that bombs were not just rained onto the advancing Germans, but well into the communication lines keeping the German advance on track as well.

The reality for those involved was becoming all the more violently detached from such reporting. Bill Keighley took off in his Blenheim to bomb oil refineries around Hamburg on July 29th.[37] Keighley was setting out on his ninth operation and was already well aware of the fact that it was unwise to speculate too much about the future. He had arrived at 82 Squadron without much knowledge of Blenheims and had certainly never flown one with a full bomb load. But even with the small number of nine operations under his belt he was a bit of a veteran, so steep had been the losses.

Out over the North Sea the clouds disappeared. This made up his mind. Keighley knew he would face a maelstrom over Hamburg and so he decided to attack the second target instead, Leuwarden airfield in Holland. After the attack he pulled away for home; at that moment two Messerschmitts came into sight closing fast. The only way to escape such an attack in the slow Blenheim was to pray for cloud cover. Keighley headed towards the nearest cloud, but the fighters were too quick and a burst of fire hit his gunner. Turning back for the kill the Messerschmitts raked the Blenheim, but just at that moment Keighley entered the clouds. Salvation was short lived, however, for the port engine propeller sheared off. The Blenheim was finished. Keighley looked below for a landing place and came down in a cornfield where he found that his gunner was dead. Injured, he was taken off to hospital, where a young Luftwaffe pilot inspected him – gloating over his success. After six weeks in hospital he was transferred to prison camp where he remained for five years.

Men were becoming weary and jumpy though morale remained remarkably high. Larry Donnelly realised he was probably drinking too much by late August.[38] He was exceptionally pleased to get a few weeks' leave, getting away from the monotony of the dull thud of the engines and the beeping of his Morse Code set. He was also very pleased to forget his anxieties. Having started the war as a young happy-go-lucky man he was now becoming a hardbitten veteran. When so many were lost it was too depressing to consider how long his own luck might last. Donnelly completed two tours before transferring to Coastal Command. He then fulfilled his boyhood ambition by gaining his pilot's wings and retired from the RAF in 1966.

At this moment of extreme agony for France Italy entered the war, falling on to its stricken neighbour. Bomber Command struck immediately, launching attacks on Genoa and Turin on June 11. Despite the widespread feeling that Italy had committed a cowardly and dishonourable act, not all agreed with the bombing. A leading article in the *Daily Mail* asked 'Are such attacks of vital importance at this time? While the peril in France is so acute, Italy must be a secondary consideration. At this stage the war is not going to be decided in the Mediterranean. It will be won or lost on the Western Front.'[39]

A colossal military disaster. That was how Winston Churchill, Prime Minister for almost a month, described the situation in France to the House of Commons on June 4. RAF Bomber Command had fought itself almost to a standstill, losing 147 aircraft. But the collapse of France was to prove no respite for Bomber Command. It now had to join in the Battle of Britain. The role of Bomber Command in that great struggle is not well known in the public imagination and memory, the lion's share of the glory going to the heroic efforts of the men of Fighter Command. But night after night the Command set out to smash the invasion ports, destroy barges and interrupt communications. No one doubted the need to press home attacks, no one doubted the gravity of the situation. Wilf Burnett recalled that:

> The station commander gathered all officers together one morning in August or September 1940 and told us that it appeared invasion was imminent and that we should be prepared for it. I remember the silence that followed. We left the room and I don't think anyone spoke, but we were all the more determined to make certain that we did everything possible to deter the Germans from launching their invasion.[40]

The other side of the coin was the need to continue the slowly evolving strategic air campaign against Germany. Air Ministry thinking was divided at this time, 'torn between maintaining the long-term strategic offensive against selective parts of German industry and the need to devote effort to targets which should bring immediate relief in the front line.'[41]

Bomber Command therefore tried to achieve a balance between bombing Germany and the invasion ports. 'Blackpool front', as the stretch west of Dunkirk was called, was attacked with steely determination by the Blenheims, Whitleys and Hampdens. It was almost as if they wanted to make up for the appalling experiences they had had in France. The need to smash the invasion ports was obvious and absolute. Rod Rodley had not long been a member of 97 squadron.[42] His first mission was against invasion barges at Calais. Being so close to England he was confident of finding it on a bright, moonlit night. Sure enough twenty minutes out from Beachy Head he saw the fingers of the jetties and quays. His bomb-aimer carefully lined up the barges and they bombed from 15,000 feet, feeling the aircraft surge upwards as it lost weight. But after completing his mission he became lost and did not get home for another six hours and had to face the wrath of an angry Wing Commander.

At the same time Bomber Command headquarters was trying to devise a plan for more effective bombing of Germany itself. During June and July 1940 the Air Ministry drew up a whole series of directives none of which could boast consistency as a plus point. Portal himself was also caught in two minds. Though originally wedded to the idea of attacking the synthetic oil plants, careful analysis of the bombing raids was raising the spectre of failure. He was reluctantly coming to the opinion that it was beyond the capacity of Bomber Command to regularly find targets and bomb accurately by night. On June 4 the Air Ministry instructed Portal to continue the oil campaign, but told him he should attempt to achieve the 'dislocation of German war industry'. In the next paragraph however it announced 'in no circumstances should night bombing be allowed to degenerate into mere indiscriminate action, which is contrary to the policy of His Majesty's Government.'[43]

On June 20 a new directive placed oil targets third and communications and the army's forward concentrations first. A few weeks later still, July 4, the directive changed again, this time German shipping and ports were first priority. By July 13 the aircraft industry was the primary target. Portal reacted to this with some plain speaking about the ability of his crews to hit targets at night. Instead he advocated attacks over a wide area, for 'it largely increases the moral effect of our operations by the alarm and disturbance created over the wider area.'[44] In other words Portal was considering an attack on the morale of the German people *before* the blitz encouraged any sense of reprisals. But Sir Richard Peirse, Vice Chief of Air Staff at the Air Ministry and soon to be Commander in Chief Bomber Command, was committed to the principle of precision bombing. He told Churchill the effectiveness of British bombing lay in the fact that it was thoroughly planned and that raids were dedicated to destroying a particular target.

Just what the RAF should be trying to bomb and what it could bomb was a subject on the verge of becoming a public debate thanks to the German blitz on Britain. In August the Germans changed tactics in the Battle of Britain and started bombing British cities, beginning with London. Churchill immediately ordered a retaliatory raid on Berlin. The press, too preoccupied with the raids on Britain, barely noticed this. Raids on Berlin only seemed to capture the imagination in the autumn and winter of 1940 as the need to hit back became greater. By the time the 'mini-campaign' against Berlin had gathered speed Bomber Command had a new commander. On October 5 Sir Charles Portal took up the post he was to hold until the end of the war, Chief of Air Staff at the Air Ministry, while Sir Richard Peirse moved in the other direction from Vice Chief of Air Staff to Bomber Command. Just over a month later Sir Arthur Harris moved from command of 5 Group and took up Peirse's old post at the Air Ministry. Peirse was determined to use Bomber Command as a precision bombing force, but his admirable sense of mission was not matched by reality. Bomber Command simply did not have the capacity, navigational equipment or bombs to carry out a crippling blow against Nazi war industries in this period.

In the meantime the press busied itself with a debate as to the correct objectives of British bombing, and in particular the question of Berlin. Leader writers scrambled to make definitive statements. On September 25 the *Daily Mail* announced British moral superiority: 'Berliners are learning that their city is no more immune than is London from large-scale bombing. The one difference is that our airmen select their targets and concentrate on objects of military value. We hope to see Berlin bombed again – repeatedly.'[45] The same day the *Daily Sketch* waded in with reflections on the questions of reprisals. It warned against relying on the methods of the terrorist as the Germans had done. However it was argued that the morale of German people was susceptible to bombing. In the first instance it advocated the bombing of German military targets. The piece concluded with the statement: 'When this has been fully accomplished we can think again – if it should still be necessary and if he [Hitler] is not already whimpering in fear of the wrath to come.'[46]

Resistance to mere reprisals was the common theme. The *Daily Telegraph* said such attacks would be 'contrary to sound strategy' and 'to adopt such a course at the expense of the main objective, which is to weaken the enemy's power of mischief by attacking his bases and factories.'[47] A month later the same leading column told Londoners 'who have endured the frightfulness of persistent indiscriminate bombing night after night, with its wanton slaughter and torture of civilians, will see in these effective attacks on the military objectives in Berlin, the most deadly form of counter-stroke.'[48]

The clear implication was that British strategy had a moral superiority and that *the RAF had the ability to carry out a strategy of precision night bombing.* Whatever the leader writers might have argued, and whatever they thought the RAF was capable of, there was always the simmering feeling of revenge in the air. A defence of British policy in the *Daily Mail* was rounded-off with this rather more ambiguous statement: 'The ruined homes and broken lives of Britain will be avenged. When Hitler has spent his fury in his useless effort to bring this country to her knees, the hour for attack will come. Then Britain must launch against Germany the most devastating offensive that has yet been seen.'[49] Similarly, the *Daily Mirror* said British operations should never be associated with the word 'reprisals', but then thundered 'in war when you're hit, you hit back. Hit of course. That, dear friends, you must do.'[50] Over the next few weeks its attitude hardened even more: 'we must continue with the skilled job of driving Berlin into its shelters – remembering that war **must** be carried into Germany, and that we **must** pass, as rapidly as we can, to the offensive.' [original emphasis] On September 12 the *Mirror* leader came up with the most interesting comment made in the British press on the bombing war. Fascinatingly, it accepted the idea of unrestricted aggression, called for a 'gloves off' approach and destroyed the distinction between civilian and soldier, implying that it was redundant in modern war:

[On bombing Berlin] This is the only policy. This is the only effective method available to us in self-defence. This is the **offensive**… Bomb for bomb and the same all round! The only policy.

And the only policy on which our dauntless suffering people **insist**. If the Air Minister doesn't agree with them he must clear out. The air war is no time for lecturers, and gloved persons wishing to live up to a high standard of ancient chivalry. The invention of the bombing plane abolished chivalry for ever. It is now 'retaliate or go under'.

We are not dedicated to passive and polite martyrdom. We **must** hit back…

Also the dislocation of German communications and nerve-centres is essentially a 'military objective' – if really it is reasonable to go on making this almost obsolete distinction.

A distinction that wears very thin. People are killed, in the devilish war of today, everywhere, anyhow. People killed are, in tens of thousands, useful workers; mainly war workers. They are in the war. Everybody matters. Maybe everybody is a victim. [original emphasis][51]

'Opinion', the leading column in the *Express*, urged 'Bomb Them Portal!/ Go to it Sir Charles Portal' in November.[52] After the bombing of Bremen in January 1941 the same paper pointed out that the RAF had hit Bremen's industries, but also crowed that it 'lies heaped today with more fire-blackened ruins than the City of London.'[53] When the King and Queen visited a Bomber Command station in December, accompanied by Peirse, British Movietone News seemed to stress the revenge element and how easy it was for the RAF to carry this out. The commentary homed in on the new volunteers and added that lots more were needed because Britain was set on 'bombing Hitler as he deserves'.[54] Of course the King stayed until the planes returned from their mission and reported a successful sortie over German territory.

The RAF itself was keen to avoid any charges of being a revenge force. When the BBC visited a station to broadcast the preparations for a typical mission listeners heard the Intelligence Officer state emphatically: 'Your primary target, and your primary job, is the attack on the Stettiner railway station. I want everybody to definitely understand that. There's nothing else – there's no red herring to drag you away from your main objective.'[55] Ensuring a policy on the presentation of the work of Bomber Command was a concern which stretched to the very top. In January 1941 a conference with representatives from the BBC, the Foreign Office, the Ministry of Economic Warfare and Bomber Command was held at the Air Ministry. Peirse said that 'there was general misconception as to the scale, purpose and effect of our bombing', and he thought that it was 'advisable wherever possible to mention specific targets that have been attacked or hit because if this was not done the impression that our bombing is indiscriminate or inaccurate is at once produced.'[56] No one asked whether this was in fact the case. Informing the public of the nature of this campaign caused friction. A secret BBC report to the Director General on the same meeting revealed much more than the rather laconic Air Ministry files. The BBC delegates were immediately aware of an argument that had been going on behind the scenes. They reported the tense atmosphere between the Foreign Office and Ministry of Economic Warfare on the one side and the Air Ministry on the other. It was said that they had been sniping at the Air Ministry over its claim to be successfully bombing Germany. The Ministry was reminded of how dangerous it was to overstate successes for it caused others to question the validity of British propaganda and information. The BBC representatives felt that Peirse sympathised with the critics, which put his own propaganda and information officers on the defensive.

But Peirse was not prepared to concede too much for he told the meeting that he was about to launch a far more intensive raiding campaign against Germany. He foresaw a problem with the presentation of this for he was unable to 'see how the Air Ministry news draftsmen could do justice to these forthcoming operations after the way they had been sending the flames hundreds of feet high, and laying waste the target areas' in their earlier reporting of relatively small attacks.[57]

They all agreed that particular care had to be taken with the case of Berlin. Neutral reporters (who remained unidentified in the report but presumably referred to Swiss and Swedish journalists) had undermined British propaganda by exposing the lack of damage done to the central railway stations of the city. It was added that some of these neutral parties might be fictions of the German propaganda ministry, but no names were given.

The report revealed many elements that were to dog the Command and its subsequent campaigns and images. Firstly it seems clear that there was very little liaison with other ministries as to the most effective way of mounting the bombing war. Secondly, the claims made were often fantastic and so created disillusion when the truth was revealed. Finally, despite a great deal of evidence warning against such sanguine judgements, there was the persistent belief of the Commander that his men and machines could and would do better. In a war and a world dominated by media images Bomber Command was failing.

Matters were complicated still further for on the night of December 16/17 the War Cabinet authorised a general attack on a German city in retaliation for recent heavy raids on British cities, particularly Coventry. Mannheim was chosen and was attacked by 134 bombers. Wellingtons led with incendiaries, the fires started were supposed to act as a guide to the supporting bombers. Bomber Command was deliberately aiming at a target that was not primarily industrial in nature, i.e. the general area of the centre of Mannheim. It was another step towards the 'area attack'; a process that had started long before Sir Arthur Harris took charge of the Command. Little damage was actually caused to Mannheim for the Wellingtons failed to start a concentrated blaze. Having failed to create a sufficiently obvious major aiming point the bombers fell into the usual pattern of scattered and inconsistent bombing.

Such a raid was generally against Peirse's conception of the role of the force. By late 1940 he had established a pattern of waiting for the full moon period and then putting up the largest force he could muster. He left the rest of the month pretty quiet. In this way he hoped to achieve fewer, heavier, better quality raids. To a certain extent Peirse was merely following logic, for the weather and the numbers of serviceable aircraft were set against him. By this manner the bombing war fell into a bit of a lull before resuming in the spring of 1941.

From September 1939 to February 1941 Bomber Command flew 19,961 sorties; 517 aircraft were lost or 14.8 per cent of those despatched and 11,288 tons of bombs were dropped. The war had not turned out the way the peacetime planners had foreseen. During this period Bomber Command was forced to start a rethink of its strategical and tactical appreciation of the conflict. This led to confusion and contradiction. In turn it made the presentation of the bombing war to the British public a rather confused affair. The foundation of so many of the legends, popular memories and popular prejudices about the bombing war – still current to this day – slowly started to evolve during this period. The main confusion was over the role and effectiveness of Bomber Command. Was it a weapon of mass destruction dedicated to revenging the blitz or was it a weapon capable of precision bombing? At that particular moment it was neither, but few were prepared to admit it. It is no surprise that confusion over its role should have reigned. Even the most well-educated and well-informed of laymen had no chance of making sense of the British bombing war for the simple reason that both the Air Ministry and Bomber Command themselves were equally confused and in the dark. By the spring of 1941 the RAF had been forced to scrap all its pre-war plans. Sir Charles Portal at the Air Ministry, taking note of the lamentable scraps of intelligence pointing to a lamentable lack of accuracy and penetration in British bombing, was coming over to the idea that the general attack was the only possible alternative. At the same time Sir Richard Peirse was hoping that given more machines, careful husbandry of his existing stock and greater experience, his crews could do serious damage to German war industry by precision bombing. All the while the British people were being heavily bombed and no matter what they might have thought later on there was a desire to 'dish it out' to the Germans. But the position had clarified in some ways. Gone was the squeamishness about attacking Germany, gone was any sense of a negotiated peace or phoney war. Bomber Command had 1941 to try to thrash out a new policy and write something big on a new slate.

CHAPTER THREE

Committing Britain to a Bomber War, Spring 1941–Spring 1942

When Robert Kee, a Bomber Command pilot, looked back over his diary for 1941 he found that it made depressing reading.[1] Most of the operations he took part in could hardly be labelled successes. A raid over Brest ruined by patchy cloud and flak. His bombs probably fell uselessly into the sea. An attempt to bomb Brunswick stifled by not gaining a whiff of where the city actually lay. A few incendiaries on what might have been Hanover. He missed anything of significance when bombing Düsseldorf. For three nights in succession he flew over Kiel; each raid was a waste of time thanks to poor weather. One raid saw him forced to bring back his 2,000-pound bomb having found no opportunity to drop it. Mannheim was covered in cloud too. But there was the odd success. One night over Hamm he and his crew managed to stoke up a big fire engulfing a marshalling yard. Many years after the war Robert Kee was not surprised to learn how inaccurate most RAF bombing was. But this was the force the British people had to rely on during long nights of standing alone against Nazism.

Winter weather with its cold and storms grounded much of Bomber Command. This gave it a chance to recover from the exertions of the autumn. With spring came the chance to relaunch the campaign in what appeared to be much better circumstances. For a start there were no allies to be helped strategically or tactically, and there was no military action in the west demanding direct intervention from the Command. Then there was the fact that more machines and crews were arriving. Finally, Bomber Command had the trust and confidence – despite its lack of a clear direction – of the British people and the Prime Minister. As the shoots and buds of spring began to show themselves Bomber Command sat in the proud position of being the weapon which would take the war to the heart of Germany. Bombed, rationed, and alone the British people were spoiling for the chance of cheering on the boys who could hit back at the Nazi empire.

Though bomber production was indeed picking up pace this was not entirely good news for Bomber Command. Many bombers never actually arrived. Instead they were consigned to the Middle East, the only theatre where British ground troops were taking on the Axis, and Coastal Command. 1 Group had returned from France and was firmly back within the Command's structure having long since ceased to be an advanced tactical bombing force. The Fairey Battles with which this Group was equipped had been completely outclassed and it was therefore converted to Wellingtons. By March Air Marshal Sir Richard Peirse, Commander in Chief of Bomber Command, had gained 17 new squadrons to the 29 available in the winter of 1940. The great irony was that despite the excellence of the pre-war training programme the Command was desperately short of crews. In April the standard summer courses in Operational Training Units were reduced from eight weeks to six. Introducing this method created a short term glut of crews. But by the winter this policy was scrapped for it resulted in a rather shocking increase in accidents and losses on operations. In May 1941 a new group, 7, was created in order to oversee the work of the bomber OTUs. As Bomber Command spread its net further it swallowed more and more men from the Dominions, plus the survivors of the air forces of the occupied nations. As early as September 1940 Bomber Command had two Polish squadrons, two more followed swiftly, and a Czechoslovakian squadron. A distinctly cosmopolitan and exotic atmosphere was to infuse the Command for by 1941 it could also boast squadrons from across the Empire. Many squadrons were sponsored by countries and districts within the empire. The sponsoring country or district sometimes supplied the cash for the running of the squadron, but many sent men too. Bomber Command was truly an imperial effort. Madras Presidency, the United Provinces, Ceylon, Hyderabad, Rhodesia, New Zealand, Hong Kong, the Straits Settlement, Jamaica (which kept its squadron supplied with West Indian rum too), East India, the Federated Malay States, Gold Coast, Canada and Australia all had squadrons. In time Canada would even run its own Group.

New aircraft were also coming into service by 1941, as well as modified versions of the bombers already available. Experience had taught that the Wellington needed more armour and waist guns. The Whitleys were also carrying more armour, and, importantly, self-sealing tanks had been added. Slowly, very slowly, the new generation of bombers planned back in 1936 started to appear. The Short Stirling made its debut on February 10/11, on 24/25 the Avro Manchester, on March 10/11 the Handley Page Halifax. All of this was reported with a great deal of gusto by the press. On March 12 the *Daily Mirror* announced with excitement that 'the Hampdens, Wellingtons and Whitleys are now more powerful, but they are being replaced by the Stirling, the Manchester and the Halifax, twice the size, faster with heavier defence.'[2] The *Daily Telegraph* could boast that 'Bomber Command now has more aircraft than ever before, some of them capable of carrying much greater loads than any of the types which were in service last spring.'[3] A few months later, on March 14, the leading article noted that the raids on Berlin the night before were carried out by 'new and more powerful bombers than ever before… carrying very heavy bombs.'[4] Greater loads could indeed be carried and it was a different type of bomb. The 500lb medium capacity bomb was replacing the earlier 250lb general purpose bomb. New incendiary bombs were also coming into production.

All of this activity represented a huge commitment by British industry, capital and labour. The reasons for this commitment were simple. Britain did not have any other way of hitting back at Germany. Any sort of invasion of the continent was an impossibility. After the debacle in Norway and France the BEF was not ready for such operations, nor would it be for a long time. The only 'western front' available to Britain was in the air and this made up the mind of Churchill. As early as July 1940 he had clutched at the bomber as the means to hit back; he wrote to Lord Beaverbrook, then Minister of Aircraft Production:

> We have no Continental Army which can defeat the German military power. The blockade is broken and Hitler has Asia and probably Africa to draw from. Should he be repulsed here or not try invasion, he will probably recoil eastward, and we have nothing to stop him. But there is one thing that will bring him back and bring him down, and that is an absolutely devastating, exterminating attack by very heavy bombers from this country upon the Nazi homeland. We must be able to overwhelm him by this means, without it I do not see a way through.[5]

Churchill probably did not believe that bombing alone would win the war, but in 1940 and 1941 there were very few other options available to him. But, having taken the decision to back Bomber Command, Churchill flung his full weight behind it and urged his government and people to give it every assistance. Churchill had summed up the nation's feelings. It is doubtful whether people did believe that bombing alone could do the whole job, but it was the only tool to hand and it therefore deserved all their energies and attentions.

Peirse had certainly been considering the situation and had been moving towards the idea of the general area attack since the previous winter. It was hardly an innovation. Portal had considered the general attack during his brief tenure of the Command. Peirse, however, had not yet arrived at a clear strategic decision. But it is hard to blame him. Bomber Command had failed to live up to any of its pre-war promises in 1939 and had not achieved much by the winter of 1940. No one had been considerate enough to leave Peirse an alternative plan should everything else fail. His main belief, based upon directives from the Air Ministry, was in fact a compromise. On moonlit nights he would try to achieve accurate bombing. On the dark nights he would attempt the area attack. A directive of October 30 1940 called for 'very heavy material destruction which will demonstrate to the enemy the power and severity of air bombardment and the hardship and dislocation which will result from it'.[6] On cloudy nights he ordered his bombers to carry heavier loads, further into Germany, in order to achieve this. Inadequate pre-war planning was making the area assault on German lives, property and morale inevitable.

In January 1941 the Air Ministry supplemented these guidelines with a new directive which ordered further attacks on Germany's synthetic oil production, 'the most concise, clear and forceful directive yet produced.'[7] Therefore the spring found Bomber Command with a slightly clearer strategy, part precision, part area bombing. Morale was up for there were high expectations of new machines and, despite the hiccups, more crews. Public support was also tremendous. For the British people the bomber force was shaping up to be a key weapon in chastising Germany and achieving victory. For the *Daily Mirror* it was also the service of modern war, the service least attached to old fashioned and out-dated ideas. In March 1941 a leader, entitled 'Salute Our Airmen!', perfectly caught the sense of expectation which was growing within the British people:

> [The bombing campaign was] The only form of fighting that cannot be concealed from the Germans! The assault that cannot be called their victory! We are hitting Berlin, Hamburg, Bremen, Cologne, the big industrial cities. We shall go on.
>
> The Germans were told that this could never happen. Even their mass-produced minds can grasp the contradiction between that promise and our bombs. We are attacking…
>
> Here, in this war, we have a service fortunately free from the grip of stale ideas and aged traditions. This service is our RAF. And every month, every week shows that, as the war passes more and more into the air, it displays its brilliant skill, the daring, the endurance of our airmen…
>
> We shall lose brave men and fine machines. We have suffered much. We must suffer more. But who can doubt, in reading of our achievement, that the spirit of the RAF is unconquerable, that our ascendancy in the air is not remote, and that it must mark the beginnning of the end of the New Order of the old brutality.[8]

But problems raised themselves straightaway. Though given a new directive Peirse hardly had time to act on it before he was ordered to break off and attack different targets. With the German domination of the Bay of Biscay the range and effectiveness of the German surface fleet and submarines was greatly increased. All of which led to an upsurge in the ferocity of the vital Battle of the Atlantic. Britain's survival was absolutely dictated by its ability to keep open its maritime trade routes in order to feed itself and supply its war industries. Therefore on March 6 Peirse was ordered to attack French ports and other maritime targets. Raids on German warships and naval installations began.

The air over France was positively swarming at times for Bomber and Fighter Commands also continued their policy of 'Circuses'. The aim was to send over mainly light day bombers with fighter escorts in order to lure the German fighters into the air. This, so the argument went, would achieve an attrition of their number. In addition a policy of blocking the English Channel to all enemy shipping plying up and down the French coast was instigated on April 28 under the dramatic title 'Channel Stop'. In the event both policies often proved to be either frustratingly inconclusive or downright terrifying.

Flying his Hampden at a slow 145 miles per hour at 10,000 feet as part of a circus made Wilf Burnett very nervous.[9] The Hampden was extremely vulnerable to anti-aircraft fire and it was actually a relief to him and his crew when they reverted back to night missions after five or six of these sorties. It fell to the Blenheims to carry the bulk of these operations again. These aircraft were very uncomfortable to fly and had a poor accident record. Having an inadequate generator they could not power heating units for the pilot and so he froze. Their unstressed glass windscreens often shattered under the tiniest pressure. Pitched into the circuses against modern German fighters seemed to prove to the crews that the RAF High Command had learnt little in two years of war.

Luckily the service still had some excellent leaders who set an example to their men and helped them through. Charles Patterson joined 114 Squadron flying Blenheims in 2 Group.[10] His Squadron Leader was the South African 'Bok' Hull, whose personal bravery was an inspiration to his men. The station commander was Paddy, Earl of Bandon. Always friendly and chatty, he helped young crews settle down and smoothed over any friction that might arise between them.

Patterson found himself promoted to Flight Lieutenant after only a dozen operations. Such promotions came about thanks to the shocking losses. Anyone who survived about 15 operations was made a Squadron Leader. Charles Patterson went on to complete two tours of daylight operations.

On a summer's afternoon Patterson joined a circus due to attack a power station at Rouen. Spitfires and Hurricanes dipped up and around protecting the bombers and looking for trouble. Once over France the flak barrage hammered at the aircraft, but Hull kept his flight together and set a pattern of gentle weaving. Having a good commander who both led from the front and led wisely was vital to the success of a squadron. Eventually they reached the target and dropped their bombs. Maintaining a strict formation and protected by an umbrella of fighters the circus returned home.

A week later Patterson realised he was on a circus shipping sweep when he saw semi-armour-piercing bombs loaded into his aircraft. (The SAP bomb was used to blow holes in the plates of ships.) After a long and exhausting sweep over the North Sea no convoys had been spotted and he was about to turn back. One of the aircraft spotted fighters so Patterson climbed for the nearest cloud. On coming out of the cloud he spotted the Frisian island of Ameland. Without considering the situation or consulting his crew Patterson put the Blenheim into a dive straight towards a German flak position. Fortunately his crew realised what was happening, his gunner opened up and his bomb-aimer put their load right on to the enemy emplacement.

Patterson came back to a broad grin from Group Captain Bandon. But his stories are the exceptions that prove the rule. By the summer of 1941 2 Group casualties were so high that the average crew survival rate was seven-twelve operations. Patterson provided proof of this by becoming a Squadron Leader nearly two months later aged only 21. He had risen through the ranks thanks to his skill, luck and the desperate drain of his colleagues.

Two facts do not seem to have made themselves sufficiently clear to both Bomber Command and the Air Ministry. Firstly, the daylight light bombers had proved themselves to be incredibly vulnerable to attack during the battle for France. Speed and armament were definitely against them. Secondly the Luftwaffe experience in the Battle of Britain had shown how hard it was for fighters of limited endurance to act as escorts at the extreme of their endurance. Why should the Spitfires and Hurricanes have had any more success in protecting bombers over France than the Messerschmitt 109 had had over Britain? When Bomber Command had altered so much of its initial strategy because of the perils of daylight operations it is utterly mystifying as to why such operations were allowed to go ahead. It was partly to do with totally unreliable intelligence reporting. It was over optimistic and worse it was believed. The Command believed that Channel Stop sank or seriously damaged 200 ships between April and September 1941. After the war German records revealed that the actual total was 50. The operation also had a direct political reasoning. Britain was hardly on the offensive in the summer of 1941. Churchill wanted action to prove that the island may have been under siege, but it was capable of offensive sallies from its fortress. Hence the determination with which the policy was urged and pursued. It was an attempt to write large the fact that it was the ENGLISH Channel and not just a channel.

Fortunately, the raids on French port installations, and on the German warships taking refuge in them, were not half so costly. But by the same token little damage was done to most of the ships. The *Prinz Eugen* and *Scharnhorst* were largely unaffected. Sergeant Basil Craske took part in a raid on the *Scharnhorst* and *Gneisenau* when they were in Brest.[11] He remembered how well camouflaged the ships were and the hail of flak the Germans sent up to protect them. The *Scharnhorst* was moved to La Pallice, a considerable distance further south presumably to make an attack on her more dangerous still. Undeterred Bomber Command continued its attacks. Craske's Whitley was fitted with additional fuel tanks to allow it to make the extra miles. Carrying so much extra weight in its auxiliary fuel tanks the Whitley got off the ground only sluggishly. He came in from over the sea and avoided the worst of the flak, but the bombing was erratic and little damage could be seen. The raids continued without causing much damage but they did at least let the Germans know that the British were alert and aware of the movements of their enemy. Eventually, a Coastal Command crew managed to cause appreciable damage to the *Gneisenau* by putting a torpedo in her stern, but this was achieved by reckless bravery and the sacrifice of their lives. For this operation Flying Officer Campbell was posthumously awarded the Victoria Cross. But, as Harris was to write of another action, 'any operation which deserves the V.C. is in the nature of things unfit to be repeated at frequent intervals.'[12] A week later Bomber Command added to this damage with four hits putting the battleship out of action for several months. Finally, in this effort to help out the Admiralty, Hampdens were also put to work on expanding mining operations along the Biscay Coast.

There is little doubt that Peirse regarded the 'Maritime Diversion' as a nuisance. He was just reaching the point where he felt the lessons of 1940 could be put to good use. He had a clear directive to attack German oil production, which he was fairly confident Bomber Command could do in the right conditions. He also had alternative instructions to follow should the weather be against him. A strategy seemed to have been cobbled together and he wanted to test it. Just as he could have expected better weather he was stopped by the need to help the Admiralty. Peirse was not happy at this and his mood only improved once he was relieved of the burden of assisting the Admiralty. However, this does not appear to have been the case throughout the service and in the Air Ministry. Sir Charles Portal appears to have lost confidence in the oil directive. The weather had already made a hash of Peirse's confidence of continuing any sort of precision campaign. Between January and March 1941, before the maritime directive was issued, only 221 sorties were flown against oil targets as compared with 425 in the last quarter of 1940. Further it was estimated that some 3,400 sorties would be needed to see the directive through! Portal expressed 'serious doubts about the soundness of the calculations upon which our oil policy was based' and thought 'that the next best policy to the attack on oil, if the latter is discarded, would be mass attacks on industrial areas.'[13] For Portal the directive to support the Admiralty was therefore a perfect opportunity to break off an already failed policy. Showing the shrewd and flexible mind he was famous for Portal had probably guessed that the oil plan was wasting more British aviation fuel than it was destroying German. The Admiralty plan was an excellent way of calling off the oil raids without its appearing like a defeat. While the attacks against German shipping were continuing the Air Staff had a chance to reconsider their plans for battle. At the same time others, outside the Air Ministry, were also thinking hard about the bomber offensive and when they expressed their views to the Prime Minister it was to support a crude but clear plan of mass destruction.

On July 9 1941 Bomber Command received a most important and interesting new directive. The wording of the directive made it clear that an attack on enemy morale was considered to be the most important objective, for it stated that:

> the weakest points in his [the enemy] armour lie in the morale of the civil population and in his inland transportation system… I am to request that you will direct the main effort of the bomber force… towards dislocating the German transportation system and to destroying the morale of the civil population as a whole and of the industrial workers in particular.[14]

The directive was no more than a summation of a long-term drift in thinking and was not an entirely new departure, but it was much more clearly stated. Even the maritime directive had made allowance for an attack on morale. Air Chief Marshal Sir Wilfred Freeman, Vice Chief of the Air Staff, had written into those instructions that: 'Priority of selection should be given to those [targets] in Germany which lie in congested areas where the greatest moral [sic] effect is likely to result.'[15] When Harris, the Deputy Chief of the Air Staff, came to make a few amendments to these instructions on March 18 he wrote on the importance of attacking the u-boat plants in Stuttgart and Mannheim: 'Both are suitable as area objectives and their attacks should have a high morale value.'[16] It was a policy designed to confuse, disorientate and disorganise the enemy war effort by dehousing workers, to destroy their place of work, to destroy the administrative offices, to destroy the essential sanitation, lighting and power services of a city. It was also a policy designed to kill civilians. It was impossible to carry out such a strategy without killing civilians.

The reasons why Britain considered such a policy are easy to understand. The enemy was brutal and powerful and it needed to be crushed before it destroyed Britain. For Churchill it was a case of brutality to ensure national survival. He was as dedicated to the cause of killing Germans as the British people. The Germans had made the world suffer and now had to suffer themselves. It did not matter whether they starved to death, were burnt to death or blown into a thousand pieces, they had to be killed. It did not matter if they were men, women or children, whether they were old or young. For Churchill, as for so many British people, the Germans had started it all and now had to suffer the consequences. If the Germans did not want to die then they could surrender and have done with it. Once the war was over the British would be fair to the Germans, but while it was going on they would attempt to kill them all. The Germans were to be smashed crudely, incessantly until they were begging for mercy. The British were going to unleash savagery to protect civilisation. But could the RAF do it quickly enough and effectively enough to avoid any further military commitments?

Like the oil directive Freeman's order to attack German industrial cities had the advantage of being clear and succinct. During the moon period the Command was to attack the Ruhr and attempt to sever its communications with the rest of Germany. On moonless nights the bombers were to go into the general attack on Cologne, Düsseldorf and Duisberg. When the weather precluded attacks on the Rhine cities more distant targets were to be hit including Hamburg, Bremen, Hanover, Frankfurt, Mannheim and Stuttgart. The whole directive was given added importance by the German invasion of the USSR on June 22. Britain suddenly found itself with an ally and Bomber Command's efforts were designed to give assistance to the Soviet forces by drawing off as many aircraft as possible from the eastern front.

Was this the moment then for Bomber Command to begin its task of smashing Germany's capability to resist by whatever means possible? Peirse managed to drop more tonnage on Germany between August and October 1941 than in any previous period of the war. But it still was not enough. The effort was not as big as that expected by the government. The government believed it was pouring every effort into helping the campaign and wanted immediate results. Why were the results not as dramatic as those hoped for? It was well known that the smaller the raid the easier it was for the German defences to handle. Bomber Command needed to saturate those defences with mass attacks. After all Peirse now had 45 operational squadrons, with an average availability of 450 aircraft and crew. But the composition of these squadrons starts to tell the real story of this period of the war. Twenty-one were equipped with Wellingtons, two squadrons had Stirlings, two had Halifaxes and two had Manchesters. What had happened to the expected stream of new generation bombers? After the expectations of the spring it was dispiriting to find that British industry was capable of delivering only 54 per cent of those planned between March and June. The force was caught in transition. Some new aircraft had arrived, but not enough. There was also a catalogue of teething, and bigger, problems, with the new aircraft.

The Stirling was already proving vulnerable. Though a sturdy aircraft, it was well armed, achieved a good speed and carried a good bomb load; it had one massive defect, a low ceiling. Flying at lower levels than the other bombers it was always going to attract more attention from the enemy defences, or even become a victim of comrades bombing from a higher level. The Halifax was simply not available in large enough numbers. Much more serious was the problem with the Manchester. Its twin Rolls Royce Vulture engines soon proved to be unreliable and lacked sufficient power for an aircraft of such size. The engines were never made reliable either, no matter how much they were tinkered with. Wilfred Lewis felt the basic construction of the engine was flawed.[17] He remembered one Manchester blowing two pistons right out of one of its engines thanks to suspect bearings. Only 209 were made, production coming to a halt in November 1941. It was a disaster for such aircraft had been conceived back in 1936, factories had been made ready to produce them, but before they could get into their swing the design was being withdrawn. The waste of time and effort seemed incalculable. Fortunately, the designer of the Manchester, Roy Chadwick of Avro, had a brilliantly flexible mind. He quickly redesigned the plane to accommodate four Rolls Royce Merlin engines, the best of their time, and the Manchester was relaunched as the Lancaster. But no Lancasters were available for operations before 1942.

Further, no new navigational devices were available. Crews were still relying on dead-reckoning, astro-shots when skies were clear, and the odd glimpse of something on the ground. In May 1940 a Whitley crew had set out to bomb the Ruhr. Like many other crews their navigation had become confused and so they had bombed the second target instead, an airfield in Holland. After they had turned away they became even more confused when the Dutch coast failed to appear. A wireless fix was eventually obtained and they found they were over England. When they landed they had the terrible suspicion they had bombed a British airfield instead. This was confirmed when the Air Ministry revealed that the timing of the bombing coincided exactly with a mystery attack on RAF Bassingbourn near Cambridge. Fortunately, there were no casualties, though the unfortunate crew had to suffer hours of leg-pulling including the dropping of home-made iron crosses by aircraft from a neighbouring airfield. More seriously it led to the demotion of the skipper. On a wider level the story highlights the appalling navigational problems and the lack of success in finding a simple solution. Even if a crew reached the vicinity of the target they then had to make a fix on the target itself before attempting to bomb it with an inadequate bomb-sight. In order to help assess raids better Bomber Command was to fit night cameras. By April 1941 693 were scheduled to have been fitted, in reality only 165 had. When a crew became lost they had little option but to fall back on their alternative orders, which were to bomb a SEMO [Self Evident Military Objective] or a MOPA [Military Objective Previously Attacked]. However, even these rather vague instructions sometimes proved impossible to carry out.

Peirse was therefore almost back to where he started. In fact throughout the entire period 1939-early 1942 it is hard to escape the impression of confusion compounded by bad luck in every aspect of the work of Bomber Command. When directives seemed to be clear the weather was bad. When the weather was suitable the aircraft weren't available. When they did raid it was unclear exactly what had been hit and how hard. It was a metaphor for the way the entire war was going for Britain during this period.

Despite the lack of activity and a dearth of exciting stories the level of public debate about British bombing remained high. For the historian, aided by all the advantages of hindsight, it is incredible to find that British newspapers and journals were conducting a full scale debate about the targets, nature and morality of British bombing. What raises this incredulity is the fact that nearly all the arguments assumed *that Bomber*

Command was carrying out some form of devastating assault on Germany. The arguments of all the pundits and commentators, whether for or against bombing, were conducted on the assumption that the RAF was conducting an all-out campaign against Germany. The journalists and public had taken the promises of Bomber Command expansion to heart and were working within that framework.

One wonders what the British people would have made of the campaign had they been privy to the information that was about to come out in a report on British bombing by the civil servant D.M. Butt. In one sense the British people were not being deliberately misled because the vital prerequisite for such a deception was a Bomber Command strategy that needed to be concealed for whatever reason. It was this prerequisite that Bomber Command was lacking. At the very highest levels of the service there was an atmosphere of confusion and misunderstanding. Peirse and Portal had differing ideas as to what the campaign was capable of and what it should be directed at. If this was the case at the command level why should the British people have been clearer? What they shared with the Air Ministry and Bomber Command was a confidence in its power. The major difference being that the public believed it had already been unleashed, or was extremely close to it. While the official side of the fence was erring more and more on the side of unleashing its potential power once all the teething troubles were overcome. In all this the Butt Report was to be both an incredible shock and an incredible scythe, paring down the role of Bomber Command, clearing away much dead wood and choking weeds.

The gestation of the report can be found in the employment of D.A.C. Dewdney, an oil expert, by Portal when he was Commander-in-Chief. Dewdney found that there was no clear evidence upon which he could work. Photographs were vital, but few were forthcoming. Instead, by a set of estimations as to how many bombs could be expected to hit a target, he began making theoretical calculations. At first his method, based almost entirely on abstract mathematical calculations and probabilities, suggested that Bomber Command was making reasonable progress against the German oil industry. All this was to change with the raid on Mannheim on December 16 1940. A Spitfire of the new Photographic Reconnaissance Unit succeeded in photographing the city, a city the crews had claimed to hit bang in the middle and set ablaze. Instead the photographs revealed a scattered attack with many fires blazing outside the target area. On Christmas Eve some excellent photographs were taken of the two oil plants at Gelsenkirchen, which showed that they had received no hits. Dewdney immediately told Peirse that the bombing error was greater than 300 yards. He followed up these investigations with a tour of bomber stations in order to canvass the views of the crews themselves. By the spring of 1941 Dewdney had come to the conclusion that the campaign was little more than a ragged, random assault.

The need for night bomber and reconnaissance photographs identified by Dewdney was exactly the theme taken up by Lord Cherwell, Churchill's scientific adviser. He instigated a systematic analysis of the bombers' own photographs taken in June and July 1941. D.M. Butt took charge of the survey and about 630 photographs together with the relevant orders and reports. Butt's conclusions were truly shocking. He had studied only the two-thirds of crews that claimed to have bombed on target. Of these 'accurate' bombers he found that only one-third came within five miles of the aiming point. When it came to targets in the heavily defended Ruhr – a region almost permanently obsured thanks to its industrial haze – the figure fell to one-tenth. Two crews in five came within five miles of the target during the full moon period, but only one in 15 did during the dark period. Men risked their lives and yet did not inflict any damage on German industry. This evidence makes it hard to read recollections of the early part of the bombing war without extreme scepticism. Larry Donnelly's memoirs provide summaries of 4 Group's operations for each month until the end of September 1940. If June is taken as an example it can be seen that the Group bombed targets in Germany and France every night. No raid was aborted entirely and most aircraft dropped their bombs. Without in any way doubting the courage, honesty or endurance of those men it must be assumed that their efforts were wasted. This was something the British people were not allowed to find out. Now there was something to be kept back in its entirety.

Peirse, unlike Churchill, simply refused to believe it. Strange given the fact that Dewdney had told him something similar months earlier. Portal had some doubts, but did not waste much time debating them. Instead he threw his weight behind the development of new navigational aids and to simplify strategy into an area attack, based on fire-raising. For Portal Bomber Command could still win the war given an even greater commitment from British industry. At last that commitment was to be tied to one simple strategy, the smashing of German cities. Peirse, on the other hand, probably still hoped that given enough resources and a bit more experience his Command could carry out a precision campaign against specific German industrial targets.

Portal wrote to Churchill in an effort to maintain his confidence in the Command and the bomber as a war winning weapon. According to Portal Germany could be reduced to surrender within six months if 4000 bombers were made available to pound German morale into the dust of their ruined cities. Ironically, given Churchill's earlier enthusiasm for bombing, his reply was cool. He pointed out some details about the limitations of bombing and left it pretty much at that. Such a response must have stung Portal for he wrote back once again reminding the Prime Minister that an expanded Bomber Command offered the prospect of 'bombing on a scale undreamt of in the last war'.[18] Churchill's reply was studious. He maintained his, and the country's commitment, to Bomber Command, but he put a condition on it, 'it is the most potent method of impairing the enemy's morale *we can use at the present time*' [emphasis added].[19] With foresight he said that should the USA become involved in the war the ways and means of attacking Germany would become more varied. Further, it was unrealistic to expect a total paralysis of the Nazi empire when its sheer size allowed for vital production to be spread across a vast area. Churchill was merely reacting to strategic developments. Britain had one new ally, the USSR. The hope was that the USA would come down in Britain's favour sooner rather than later. This opened up more options than the bomber. However, Churchill did not divert British industry from its commitment to bomber production. The Command still had the chance to do something big.

Something big now meant to Portal a very definite commitment to the area attack. Experience, reflection and observation all pointed to this as the only possible option. In October 1941 the *Sunday Dispatch*'s air correspondent penned an article, 'A Year of Portal', seemingly based on an interview.[20] The ability of Bomber Command to hit hard was damned by the statement that raiding would continue 'to the best advantage considering equipment available'. This sounds like a very poor show. But then came the big point for the strategy did 'not embrace continuous reprisal raids *until they can be carried out on a permanently expanding scale.*' [emphasis added] Portal's mind appears to have been on his plan for 4000 bombers and a systematic smashing of German cities exacting at least the price in civilian lives achieved by Luftwaffe raids on Britain. Regardless of what other commentators have said it must be concluded that Portal was committed to the area attack as a way of killing civilians and reducing German morale. The ultimate effect would be the paralysis of German war industry.

Sir Charles Portal was not a vicious man, but he was a shrewd one and he was committed to the job in hand. Tall with thinning hair and an angular nose, a glance at his photograph shows the face of a man able to accept the realities of the situation. Here was no theorist making abstract predictions based on laboratory conditions. Portal was a man of great pragmatism. At this moment in time it was an asset. Later it seemed to become a handicap. He had realised that Bomber Command was not able to carry out its pre-war plans and devised a strategy that could be enacted. For Portal, like Churchill, the life of an individual German meant nothing. It was war, a war in which the Nazis appeared almighty entirely because they had the power to terrorise. Portal was out to fight fire with fire.

Unlike Ludlow-Hewitt and Peirse, Portal was a good communicator. He managed to get his ideas across both verbally and in writing. He knew Churchill wanted an offensive and had a clear idea of the way to deliver it. There never was a debate about the morality of the British bombing campaign. Why should there have been? Britain was up against the wall and like a penned animal it became vicious.

As Downing Street and the Air Ministry were finalising these plans a public debate about British bombing had started. But it was a debate that had 'jumped the gun' for certain commentators assumed a full-on offensive against morale before it had even been completely accepted by all in the Air Ministry and Bomber Command.

In the spring of 1941 the German blitz against Britain was tailing-off. It had been indiscriminate and awful. It had also fostered a wide range of opinions as to the best way of bringing the war home to the Germans. As the British came out of their shelters 'Reprisals' became the word of the hour. Every newspaper seemed to be conducting a subtle survey as to their readers' opinions on this matter. A *Daily Telegraph* leader in March took on an Old Testament line: 'As their [Bomber Command's] numbers increase, we shall come to the day when the command of the air will give us "Fire to scourge the foe, steel to smite and death to drive him down the unreturning way".'[21] Raids on Cologne in July had brought forth an equally strong response from the *Daily Express*: 'Cologne Gets It Back!' and under this headline, 'This is the news you have been waiting to read – how the face of Germany is showing the scars of the daily increasing blows with which the RAF is repaying the punishment Britain's cities so resolutely withstood.'[22] In September the *Daily Mirror* reported rather gleefully that RAF raids on Berlin had made Berliners 'squeal' and that Goebbels had 'turned on the sob stuff about poor little innocent Germany being cruelly bombed by the big, bad RAF'.[23] The *Daily Mail* took a dramatic stance on this attack on Berlin.[24] It crowed to its readers that Berliners had been turned white with fear and emphasised that they got to work shaken, withdrawn and subdued. They were also very, very tired having experienced 'the most terrifying RAF raid since the war began'. British hearts were cheered to learn the mood of Berlin was depressed and fearful. Just as Bomber Command had intended it was said to be a city without a future. The Nazis had wiped out towns and cities across Europe – what did it matter if the capital of it all was consigned to history?

In October the second capital of Nazism, Nuremberg, was hit. It was a further snub to Goering who had boasted that not a single enemy bomb would fall on the Reich. These were 'smashing blows... particularly deadly to confidence in the Nazi boasts that the Luftwaffe would always rule the air and keep Germany immune from bombs', according to the *Telegraph*.[25] It was important to repudiate the claims of Nazi leaders for such raids were a demonstration 'that Germany was not invulnerable (as her leaders had led her people to suppose) and that Britain was neither down nor out'.[26]

The *Telegraph* became a forum for much debate about bombing and attracted letters supporting many differing views. J.M.L. Service wrote in to advocate bombing of Berlin and all Germany's regional capitals to teach the Germans a lesson.[27] In the same issue C.D.L. Enoch wrote that: 'We ought, with utter impunity, to bomb Berlin and bomb it unmercifully.'[28] In order to avoid unnecessary bloodshed he said the RAF should announce these raids in advance thus allowing civilian evacuation to take place. 'A Medical Psychologist' took up the theme that seems to fascinate Anglo-Saxons, the Teutonic character.[29] The conclusion this correspondent reached was that Geman morale was extremely susceptible: 'they [the authorities] don't seem to realise that what merely stiffens our backs flattens a German.' Seeing as this was the case the best thing to do was to 'whip them as they have whipped us'. 'There must be thousands in this country,' wrote B.M. Maynard, 'who feel with me that until the people of Germany themselves are made to feel and suffer what they are willing to make others suffer it will be a very long time before we can shatter the prestige which the Nazi regime continues to enjoy.'[30] G.L. Braidwood added that: 'Civilian morale is the most important of all strategic objectives in this war and may ultimately be the crucial one... Berlin and Munich in ruins would shake Nazism more profoundly than the next twelve month's bombing of "military targets".'[31]

Such views cannot be dismissed lightly, as has often been the case with those anxious to prove the British were not interested in reprisal raids on Germany. Winston Churchill himself publicly encouraged a spirit of reprisals and revenge. On July 14 he reviewed the London fire and civil defences services in Hyde Park and then attended a luncheon at County Hall. His speech referred to what the people of Britain and other nations had suffered under Nazi bombers, he then proclaimed that:

If tonight the people of London were asked to cast their vote as to whether a convention should be entered into to stop the bombing of all cities the overwhelming majority would cry, *'No, we shall mete out to the Germans the measure and more than the measure they have meted out to us'* [The Decca recording of this speech reveals a good deal of table-rapping and noises of assent when this line is delivered]... Every month will see the tonnage increase and as the nights lengthen and the range of our bombers also grows, that unhappy abject, subject province of Germany which used to be called Italy will have its fair share too. [emphasis added]

Opinion against British bombing was of a relatively homogenous sort. Most people in this camp were not against bombing *per se*, only bombing deliberately designed to terrorise or as a reprisal. In May 1941 the *News Chronicle* report published a Gallup survey of attitudes towards bombing.[32] Gallup asked people across the country, 'Would you approve if the RAF adopted a policy of bombing the civilian population of Germany?' The results proved 'the people of Britain are in favour of reprisal bombing of Germany', but it was not as clear cut as that conclusion seemed to suggest. It was found that people living in areas away from the main German attacks, in the rural north west for example, were far more likely to support the idea of reprisals than Londoners. The actual figures quoted in the *News Chronicle* read as follows:

District	Approve of statement	Disapprove	Don't Know
Inner London	45%	47%	8%
Outer London & SE	51%	37%	12%
West Riding	65%	28%	7%
North Riding, Cumberland and Westmorland	76%	15%	9%
Glasgow and Clydeside	53%	43%	4%
Midlands	49%	40%	11%

'It would seem that sentiment in favour of reprisals is almost in inverse ratio to the amount of bombing experienced,' the survey concluded. A similar survey conducted six months earlier had found a much more even spread across the country with 46 per cent saying they approved of reprisals, while 48 per cent disapproved and 8 per cent did not know. The ensuing period had the effect of raising by 7 per cent for the whole country those in favour of reprisal bombing.

In revealing that most people did not like the idea of reprisals – most people who had actually been bombed that is – it made no statement about whether people believed all bombing was wrong or ineffective. Indeed, according to some sources the public had not rejected the idea of reprisals at all. Two months earlier Home Intelligence had reported to Churchill that 'people will want a lot of convincing that really heavy raids on civilian centres in Germany are not our most efficacious weapon.'[32]

Uneasiness about the idea of reprisals had first come to light in April, when the story got out that the RAF would flatten Rome if indiscriminate bombing of Athens or

Cairo was instigated by the Axis. This had the effect of forcing George Bernard Shaw and the Classicist Gilbert Murray to make a statement. In a letter to *The Times*, they made it clear they were not advocating any sort of armistice, but wanted to question the military effectiveness of night bombing. Statistics were produced to buttress their argument: 'If raids could be maintained nightly and each raid killed 1000 persons half of them women, it would take over half a century to exterminate us and a century and a half to exterminate the Germans.'[34] A rational argument, largely removed from morality, was therefore introduced to the debate. However, there can be little doubt that the morality of night bombing was impugned. The Labour MP for West Bermondsey, an area of London that had suffered heavily in the German blitz, Dr Alfred Salter, declared in the Commons that Britain's policy was one of revenge. He was listened to in polite silence, but nothing was done and it is doubtful whether many people outside of Westminster were aware of his comments. Consciences were stirring, not the least of which came from within the Church of England. Bishop Clifford Woodward of Bristol and Bishop George Bell of Chichester soon made their views known. When the Bishop of Bristol declared his doubts about the morality of night bombing he was condemned by the Mayor of Bristol. The *Daily Sketch* reported he had pointedly told the bishop civilians should not interfere in military matters.[35] The *Sunday Dispatch* took up the theme of the bishop's lack of military knowledge: 'he suggested that Britain – fighting with her back to the wall against the greatest gangsters in history – should sacrifice the weapon which will most help her to victory. If the battle of the darkness were to stop tonight it would mean that a war of attrition would last years longer.'[36] This was indeed a potent argument. Running throughout British life in the twenties and thirties was the shadow of the Great War, and in particular the memory of the appalling battles of the Somme and Passchendaele. Most Britons held a deep-seated fear of a repetition of such a struggle. Bomber Command was the answer, it would reduce Germany to submission without the need for a protracted land campaign.

Interestingly, the responses of the bomber boys themselves were never canvassed. Leading strangely insulated lives on their stations, popping into the nearest village or town for a good drink on their days off, they were far removed from the debates. Most crews treated the job with a sense of detachment. They bombed according to their orders and rarely saw anything on the ground. They tried not to imagine the effects of their bombs and were given the chance to avoid it by the massive effort of concentration required to fly their machines across enemy territory and back again. In any case they rarely felt pity for the Germans. This is not hard to understand. Every night the Germans used all their abilities to try to kill them. Every German knocked out was one less German to fight, every factory that lost a day's work was one less cannon shell in a flak gun. But these men could never judge for themselves the accuracy of their raids, nor tell if the enemy really was suffering. They relied on being told by their commanders. Ironically the civilian population all seemed to be experts and were busy giving their opinions to all who would listen.

But the controversy did not go away. Bishop George Bell wrote to *The Times*. A few weeks later the highbrow *Fortnightly Review* reprinted his original letter and threw open its pages to various figures.[37] Bell's argument accepted that British airmen did not target civilians, but their missions sometimes meant that civilians were accidentally killed. He wondered whether some sort of convention could be entered into and whether daylight attacks would be militarily more effective. The invited respondents then gave their views.[38] The Marquess of Crewe, a respected Liberal politician who had reported on alleged German atrocities in the Great War, doubted whether the RAF could do more to avoid accidental civilian casualties. Viscount Sankey, an expert on international law and arbitration, produced a dense, philosophical argument. He quoted international law, citing its edicts on the rules of war (which outlawed the bombing of civilians), and the seventeenth century English philosopher Thomas Hobbes. Sankey picked his way through Hobbes' complex theories on man's essential selfishness and the construction of the state and its powers which were invested in one individual empowered to act in its defence. Sankey therefore concluded that the complex issue of bombing policy was best left to Churchill. Lord Esher produced the argument that would be put forward by the apologists of a campaign against cities: in modern war there was no such thing as a non-combatant. Storm Jameson, a novelist with an interest in internationalism, opined that bombing was not effective, but then contradicted this conclusion by saying it would probably lead to the devastation of Europe leaving 'its fields soured, and its energy spent for a generation or more'. Dorothy L Sayers said it was pointless trying to come to any sort of convention with a man like Hitler, Henry Nevinson produced much the same point. According to St John Ervine the writings of Hitler, Rauschning and Clausewitz told a great deal about the German national character, he also claimed area bombing would reduce the morale of the German people. Richard Stokes, Labour MP for Ipswich, opined that night bombing besmirched the British cause: 'The guerillas in their tribal wars have made more sense than the leaders of our civilisation today... Bombing alone will not win the war and more destruction and the spirit of vindictiveness will ultimately get us nowhere. We should set an example to the world, not follow others down the slippery slope of abandoned principles.' This was the most interesting piece in the collection for Stokes was a passionate supporter of the idea of tactical bombing and the righteousness of the cause. Moreover he was a veteran of the Great War, winner of the Military Cross and the Croix de Guerre, no rarefied Bloomsbury philospher pontificating from an ivory tower.

One element united virtually all of the respondents and that was their disbelief at Bell's naivety. Bell was, ironically enough, one of the great believers of Bomber Command's claims to be a precision instrument. His criticism was built on the belief that in daylight and against areas declared to be legitimate military targets – therefore giving the Germans the chance to empty them of their non-combatants – the RAF would be able to conduct a brilliant campaign. On exactly how all this was to be achieved the bishop made no comment.

The *Spectator* invited J.M. Spaight, a civil servant at the Air Ministry, to express his views.[39] He argued that bombing was an extension of naval blockade and so was a typically British strategy. In supporting this he drew upon Admiral Alfred Mahan (1840-1914), an American expert on naval affairs whose books on strategy had influenced many in

North America and Europe. At times his argument was weak for he believed Hitler had invaded the USSR because British bombing had forced him to look for the raw materials and plant he had lost. However, he was right when he suggested the British had put far more thought into a strategic air war than the Germans, he noted that it was a 'British speciality'. At a point in the war when the British were showing that very little else was their speciality it was exceptionally important to continue with the campaign. Spaight thundered against those who wanted to compromise Britain's only powerful weapon:

> We cannot allow the weapon in which we excel to be blunted by people who see only the suffering which bombing and counter-bombing inflict, and, like the Bishop of Chichester and others, urge the abandonment of the night bombing which constitutes the main part of our strategic bombing... The bombing of factories cannot be stopped because women and children in the vicinity may suffer if they remain in the vicinity. They suffer also under the blockade.

But, just as the press had played host to a variety of correspondents calling for Bomber Command to wreak havoc on Germany, they also printed opposing views. E. Armstrong wrote to the *Telegraph* to say Britons were proof that morale bombing would not work. The unwritten subtext of his letter was that the Germans would react in much the same way as the British, and he added 'let us fight in as clean a manner as modern warfare can be fought'.[40] 'A Yorkshire Woman' shrewdly pointed out, also in the pages of the *Telegraph*, that the gestapo would ensure the obedience of the German people regardless of the effects of bombing.[41] German characteristics were referred to by 'Target' in a letter to the *Spectator*.[42] He quoted the diplomatic correspondent of *The Times*, who had written of 'the traditional force of German discipline in the face of hard tasks', all of which led 'Target' to believe there was 'no justification for the assumption that the enemy's morale will be undermined any more than that of this country.'

Others found the idea of reprisal and morale bombing unEnglish. Lord Queensborough, President of the Society of St George, wrote in the August edition of the society's journal that revenge was not true to the spirit of St George.[43] But he did advocate bombing of Germany to achieve the destruction of its war industries. Gallup's survey found a respondent who stated that reprisal bombing 'was not English... We're not Nazis. Let's keep our hands clean'.[44]

In November Richard Stokes gave his support to a petition against night bombing. Though it gained many sympathisers it also revealed the problems people had with the idea of giving up the advantage they believed the RAF held. A correspondent to *The Times*, John Derby, wrote of his inability to sign the petition.[45] He admitted he found the idea of bombing barbarous, that if a way round night bombing could be found he would support it. But he had reluctantly come to the conclusion the campaign had to continue, with the proviso 'that, whatever the provocation, we may never allow ourselves to depart from the standards which we have thus far maintained.' Retired Captain R.W. Keay pointed out the military realities in a letter to the *Telegraph*.[46] Having no long range fighter protection the RAF was forced to bomb at night. This simple fact he believed would silence the Committee for the Abolition of Night Bombing (as the group pivoting on Stokes, Bell, Shaw and Vera Brittain had named itself). A burning anger was never too far away, however. A.N. Bowyer declared he had read 'with astonishment and despair of the petition… Every bomb we drop on German territory by night or day is so clearly a blow struck for the simplest principles of humanity that the "tolerance" which deplores such blows reveals a weak, degenerate and shambling state of mind that would be pitiable in the ignorant, but is incomprehensible in thinking men and women.'[47]

In the middle of this debate a film was released which was to have a huge effect on the way the British people viewed the war generally, and the bombing war in particular. Official British propaganda cinema had not made much reference to the bombing campaign, especially when compared with the amount of attention the press was giving to it. Much of the efforts of the Crown Film Unit of the Ministry of Information had thus far been taken up by stoic 'taking it on the chin' films, such as Harry Watt's *London Can Take It!* (1940) and *Christmas Under Fire* (1940). Watt himself admitted they needed to be complemented by what he called 'a hitting back film'. This coincided exactly with Air Ministry feeling. An undated memo, probably of late 1940-early 1941 argued the need for the MoI to produce a good Bomber Command film. A list of suitable subjects and themes was drawn up, these included: showing the soundness of Trenchard's judgement on the need to impose an air blockade; the skills and training of bomber crew including how great a role teamwork and camaraderie play; the lessons taught in 1939 and the undoubted ability of Bomber Command to take the war to the Germans.

Much of this came together in Harry Watt's celebrated documentary *Target for Tonight*, a title taken from the jargon of the RAF. Watt was an established documentary maker by this time, his hallmarks being an ear for an accurate script and the use of real people performing their real tasks. Once Air Ministry approval was forthcoming Watt and the Crown Film Unit set about their task of making Bomber Command's work truly accessible to the public. Watt and his crew did most of their actuality shooting at Mildenhall, where Powell had earlier gained his footage.

The aim of the film was to be a realistic slice of life within the Command centred on the planning and execution of one raid. There was to be nothing out of the everyday routine, as Watt said it was to be 'utterly straightforward'.[48] In order to achieve this he trawled thousands of Operational Record Books and spent weeks just talking and listening to servicemen and women at Mildenhall. When forced back into the studio he laid great stress on getting the scenery and props absolutely right. An Operations Room was therefore reconstructed as a perfect replica of that at Bomber Command's High Wycombe headquarters. Then came the final coup, Sir Richard Peirse was persuaded to come along, with his number two, Air Marshal Sir Robert Saundby, to recreate in front of the camera initial planning stages for a raid.

Planning is, in fact, a crucial part of the documentary. A great deal of stress is laid on the fact that detailed information and intelligence flows through every level of Bomber Command and nothing is left to chance. When the target for tonight is chosen by Peirse and Saundby, they are seen to have a great deal of information about it. Friehausen is said to contain docks and a barrack complex and the latest photo reconnaisance has identified a secret oil plant hidden in the nearby forest. When details of the raid are passed down to the various squadrons ever more layers of intelligence are put down. The crews are given exact instructions as to map-reading, type of bombs, height at which bombs should be dropped and timings for the raid. This accorded entirely with the earlier Air Ministry memo which stated that: 'everything is done according to a long term and carefully prepared plan. The one word that can never be applied to British bombing is haphazard. Every bomb has its mark worked out for it perhaps weeks in advance.'[49] Indeed the Wing Commander warns his crews that: 'You must definitely locate the target before you bomb.'

Watt concentrated on one crew, *F for Freddie*, and assembled an eclectic bunch to emphasise the cross-class and multi-national flavour of Bomber Command. The crew contained three Englishmen, a Scotsman, a Canadian and an Australian. The understated, clipped, business-like speech is probably representative of the idiom of Bomber Command.

F for Freddie took off only after all the preliminary tasks of arming and fuelling, this stressed the wider teamwork involved. The British people received the message that it was not just a war of aircrews. They are seen to be reliant upon their comrades on the ground. The bomber flies through the night dodging flak and searchlights. There are some excellent and highly effective shots of the Wellington flying in the night sky, specially shot by Watt. But it was not just a film from the British side for the Germans are seen manning their flak guns and shooting. There is an acknowledgement that not everything is simple for the wireless set breaks down and they sustained a casualty. But the bombing is carried out with mathematical precision and only once the bomb-aimer is absolutely happy. The marshalling yard and installations explode into balls of fire. The crew then flies home to a short debriefing, in which they confirm that they have hit the target: 'Caused a hell of a big fire. Buckets of smoke. Visible, oh about 50 miles away.' As the crews shuffle out the intelligence officer and squadron leader make out their preliminary reports, and the film ends on the understated air of relief, satisfaction and tiredness summed up in: 'Well, old boy, how about some bacon and eggs?'

Reaction to the film was unanimous. Never had a film so accurately shown the nature of war and the quiet understated way with which Britons and their Commonwealth brothers go about it was the essential reaction. Watt stated that the trade show went very well, with the *Daily Express* critic asking to see the film again. However, this was the result of a near disaster for the press boys had all arrived late and tipsy after coming from the press show of a Hollywood production supplemented by free alcohol. The critics had mostly arrived late and miffed at being forced to leave their drinks. But, next day the *Express* labelled it 'the Greatest Story of the War' and argued that all cinemas in Britain should show it regardless of distribution deals. Within a couple of weeks it was carrying the story in serial form accompanied by stills from the movie. *The Times* praised its understated heroism, as did Graham Greene and William Whitebait. Dilys Powell called it 'a superb unemphatic statement of the work of Bomber

Command.'[50] It was a huge success with the cinema-going public too, making the Treasury a tidy profit on its £6000 investment, taking £73,000. Churchill, too, stated his approval. Quentin Reynolds of *Collier's Weekly* and narrator of Watt's blitz films, witnessed his reaction: 'Churchill was as tense as any movie fan when things looked bad for the bomber that was over Germany. He chuckled when its bombs hit the target.' Once again Commonwealth and allied countries reacted favourably, with Stalin receiving a print as a gift. In the USA the reaction was incredible given the fact that it was still a neutral country. Bosley Crowther, chief film critic of the *New York Times*, was fulsome in his praise. He told his readers of the ordinary way in which heroic events were carried out. He was clearly impressed by the stoic British and their ability to hit back at the enemy. Obsessed with American opinion, Churchill must have been happy the film met with such a warm reception. Bomber Command was the only proof that Britain was down but not out.

But what must have been of greater importance to Watt was the fact it was a success in the RAF itself. Three shows were put on at Mildenhall itself and each one was packed solid. It was then screened for the Air Ministry, at Fighter Command (twice) and at Bomber Command HQ (twice). Later the film made a circuit of various Bomber Command stations.

However it was hardly a real documentary, it hardly achieved realism and was hardly an accurate portrait of the capabilities of Bomber Command in 1941. *Target for Tonight* was obviously a great shot in the arm for the British people and indeed for RAF Bomber Command, which was feeling neglected by the Ministry of Information, but was already swallowing up so much of the British war effort. Watt himself half-admitted that the success of the film was due to the fact that it was simply the right thing at the right time:

> To give the real reason for its success one must realise the emotions of the people of this country at the moment it came out. All propaganda had been geared to encourage us to bear up, to stay cheerful and optimistic under bombs, mines, torpedoes, rationing and cold, while a constant stream of success stories came from the other side. There was no sign of cracking, but I believe, away back in many people's minds, there had arisen the doubt that we could ever win, although I am sure we would have fought to the end. Then came this film, actually showing how we were taking the war into the heart of the enemy, and doing it in a very British, casual, brave way. It was a glimmer of hope, and the public rose to it.[51]

The reality of *Target for Tonight* must therefore be questioned. One of the reasons for its success among Bomber Command must have been because it reassured them they could actually do something successfully. For crews unsure of what they were hitting down below it was good to see the Germans rocked. In its own way therefore *The Lion Has Wings* was more accurate because it had the excuse of showing what the war was like according to RAF planning before it had been changed by experience. *Target for Tonight*, by contrast, was more like wish-fulfilment. It was a dream that was a long time in the dying.

Bomber Command took up much attention that summer, for not long after *Target for Tonight* was released came an official history of the campaign so far, *Bomber Command:*

*The Air Ministry Account of Bomber Command's Offensive Against the Axis, September 1939 –
July 1941*. The book was nicely produced, containing many illustrations and was
designed to answer many questions about the campaign and ensure continued support
for it. Keeping people committed to the bomber war was subtly achieved by the admission that the campaign had not been entirely successful. Instead it was admitted that in
the early days the bombing war was not that good: 'the picture is sombre in places.'[52]
Truthfully, the work also admitted that by the winter of 1939 it had become clear 'that
we should have to accept heavy casualties if we attacked in daylight areas protected in
strength by shore-based fighters.'[53]

No one was allowed to doubt it was the Germans who had started the bombing war.
Included in this report was a defence against the charge that the British had started to
bomb civilians first. Readers were told British bombers did not fly against Germany
until May 11 1940, two days after the first German bombs had fallen on Britain, 'these
are the facts'.[54] Rather more powerful than these facts was the list of German attacks
on peaceful cities, Rotterdam, Warsaw and Belgrade. 'When the chances of retaliation
were nil or small the enemy did not scruple to slaughter helpless men, women and children by the thousand.'[55]

When it came to describing British bombing, a certain sense of ambiguity entered
the story. Though the attack on sites of economic importance was maintained it was
also admitted that larger areas were subjected to assault. From December 1940 it
stated, 'the weight of our attack began to be directed to special areas where industry or
transport was concentrated and where in consequence the greatest amount of damage
could be inflicted'.[56] Whether the Command was pursuing a campaign against German
morale was not made clear. Instead a strange, contradictory compromise was reached.
On the one hand: 'There are no outward signs of any break in morale, and it would be
rash to prophesy the moment at which they will appear.'[57] But it was also claimed that
'German morale has suffered, that it will go on to suffer is quite certain, that it is fast
cracking under the strain is, however, not yet true.'[58] Though a compromise, it represented nothing more than the truth as perceived by the realists at the Air Ministry and
Bomber Command. It was a rare and bold move, for it was a statement of truth aired in
front of the British public. It was indeed a rarity when so much of the public comment
on the campaign was either inflammatory, conjecture or both.

However, this refreshing strain of honesty was juxtaposed with some very wishful
thinking. According to the text British bombing of places such as Hamburg was so
accurate as to have no adverse effects on German civilians for only places of absolute
military importance were attacked. 'Knowing that our objectives were in the harbour
area, some of them [the people of Hamburg] with the connivance of their wardens
were in the habit of watching raids from afar off.'[59] German civilians were hardly likely
to be able to watch British bombing with interest for clinical bombing was well beyond
the capability of any air force in this period.

Having examined the problems of the early days of the war, stressing the lack of
numbers, the book ended on an up-beat note: more bombers, more crews, more
bombs. People were persuaded into continued support of the campaign by being told it

had suffered a couple of false starts and so could be neither judged nor written off. In fact Bomber Command, according to this approach, was just about to start its real work: 'One thing is certain. Bomber Command will allow no pause, no breathing space. Our attack will go on, fierce because it is relentless, deadly because it is sure.'[60] An element of romance was also allowed into this final summing up, a romance based on the conquest of the air, British racial traits and British history:

> Determination and endurance are said to be among the distinguishing qualities of our race. These they [the airmen] possess in full measure. They are of the same breed as the men who each evening notched their dragon prows into the sun's red rim on the first voyage to Labrador, who braced the yards of the *Golden Hind* to round Cape Horn and who stumbled with Scott from the South Pole.[61]

The reviewer in *The Times Literary Supplement* was impressed by it, especially for not claiming to be a chronicle 'of unchecked success'.[62] Having admitted weaknesses it made the predictions of future success more credible. The problem remained in Bomber Command and the Air Ministry, for they still had not quite decided on one single strategy. Matters were to come to a head in the disastrous autumn and winter of 1941.

In the winter of 1940 the Luftwaffe had been no more prepared to fight a night battle against bombers than the RAF had been. But during 1941 the German defences increased and became more effective. By the summer of 1941 Bomber Command was to find it was losing on two fronts. Not only did the force still lack a coherent, overall strategy, it was also being hit harder when it did attempt operations. The German invasion of the USSR did draw off much of the Luftwaffe, but it did not mean the west was left undefended. Indeed part of the Air Ministry's strategy was to raid more intensively in order to drag back aircraft from the east. German night-fighters gradually increased, by July there were 134 twin-engined fighters with trained crews in the west.

The commander of the German night-fighters, General Kammhuber, established a continuous belt of searchlights behind the coast and away from the main coastal flak batteries. The idea was to allow his fighters to attack British bombers without fear of being hit by their own flak. In practice this technique did not work too well, so Kammhuber worked hard on refinements. He developed a chain of radar boxes making an invisible grid of the night sky. In those boxes fighters could be controlled from ground stations and directed on to individual bombers passing through that box. When this was coupled with the introduction of radar sets to the fighters themselves German defences became far more effective.

Peirse now had a real problem on his hands. From July 7/8 to November 10/11 Bomber Command lost 414 night bombers and 112 day bombers, an awful statistic. Since the start of the war the Command had suffered nearly 5000 deaths on operations. A campaign devised to avoid the Somme and Passchendaele was in danger of becoming a repetition. New production was negated by losses. On top of this came the

Butt Report. Peirse's reaction was two-fold and contradictory. Firstly, he steadfastly refused to believe the report was a balanced account of events. But, he then seemed to change his approach. Desperate for success, Peirse actually turned away from the hardest and most important targets. Instead he put his crews to work hitting lesser targets. Hoping defences would be weaker too, he sought to provide his masters and doubters with proof of his ability to achieve results. But, if he was convinced the Command could continue with a precision campaign, albeit of a reduced and limited nature, why did he not press on with it? His double-edged approach looked like duplicity.

Sir Richard Peirse is a difficult character to understand and warm to. The face of a competent but uninspirational school master stares out of the photographs. Lacking good communication skills, he was hampered still further by taking charge of a weapon struggling to recover from a host of difficulties. He undoubtedly forfeited the confidence of his crews by his inconsistent policies. This, again, was not entirely his fault. A barrage of contradictory directives had left him little room to manoeuvre. But when he ventured from his headquarters his irritable, seemingly arrogant, detachment from reality could jolt his men. Sam Hall, a navigator, met his Commander-in-Chief soon after a disastrous raid on Berlin.[63] As a young man he was nervous at coming face-to-face with the boss. Peirse strode up to him and immediately created an awkward atmosphere by asking where he had been the night before as if he had no idea of his own orders. Having reminded Peirse that it was Berlin, Hall was asked how he had found it. Not wanting to say 'terrifying', he said, 'Very interesting sir.' Peirse then proceeded to ask how many raids he had been on. Hall was proud to have survived four and said so. Then came the crushing moment. Peirse turned on his heel and said out loud to the squadron commander, 'I'd like to speak to somebody with a bit of experience,' and walked off. Here was no great motivator. Crews were not likely to press on despite all difficulties if this was the response they were to face.

Peirse needed to gain some successes and having devised a new policy he was determined to get them. But he faced more problems. Poor weather continued to hamper operations and declining confidence among the crews meant that few were prepared to tough it out in order to bomb primary, or even secondary, targets. Matters reached a head on the night of November 7/8. Peirse decided to mount an all-out assault on Germany. He persisted in this plan despite a late weather report warning of storms, thick cloud, icing and hail over the North Sea, which would hamper the main part of his plan to attack Berlin. In every sense this was Peirse's attempt at a rebuttal on Butt for Berlin was not the only target, Cologne and Mannheim were also included. In total 283 aircraft were to be involved in these main assaults, with a further 99 on smaller operations. The attack, particularly that on Berlin, was a disaster. Of the 169 aircraft sent to attack Berlin, 21 were lost and seven Wellingtons were lost of the 53 despatched to Mannheim. The total cost for the night was 37 aircraft, or 9.7 per cent. This high averaged-out total covered the worse statistic of 12.4 per cent for the attack on Berlin.

Such a disaster would take a lot of explaining. The poor weather conditions were partly to blame, but they were made the full explanation by the press. Poor weather made reassuring copy, for it deflected from its significance as the final blow to a force which had been suffering heavy casualties for a long time. The *Daily Express* reported that: 'Britain's great new bombing offensive against Germany will not slacken because of the loss of 45 bombers during the weekend. I was told in London yesterday that all our frontline bomber stations are again at full strength, ready for another great attack when Sir Frederick [sic] Peirse, the Commander in Chief, gives the word.'[64] Their air correspondent then went on to explain how the weather had become the greatest enemy. A similar conclusion was reached in the *Daily Sketch*, the weather was to blame and the offensive would go on.[65] The report was of a rather stoical nature. It told readers the RAF would grind on with its campaign regardless. The RAF and the British people knew that heavy losses were to be expected, and the prospect of further losses was not going to stop them. A grim message for an increasingly grim war.

Determined reactions like these were all very well, but at Bomber Command and the Air Ministry an atmosphere of crisis prevailed. Both Portal and Churchill demanded an explanation. They also decided to ground most of the force in the interests of conserving its numbers. Effectively, Peirse was no longer in charge of his command, others were making decisions for him. Churchill summoned him to a meeting at Chequers, subsequently the matter was discussed by the cabinet. Portal then took up the investigation. He accepted that on this occasion the weather, rather than defences, had been by far the worst enemy. But he wanted to know why the force had attempted to raid at all given the conditions. By way of defence Peirse said he had been given an inaccurate weather forecast. But this did not tally with the fact that Slessor, commander of 5 Group had an accurate forecast and asked to bomb Cologne instead, thus avoiding the weather over the North Sea. Peirse had granted permission for this, which was effectively an acknowledgement of the difficult conditions. Portal also found out that one station commander had, on account of the weather, permitted only his most experienced crews to go out and had been shocked when they returned with their tanks almost empty thanks to the strain of fighting the elements. This made Portal still more suspicious. Just why had Peirse allowed such a large attack on Berlin given the conditions over the North Sea? Portal sent a further list of queries to Peirse.

The raid was still being debated when, on December 7, Japan attacked Pearl Harbor. Britain had gained an ally but also a new enemy for Japan was attacking British possessions too. A week after Pearl Harbor, Hitler declared war on the USA. The war had suddenly lurched into a new scenario. Britain had two huge allies, the USSR and the USA, but this was balanced by two very powerful enemies. Churchill immediately packed his bags for a conference with his new ally Roosevelt, in Washington. Portal accompanied Churchill, taking with him all the papers relating to the Berlin raid. Towards the end of the conference Portal took the opportunity to show them to Churchill. The Prime Minister must have reached the same conclusion as Portal – on January 8 1942 Peirse was relieved of his command and packed off to take charge of allied air forces in India and South East Asia.

Peirse was also paying the price for his earlier reckless confidence and the arrogance with which he faced many critics. His distinct lack of an electrifying 'Nelson touch' with his staff and crews had brought about a general malaise. But some sympathy must be extended to Peirse for it was a malaise that had started long before he came to command the force. Portal had clear conclusions, but he had arrived at them only after studying results over a period of time. The RAF had started out with a fundamentally flawed policy and it was only after experience and time had provided the opportunity to reflect that a new scheme could be decided upon. Peirse can be condemned for not reacting quickly enough, nor decisively enough once the hard evidence started to roll in. He had never made much of a splash with the press either. News of his sacking was kept from the British public. But the *Daily Sketch* proved far more astute than its rivals.[66] Of all the British papers it was the one to notice the tailing-off of air activity over the course of the winter. On January 9 1942 the leading column picked up on Sir Archibald Sinclair's speech on recent bombing given at the Guildhall in the City of London. The leader said: 'The British public has been for some time asking what has become of our bombers. Why have they not been making the increasingly severe attacks on Germany which were expected and which we promised?' It went on to note Sinclair's comments on the increased German defences, which led the *Sketch* to consider whether too much had been expected of the bomber offensive: 'we must not set exaggerated hopes on the possibility of bringing Germany to her knees by bombing alone, no matter how large the strength of the RAF grows.' What had happened to the great optimism?

The sacking of Peirse led to a brief interregnum before the new commander could take up his post in late February. The new commander had a huge task in front of him. After two and a half years of war Bomber Command did not seem much further advanced than it had been in 1939. 1941 had been a fresh start, but the bloom soon withered. A continued lack of a clear direction hampered it, as did the lack of the promised aircraft and other equipment. But Portal at least had come to a clear decision as to the future conduct of the campaign. With Peirse gone the new commander could get on and implement it. Despite gaining two huge new allies Britain was no closer to attempting an invasion of the continent in 1942. Bomber Command was therefore still the one way to attack the enemy directly. A new commander prepared to implement not a new policy, but one that had been thus far carried out in fits and starts and without proper resources, might still achieve great results.

CHAPTER FOUR

Unleashing the Whirlwind, February 1942–August 1943

Sir Arthur 'Bert' Harris was appointed to take charge of Bomber Command on the removal of Sir Richard Peirse. But there was a short period between his appointment and his arrival at High Wycombe, during which Air Vice-Marshal Sir John Baldwin of 3 Group took charge. Harris therefore missed the debacle of the 'Channel Dash'. The German high command had become increasingly concerned for the safety of the battle cruisers *Gneisenau* and *Scharnhorst* and the light cruiser *Prinz Eugen* at harbour in Brest. It was eventually decided they should bolt for Germany. On February 12 this carefully prepared operation was put into effect. Covered by awful weather and an umbrella of fighters, the warships sailed up the English Channel. The British did not become aware of the movements of these ships until they were spotted off Le Touquet late on in the day. In the winter afternoon a frantic effort was made to bomb the ships before night-fall protected them. Unfortunately for the British the poor weather and chaotic scramble to launch an attack led to the escape of the warships to Germany. It was yet another depressing blow for the British. Caught cold by the Japanese with Singapore falling, the Germans had now managed to sail ships right under their noses through the *English* Channel.

The newspapers were filled with a mixture of anger, indignation and resignation, as was much of the country. The leader of the *Daily Mirror* announced on February 13, 'WE CAN LOSE!'.[1] In the *Sketch* the leader asked why the Air Ministry had tried to bomb the ships only after they had left Brest. They also conceded that: 'it is useless to deny it. The successful escape of the *Scharnhorst*, the *Gneisenau* and the *Prinz Eugen*... has left us in a state of mingled stupefaction, admiration and anger.' Two days later Singapore fell. The Ministry of Information's Home Intelligence Weekly Report for February 16-23 noted that the public felt that it had been 'the blackest week since Dunkirk'.[2] However there was a key difference. Dunkirk had produced a sense of solidarity. This time the mood was of recrimination and introspection. For the newspapers and the public enough was enough. The war had to be fought by new men with new ideas or else. For too long Britain had suffered from its Blimps. The war had to be prosecuted not as a gentleman's game but with all the ruthlessness and dedication of the Nazis. Right could only be made mighty by the correct application of every energy, and it did not matter too much whether the British sense of sportsmanship was over-ridden in all this. Dear old blighty might cease to exist if it remained a matter not of whether you won or lost but how you played the game. February 1942 finally proved that Winston Churchill had been absolutely right in May 1940: 'Victory at all costs, victory in spite of all terror, victory however long and hard the road may be; for without victory there is no survival.'

Harris was the man for the job. Nearly fifty years old when he came to the job, Harris brought with him a wealth of experience and fierce determination. In the Great War he had joined the First Rhodesian Regiment, having emigrated from England to become a farmer in 1910. He saw action in German West Africa before transferring to the Royal Flying Corps. By the armistice he was commander of a fighter squadron. Deciding he liked the life he stayed on in the infant RAF, serving in Afghanistan, Iraq and Palestine. He got his first real experience of bombing in the Middle East. Harris saw how effectively bombing pacified rebellious natives. He soon became convinced bombing would make the role of an army much easier. In effect it would become the servant of the air force moving in to mop up after bombing had paved the way. The army would become more of a police service than an offensive weapon. He was partic-ularly influenced by his time in Palestine, where he served alongside the young Bernard Montgomery who was commanding the ground troops. Montgomery, in his brief tenure in Palestine, made good use of Harris's air arm. In turn this convinced Harris his deductions about bombing were correct.

In 1939 he returned to Britain as commander of 5 Group, Bomber Command. His organisational skills, commitment to training and willingness to learn from experience soon led to a transfer to the Air Ministry. From April 1940 until May 1941 Harris served as Deputy Chief of Air Staff under Portal. Though committed to all aspects of the air service Harris, like Portal, was a great advocate of Bomber Command: the two most important men in the Air Ministry were therefore 'bombers'. In May 1941 Harris was placed in charge of a RAF delegation to Washington detailed to investigate the American aviation industry and then place orders with the best firms. Harris was in Washington when he heard of his new appointment. He was ready, willing and able to lift Bomber Command out of the doldrums. Harris was unquestionably the best man for the job. He had experience of commanding a Group in war; he had held an impor-tant organisational and policy post; he had a personal relationship with the commanders of the US air forces and, like Churchill, he had an absolutely unquench-able desire to win.

Harris brought all these qualities with him to High Wycombe. He also brought a simple, clear strategic insight based on absolute pragmatism. He knew that without better navigational and target finding aids Bomber Command had no chance of conducting a prolonged or widespread precision bombing campaign. Instead Harris advocated the area offensive. But it was not seen as an alternative. Rather for Harris it was a policy in itself, just as likely to be effective as a precision campaign. Harris's view was supported by Portal and the Air Ministry. Just before he had arrived back in England the Ministry had issued a new directive which stated that 'the primary object of your operations should now be focused on the morale of the enemy civil population and in particular, of the industrial workers.'[3] At last Commander and Air Ministry were in agreement. Harris wanted a general attack and the Air Ministry wanted to attack morale. This objective could be achieved only by the general attack. Harris later denied in his war memoirs that he was interested in attacking enemy morale believing the dislocation and disruption of industry was far more important. However, it is difficult not to believe this was a judgement passed in hindsight. The collapse of German morale and the collapse of German industry were part and parcel of the same strategy by this point.

All along the British public knew deep down what this policy actually meant and were glad of it. What they did not want to do was think about the real details of its implications. They shied away from the savage in them. After the war they would try to deny it altogether.

But no sooner had Harris sat down at his desk than he had to face a barrage of criticism of his Command. A.V. Hill, Independent Conservative MP for Cambridge University and one of the brains behind the development of radar, denounced the role of Bomber Command in the Commons.[4] He told those present that the idea of bombing a well-defended enemy into submission, or of seriously damaging him either in terms of morale or material, was an illusion. His scepticism was revealed in his claim that most bombs hit nothing of importance – hinting that the Butt Report had leaked some of its details. The policy, he concluded, was an absolute disaster compounded by being allowed to continue. A few days later Sir Stafford Cripps added his view that the concentration on bomber production for the European campaign had disastrously weakened the air forces in the Far East. Cripps stated his belief that a few more aircraft in Malaya and Singapore could have staved off calamity.

At the beginning of March the *Daily Mirror* surveyed the air offensive. All earlier optimism had disappeared, instead it was convinced that all was chaos and confusion. It asked its readers rhetorically: 'What *is* our plan? What *is* our air policy.'[5] Sneering at Sir Archibald Sinclair, it asked for forgiveness for doubting that the British were actually mounting an air offensive. Further, it asked whether the aerial second front in aid of the Red Army had ground to a halt making Britain an ineffective ally of a nation fighting desperately hard.

But Harris was not a man to be worried by such doubts. He had every intention of proving the worth and capabilities of Bomber Command. Crucially, his conception of the capabilities of the Command had been shaped by three years' experience of war and he knew exactly what could and could not be done.

Bomber Command therefore had a policy to follow. It was not a new policy, but one that had been unequivocally announced by the Ministry to the Commander. It was a policy about to be followed by a man who was determined to make the area offensive work. This was the new departure. Harris did not invent area bombing, but he was committed to it as no previous commander had been. As the *Daily Express* said of Harris on the announcement of his new job: 'he is credited with the saying "Crack 'em hard; crack 'em all the time."'[6]

The big fear in the winter of 1941-2 was that the bomber force would be reduced to nothing. The lull in the offensive had allowed the force to re-gather, but it was still no bigger than it had been a year earlier. Squadrons were still being siphoned off to the Middle East and Coastal Command, leaving Harris with 469 night bombers and 78 day bombers. However, the Lancasters were just about to become more numerous, as were the Stirlings and Halifaxes. But against this the Hampdens and Whitleys were being phased out. The RAF had also conducted a short-lived experiment with American Flying Fortresses, but found them unsatisfactory for its purposes. The Fortresses produced too much of a vapour trail making them easily visible during daylight operations and the Sperry bombsight was not reliable over 20,000 feet. An American bomb-aiming expert failed to place a bomb on Bremen when taken on a Fortress mission by the RAF. The fact that these aircraft went on to gain such an excellent reputation was, in fact, partly due to the improvements made to them in the light of their RAF service. The size of the Command was therefore not increasing much, but its bomb-carrying capacity was, for the new machines were all much better weight lifters. British industry was now fully committed to the bomber campaign. No other combatant nation harnessed as much industrial effort to its bomber force. Though the Official Historians estimated that only 7 per cent of the nation's manpower was taken up by the bomber offensive, this figure did not take account of the qualitative input of the nation. Each bomber took a huge number of man-hours to build, and the more sophisticated the machine the more it took. For example, each Spitfire required 15,200 man-hours; each Whitley took 52,000, but each Halifax swallowed no less than 76,000 man-hours. Occasionally, the workers were included in the glory of the RAF achievements. In June 1942 the *Daily Telegraph* said all Bomber Command successes started in the aircraft factories.[7] Gaumont News had run a special feature on a Halifax factory a month earlier. British workers were driving themselves hard. If the cost in time was high the financial cost was enormous.

The supply of crews was also picking up. The Empire Air Training Scheme (soon to be renamed the Commonwealth Air Training Scheme) was running well, and sending on a constant stream of men to the OTUs. A shrewd move was the decision to dispense with the second pilot, giving rudimentary training to a crewmember who could then take charge in the event of an emergency. Harris was against this move accepting it only once he had won the concession of an automatic pilot in every bomber. In March 1942 the so-called 'New Deal' in training was introduced. Under its rubrics the navigator was stripped of his bomb-aiming duties. Navigation was to be his sole responsibility. A specifically trained bomb-aimer (also known as an air-bomber) was introduced, but he was also given some training in air gunnery to act as front-gunner. The bomb-aimer and Flight Engineer were given some flying instruction, allowing them to act as the 'pilot's mate'. The wireless operator was trained as an air-gunner and there was one 'straight' air-gunner. Despite this reorganisation accidents at OTUs were frequent, between 1939 and 1945 5,327 officers and men were killed and a further 3,113 injured. The problem was that the aircrews who carried out the training were often tired from tours of active operations and used under-maintained aircraft.

However, this did at least mean the new crews were receiving instruction from men who had been at the sharp end and they were using aircraft with their own ingrained characteristics. Training was not, therefore, a totally sterile and unrealistic experience.

A great advantage was the development of the *Gee* navigational device. *Gee* was a device originally conceived to help blind-bombing. Though it proved incapable of doing this it was an important navigational aid. It allowed a navigator to fix his position by consulting an instrument, the Gee Box, which received pulse signals from three separate stations in England. *Gee* computed the difference between the receipt of these signals and from this the navigator was able to make a fix. But *Gee* was a line of sight device and so could not bend with the curvature of the earth, thus giving it a limited range. It was, however, a great help for bombers trying to find targets within its range, and in giving bombers a good start in the search for targets beyond. *Gee* brought the Ruhr, the Rhineland and the North Sea ports of Bremen, Emden and Wilhelmshaven within range. Though it could do nothing about seeing through cloud-cover over the target it would at least bring the bomber to the correct location. It was the perfect instrument to complement an area attack.

As Harris digested the situation, he was given a further impetus by the acceptance of the Cherwell Report. Lord Cherwell, chief scientific adviser to Churchill, carried out a survey of the extent of dehousing and lost working days as a result of German bombing of Britain. He then worked out how many bombs and bombers would be needed to reduce German industry to nothing based upon the dehousing of workers. It gave a further justification to a bombing strategy already in existence. However, not all were convinced by this. Sir Henry Tizard, Cherwell's great adversary and a father of the radar project, questioned his calculations. He said that Britain might lose the Battle of the Atlantic before the bomber force necessary to deliver this tonnage of bombs could be built. He further questioned the ability of the crews to find and hit the right towns and cities consistently. Tizard's doubts were then given additional weight by Professor Zuckerman's findings, the man who had reported on the effects of bombing on Hull and Birmingham. It was Zuckerman's statistics on which Cherwell had based his work. Zuckerman said that Cherwell had used his figures in the wrong way, he doubted whether enough houses could be destroyed and whether German morale would crack.

To a certain extent Harris was unconcerned by these arguments. He knew what he wanted to do and how he wanted to go about it. Of far more significance to him was the role and opinions of the Ministry of Economic Warfare. Naturally enough this ministry took a great deal of interest in the structure of German industry and economics. It then tried to transform its knowledge into instructions as to the most efficient bombing policy. For Harris this was unwarranted interfering in his own Command. The Ministry of Economic Warfare was forever identifying 'choke-points' in the German economy and urging Harris to hit them believing it would cause the Nazi war machine to seize-up once and for all. Harris complained that when he hit these targets no magical collapse occurred. The Ministry then changed its mind and told him he needed to hit yet another target. It concentrated on a few areas, German aircraft manufacture (particularly the vital component of ball-bearings), German submarine plants and German oil reserves. When pressurised to raid these targets Harris would do so. The first came relatively soon into his command. Augsburg with its MAN factory, producing diesel engines for submarines. Ironically this was not actually as high on the MEW's list as the ball-bearing plants and led to a fierce argument between Harris and the MEW, for they felt they had been deliberately kept in the dark and would have urged attacks elsewhere. Twelve Lancasters were despatched in a daring daylight raid deep into southern Germany. Only five managed to return to England. The Lancaster crews displayed intense gallantry and skill in reaching their target, as Rod Rodley's recollections prove:

> Our route took us from the north end of Lake Constanz across another lake, where we turned north towards the target… We were belting along at full throttle at about 100 feet towards the targets. I dropped the bombs along the side wall. We flashed across the target and down the other side to about 50 feet, because flak was quite heavy. As we went away I could see light flak shells overtaking us, green balls flowing away on our right and hitting the ground ahead of us. Leaving the target I looked down at our leader's aircraft and saw that there was a little wisp of steam trailing from it. The white steam turned into black smoke, with fire in the wing… It looked like a blow lamp with the petrol swilling around the wings and the centre section, igniting the fuselage and the slipstream blowing it down. Just like a blow lamp.
>
> He dropped back and I asked our rear gunner to keep an eye on him. Suddenly he said, 'Oh God, Skip, he's gone. He looks like a chrysanthemum of fire.'
>
> One other of our aircraft caught fire just short of the target, but kept on, dropped the bombs and then crashed. The raid was suicidal. Four from 97 Squadron got back, but only one from 44.[8]

A very heavy price had been paid, particularly as five of the 17,000 lb bombs failed to explode.

Harris's fear of daylight raids had been proved correct, and confirmed the difficulty of hitting a small, distant target with precision. But, for a public deprived of glorious incident it was a shot in the arm. The *Daily Mirror* trumpeted that: 'If anybody is inclined to ask the usual question as to whether such an enterprise were worthwhile, the answer is that anything is worthwhile which so glorifies the human spirit, and sets an example to inspire the whole nation.'[9] For *The Times* it was 'one of the most brilliant and audacious [raids] of the war'.[10] The report stressed the endurance and skill of the pilots and the technical supremacy of the Lancaster. Low-level daylight bombing by heavy aircraft was rightly regarded as a major achievement. One of the pilots later went on the BBC to tell his story, and his words were then published in a book of RAF broadcasts, *Over to You* in 1943. The air offensive was back in the public imagination.

But for Harris this was no more than a 'panacea target', as he called them. He fought a running battle with the Ministry of Economic Warfare over such targets. A great deal of pressure was put on him to attack the ball-bearing plant at Schweinfurt. American raids on the plants had already produced a formidable casualty list, when Harris sent his force in on February 24/25 1944 it also achieved only negligible results. His doubts about the demands and realism of the MEW's schemes were heightened still further. Attacking the Rumanian oilfields at Ploesti was another 'panacea target' according to Harris, and he pointed out the difficulty of flying across the width of Europe with a heavy bomb-load. Even if the raid was successful he doubted whether it would have a decisive effect. He watched the American raids on this target with deep scepticism. The high casualties the USAAF suffered seemed to prove him right.

The problem with the attack on German industry, and by extension the whole concept of strategic bombing *per se*, was that no one really knew what to attack and for how long. No one really knew anything about the Nazi war economy and no one could actually identify a genuine bottleneck or choke point. Despite reams of statistics produced by the Air Ministry, Bomber Command, the MEW and a host of other interested scientists, economists and civil servants, an accurate survey of the nature of the German economy was never produced. It was the ultimate irony of the campaign.

But this was not the only irony. The entire assumption of the British government was that the Nazi economy was dedicated to making war. This assumption suited Bomber Command for it meant any attack on Germany affected the war-making capability of the Reich. However, this was completely wrong. There was a huge amount of slack in the German economy, and a high level of chaos and disorder. 'It has been said that if Britain had understood in 1941 how powerful and how effortless was the German industrial machine, what enormous untapped potential it possessed, how widely its resources were dispersed, no one could have contemplated the overwhelming task of attempting to crush it by bombing.'[11]

When Albert Speer, Hitler's architect and one of his chief courtiers, was given the job of restructuring Nazi industry in 1942, he had to make sense of chaos. Bombing was hardly likely to have a catastrophic effect at this time for the Nazi economy was still producing things like typewriters, refrigerators, domestic wireless sets, electric blankets, electricity meters, riding boots and spurs. What did it matter to the German war effort if bombs fell on any of these targets? Speer reorganised and took-up the slack. The bombing war could be regarded as a race. Would the allies work out the real German soft spots before Speer could find ways of reorganising and methods of negating allied bombing?

But Harris did not know this, and he was convinced that bombing could work. He had a strategic objective, the dislocation of German industry by the area bombing of its major towns and cities. In order to pursue this he needed a tactical re-think too. Peirse had often split his force between a number of targets and raids had progressed over several hours. Harris, on the other hand, believed that the key to success lay in concentration over the target area and that it should be only one target area. He argued that such a concentration would overwhelm both civilian and military defences. From this point raids unfolded according to the following pattern: an initial dropping of high explosive designed to block and crater roads, thus making it very difficult, if not impossible, for fire engines and rescue squads to move around. Then would come blast bombs to smash windows and blow off roofs. Finally masses of incendiaries were dropped to burn their way through the shells of buildings created by the blast. Bomber Command was becoming a force dedicated to the god of fire.

The early weeks of Harris's command were rather reticent and sleepy, he had no intention of being rushed into action. Harris was avoiding the mistakes of Peirse. He was determined to unleash his force only when the weather was right and when he could use an appreciable number of his machines. In the meantime he got on with the job of mining. Harris believed mining was an excellent way of completing the training of his crews. It gave them combat experience without exposing them to too much danger, and helped the Navy in their war against the submarine and enemy shipping. 'The laying of these mines was critical. They had to be dropped in fairly shallow water in order to be activated. So navigation was a problem, as these operations were carried out mainly by night,' pilot Sir Lewis Hodges recalled, showing just how such activities helped to sharpen skills.[12] Harris then scored an early success against the Billancourt Renault works outside Paris. This raid was followed by the first big smash of the Harris show, Lübeck.

Lübeck was beyond *Gee* range, but the new device and the clear weather gave the force an excellent chance of success, and a success is what they delivered on the night of March 28/29. The wooden heart of the old town burnt furiously and it was estimated that thirty per cent of Lübeck's built-up area was destroyed. For some reason news of the raid did not reach the press until a similar set of raids on the Baltic port of Rostock were completed. Rostock was raided on four consecutive nights between April 23-27. Again fires spread furiously and 60 per cent of the Hanseatic port was destroyed. Goebbels used the term 'terror-raid' for the first time and public opinion in Germany was shaken.

The response in Britain was tremendous. The public had been desperate for some good news and this was good news. The *Daily Mirror* carried the banner headline 'We Smash Their Towns One By One'.[13] Here was no ambiguous statement, the meaning behind the statement was, and is, obvious. Here was the weapon that would teach the Germans the meaning of war. The *Mirror* report told its readers that a new era in aerial warfare had opened. It lionised the raids as the two most destructive of the entire war. As with many other reports about this raid the role of the new breed of heavy bombers was stressed. Such references must have cheered the workers of the aircraft industry. The people of Rostock had suffered 'an hour of concentrated fury'. The report was accompanied by photographs, with the triumphant headline 'What We Did to Lübeck and Now Same to Rostock'.[14] The *Daily Express* also published aerial photographs showing the ruins of Lübeck. A similar air of retribution pervaded its description: 'This is what happened to the city of Lubeck, where 150,000 Germans live and work, on the night last month when the RAF decided to render an English translation of the word "blitz". No city in all Britain ever suffered so much in a single attack.'[15]

The press revelled in the fact that Goebbels had labelled the British 'terror raiders'. For many this proved the attack had worked and the hypocrisy of the Germans had fully revealed itself. Goebbels also claimed both Rostock and Lübeck were of no military importance (this ignored the fact that both were used as supply centres for the eastern front and Rostock contained a Heinkel factory) and were fine examples of medieval Hanseatic architecture. The RAF was thus a gang of barbarians destroying

Europe's architectural history. He said that the Luftwaffe would retaliate with attacks on British cities of historical and architectural interest. The result was the famous 'Baedeker Raids', so called because they were aimed at towns covered by the distinguished tourist guides. This was not really regarded as a disaster in Britain, for once again it was taken as proof of the profound effect of the RAF raids. A leader in the *Daily Sketch* proclaimed that 'the RAF is going on to bomb Germany heavier and heavier this summer no matter what the Luftwaffe decides to do'.[16] At much the same time Herbert Morrison, Minister of Home Security, addressed the Commons. His attitude was one of grim determination, it epitomised the new British spirit which was coming close to the maxim 'kill or be killed':

> The Nazi crocodile tears over the destruction of certain old German buildings in British raids do not in the least impress the world which well remembers how those same Nazis openly boasted and gloated over the fires and destruction among so many of our own lovely and ancient monuments... If the British determination to attack the German war machine means that civilians and ancient buildings may suffer, we see nothing in this to boast about as the enemy did when he flaunted his bombing power in our night skies. But the foul canker of Nazism must be cut out, and until it is the body of the German nation will suffer. Let the German people themselves draw the moral. If they cannot or will not win the victory over the bloodthirsty tyrants who rule them, we will.[17]

In only one aspect was Morrison a little off course: surely there was just a bit of an element of gloating in the coverage and response to the British raids?

It was certainly felt by some, for a correspondent to the *Spectator* wrote of his unease. F.L. Jackman stated that the British raid on Lubeck was entirely concentrated on the ancient heart of the city containing few buildings of military significance.[18] He went on to ask whether 'terror bombing [is] now a recognised feature of British air policy?... either we are descending to Nazi methods or the RAF marksmanship is not what we have supposed?' The editor replied in terms very similar to the official language of the Air Ministry, a ministry reluctant to admit what it was actually up to: 'a reasonable explanation is that the RAF is pressing its attacks on military objectives even when some destruction of civilian life and property is inevitably involved. There is no evidence... of the deliberate bombing of civilians in order to destroy morale'.[19]

At much the same time as Bomber Command was re-establishing its credentials with the public an interesting film, depicting aspects of its work, was released. Powell and Pressburger's *One of Our Aircraft is Missing* developed further the partnership the two had struck-up in such memorable films as *Spy in Black* (1939) and *49th Parallel* (1941). Though concerning the crew of *B for Bertie* and also taking an official phrase for its title – the BBC would announce how many British aircraft were missing as given to them in Air Ministry communiqués – unlike *Target for Tonight* it was not really centred on a bombing raid. Rather this film concentrated on the escape of a Wellington crew from occupied Holland following their bailing-out from their damaged plane. The bomber gets into trouble on the homeward flight after it has bombed the target and set it merrily ablaze. But the film then becomes an odyssey for the crew move from person-to-person, community-to-community as the Dutch help them to escape. Finally they come to a port where the final part of their escape is engineered by a Dutch woman (Googie Withers). Just before they leave they hear the sound of bombers crossing the coast and sirens sounding. German soldiers run in all directions shouting out commands. At this point it must have been impossible for the cinema viewer not to think that British bombing policy resulted in the deaths of innocent people in the occupied lands, whose governments in exile were gathered in London. But just such thoughts were answered by the Dutch woman's stirring speech to the airmen assuaging consciences everywhere:

> You see, that's what you're doing for us. Can you hear them running for shelter? Can you understand what that means to all the occupied countries? To enslaved people having it drummed into their ears that the Germans are the masters of the earth. Seeing those masters running for shelter. Seeing them crouching under tables. Hearing that steady hum night after night. That noise which is oil for the burning fire in hearts.

At the end of 1942 2 Group used its daylight bombers to effect a daring raid on the Philips wireless factory at Eindhoven. The reaction of the Dutch was very similar to the above sentiments, for the *Daily Mirror* said that 'all the crews reported that the Dutch waved enthusiastically to them as they flew low over the fields and villages of Holland.'[20]

The final shot of the film shows the crew of *B for Bertie* standing by their new machine, a four-engined Stirling. The implication clearly is that with these new machines the British will be able to start more fires than the Germans will ever be able to put out. Bosley Crowther of the *New York Times* gave a British film the thumbs-up, he noted the realism and excitement of the film: 'Inside the plane quiet men are setting instruments for the precise job of destruction below. It is probably as close to the numbing excitement of a raid as one is apt to reach in a movie theatre.'[21] Like *Target for Tonight* it provided the American people with proof of British intentions to fight the war with deadly earnest. In Britain it met great public success. The RAF was seen as the service with most glamour, with most potential to tell the Germans the British were alive and kicking and were about to kick much harder.

Another film, this time a documentary 'short', implied a war in which civilians were being killed. *Biter Bit* was made for the MoI by the famous director Alexander Korda, with Ralph Richardson taking on the role of the narrator. Aerial photographs of German cities were used to show how much damage had been done to Germany. The commentary went on to add that the Germans were 'whining' because they were finally getting the rougher end of the deal. It was, indeed, about to get a whole lot worse for the Germans.

Lübeck and Rostock had definitely made a splash. Harris was determined to keep interest in Bomber Command high both within the government and with the general public. The magic figure of a 1000 bomber raid entered into his calculations. He sought

Portal's and Churchill's permission for the enterprise. Both men were equally electrified by the idea and it was granted with the operation given the ominous title MILLEN-NIUM. For Harris this was a chance to show what a reasonable force might achieve. Few within the Air Ministry or Bomber Command had forgotten the demands for a 4000 bomber force, a big success over Cologne would give such demands a huge boost.

Scraping up crews and machines for the operation was a gargantuan task. Harris approached everyone for help – Coastal Command, Army Co-operation Command, Fighter Command and Flying Training Command. All agreed to help. However, the Admiralty overturned Coastal Command's original decision. The reasons for this seem twofold. Firstly, the losses in the Atlantic were reaching an alarming point and every aircraft was needed on ocean patrols. Secondly, Harris's well-known disdain for the Navy and direct intervention in the Battle of the Atlantic had probably made itself felt at the Admiralty. It fostered a certain spirit of 'if you're not going to scratch my back I'm certainly not going to scratch yours'. In order to make up the numbers Harris had to throw in his Operational Training Units including pupils and instructors. The final figure was 1043 bombers, the majority coming from Bomber Command's own resources. But, as if to stress the fact that British bomber production was still lagging, the backbone of the force was the 598 Wellingtons, which were supplemented with 338 Lancasters, Halifaxes, Stirlings and Manchesters and 107 Whitleys and Hampdens.

This was a huge risk. The entire Command was committed to battle. Whatever else might be said about Harris it is impossible not to admire his confidence and clarity of purpose. If anything went wrong it would be his fault, he would be answerable to the country. In carrying out such an operation he knew he could leave nothing to chance. Yet more tactical refinement was introduced for the raid. The bomber stream was adopted. This meant that each bomber was allotted a height band and time slot that they had to stick to in order to avoid collision. This allowed the bombers to be concentrated and then forced through very few boxes of the Kammhuber line thus overwhelming the fighters within them. The German controllers could only orchestrate six potential interceptions in one hour. The next innovation was the time over the target. At the start of the war four hours had been allowed for a raid by 100 aircraft. Harris allowed two hours for 234 aircraft over Lübeck, but here he ordered the bombing to take 90 minutes. Collision was a very real danger, but it would ensure that the local defences would be completely overwhelmed.

The final requirement was a good night. Harris wanted to use the moon at the end of May. The weather cleared after an agonisingly long time, but weather over Germany was still a problem. Potential targets in Germany were severely narrowed by this hazard, it ruled out Hamburg, Harris's preferred choice, and so Cologne was chosen instead. On May 30 the bombers set off. The *Gee* equipped aircraft of 1 and 3 Groups – carrying Sir John Baldwin, the Commander of 3 Group – led the force. They arrived over the target and started fires which acted as a beacon for the rest of the force. A devastating attack then unfolded. Cologne suffered the loss of 12,840 buildings, over 600 acres were razed, 2500 fires were reported to be burning. It was another incredible jolt to the Germans. Goering refused to believe the reports of the Cologne police, but the exodus of refugees proved that the attack had hit home.

The success had been achieved seemingly at low cost, for there is some debate about the mathematics and the calculation of British losses. Forty-one aircraft lost is the usual figure, or nearly 4 per cent of the force despatched, but John Terraine calculated it at closer to 91 aircraft or just over 9 per cent.[22] Whatever the debates of historians, the important point is that at the time the lower figure was believed both officially and by the public. An amazing success had been achieved at very little cost. Harris got a publicity bonanza.

The earlier doubts of the *Daily Mirror* were swept aside. The front page carried the headline: '1,500 Planes in Biggest Raid: 3000 Ton Bomb Storm.'[23] The leader gloried in it all. Unwittingly, perhaps, it implied that Britain was now set on a path of terror, for it stated that what Goering had started the British would finish. Glorying in the fact that the British people had withstood the punishment of the Luftwaffe, it was now time to repay the loan with massive interest. A sense of awestruck wonder filled the leader. There was the definite feeling of a new start, of a tightly coiled spring flicking back with venomous power. Bomber Command was about to regain its position as the darling of the British press. The British heavyweight standing in the ring looking for all-comers. The *Daily Express* took a similar line to the *Mirror*, its headline read unambiguously 'The Vengeance Begins!' Revenge was certainly in the air – in every sense – but it had to be tempered, no one wanted to be accused of naked savagery.[24] It was carefully pointed out that Cologne was no Bath, Exeter, or Norwich. As a great German 'munitions centre', railway junction and river port it was the hub of Germany's western frontier and the gateway to its empire in France and the Low Countries. Having established the validity of the raid, the bomber boys themselves were praised. The language almost had a biblical ring to it. It was as if the young men of Bomber Command were those of Gideon's army surrounding the camps of the Amalakites and Midianites, bringing death and destruction and the righteous anger of the Lord. Goebbels' claims of terrorism were mentioned. 'Certainly the force with which we can now smite German war centres carries terror to the home of German war workers around them.'[25] However, Cologne was regarded as an absolutely legitimate industrial target and so was not an act of terror. Here was the strange game the British press and people were to play for the rest of the war. Vicariously glad to be causing intense misery to their enemies, but pretending that it was part of a simple policy of hitting vital centres of industry.

The *Daily Telegraph* quoted an air bomber who said that the blitz of London at its worst was nothing like the raid on Cologne.[26] For its leader writer the attack was a vindication of the Trenchard doctrine. For the *News Chronicle* the bombing was a way to cleanse the Germans of their blood-lust:

> The German people must be made to feel in their bricks and bones the mad meaning of their rulers' creed of cruelty and destruction... if by the ferocity of our retribution we can convince them at last that violence does not pay and induce them to become good citizens of the world – then the loss of

their monuments will be as nothing compared to the contribution to our common inheritance which their conversion to civilised conduct will make.[27]

There was a gratifying sense of the raid marking not the culmination but the start of a campaign. The *Daily Mail* told its readers that 'Cologne was just the beginning. Nothing will stop the development of this attack now. We are committed to a long-term policy of strategic bombardment. We have spent a tremendous amount of time and effort in building up a force of giant bombers.'[28] It then noted that 'the air offensive is not designed primarily to shatter German morale, though that aspect is important. It is intended to smash the enemy power at source.' Winston Churchill also took up the point that the campaign was only the beginning. On June 2 he told the Commons: 'I may say that as the year advances German cities, harbours, and centres of war production will be subjected to an ordeal the like of which has never been experienced by any country in continuity, severity or magnitude.' The BBC announced its sorrow to hear of ordinary women and children who may have suffered for the stupidity of their menfolk.[29] But it was then stressed that it was a society still following Hitler and his gang of crooks. This was followed up with a reminder of the German wickedness in the bombings of Warsaw, Rotterdam, Belgrade and Coventry. It was stated that the Germans had cheered on these bombings, had rejoiced in them. Not just some Germans but all, women and children. When that was considered sympathy evaporated. The BBC announcement made it clear that all Germans regardless of age and sex should be able to recognise evil and do something about it. In not doing so they made themselves targets of war. As with the inquisitors the British were using flames to purify souls.

The newsreels also had a field day over Cologne. Paramount covered it under the title '1000 A NIGHT ONLY START';[30] Universal called it the 'WORLD'S GREATEST AIR RAIDS';[31] Gaumont announced '1000 – RAF lets Hitler have it right on the chin!'.[32] This was a quote from Harris himself, who was also seen in the Movietone coverage giving out his message to his crews: 'If you individually succeed you will have delivered the most devastating blow against the vitals of the enemy. Let him have it right on the chin.' The commentator announced dramatically: 'The hours of darkness over Hitler's Germany are about to be made hideous... Round the clock with the RAF... Tonight is going to be very, very interesting. A thousand bomber night.' Gaumont reminded its viewers of the just retribution the Germans were receiving:

Do you remember how those jackbooted German troops marched over Cologne Bridge to re-occupy the Rhineland in 1936? That for the world was the rebirth of German lust for bloodshed and conquest. It's poetic justice that it should be Cologne that got the first raid of the Thousand Plan. What's coming to the Nazis in Germany is what they would do to us if they could: and still will, if they can... Never forget – it was Hitler's Germany that started this: we never wanted it: and since our would-be peacemakers, for all their trying, failed to keep the peace, let the men of war get peace back again in the only possible way... the hard way.

Thanks, Bomber Command! You're doing a grand job: this was Cologne, making war with factories: but the RAF has thrown a spanner in the works.[33]

Harris never missed an opportunity to get more coverage for Bomber Command and Cologne provided him with an excellent chance. He encouraged the distribution of aerial photographs showing the damage caused at Cologne and in other recent raids. He told the Public Relations Department to pick some good, clear photos for they could be quite hard to interpret. He added in his own inimitable style: 'even Service Officers in many cases have not the vaguest idea what they are looking at when viewing an air photograph... one never knows whether they are vertical photographs of air damage or the south end of a bathing beauty looking north!'[34] The last piece in this publicity jigsaw was the recollections of the men who took part. The National Savings Movement released a publicity record containing the reflections of Flying Officer Friend, who told of the immense fires and the immense number of planes over Cologne, 'they were doing exactly as we did, going in according to plan, coming out according to plan, making their way home'.[35]

The irony of Cologne was that it built up another huge weight of expectations Bomber Command could not really live up to. Every aircraft had been scraped together for Cologne. It was impossible, given the usual number of machines available, to repeat that kind of raid too often. June and July actually proved to be very frustrating for Harris, and his attacks were often made ineffectual by the usual combinations of the German defences, weather and insufficient numbers. Morale in Bomber Command slumped again after the rally of the spring, it all seemed to be slipping back to the bad old days. Harris was exasperated by continuing losses to Coastal Command, and then the underpowered Manchester just had to go, most of which were in the already depleted 5 Group. The late summer saw the Blenheims phased out and the Hampdens went over to training units, but the Wellingtons, those old faithfuls, were kept on.

2 Group was probably in the worst position. Harris had definitely set his face against both light bombers and daylight operations. Morale in 2 Group was low, re-equipment with new British and American aircraft was moving forward very slowly, but Harris did not have much for them to do. The Boston had proved to be a sturdy, powerful aircraft as had the Mitchell. The Mitchell was particularly liked for its ability to survive heavy fire and dish it out too. But the Ventura was a failure, it suffered from indifferent performance and handling. Ironically, this was one of the aircraft ordered by Harris and his team during his trip to the States. This did not stop the Group from continuing with some very important work such as mining and the bombing of the Philips factory. It would also be the first Group to use the brilliant de Havilland Mosquito, a lightly armed but very fast and strong, wooden bomber. The Mosquito was to become one of the most important and famous aircraft of the war. A good measure of the advance of the British aircraft industry can be seen in the fact that the Mosquito could carry a bomb load equal to a Wellington, but 170 miles per hour faster, 300 miles further and 21,000 feet higher. However the successes of the Mosquito were to come.

In the summer and winter of 1942 Bomber Command did not look good. Evidence of poor morale came in a variety of forms, a lack of desire to push on to the target, early returns due to 'defects' with the aircraft, listlessness and lethargy. Survival was a tough task especially as the tour system looked as if it had been designed to ensure death. Each man was expected to complete a first tour of 30 operations before an extended leave. Then would come a second tour of 20 operations. After 50 raids a man could not be forced to fly again, though he could volunteer to continue. The tour system had a fascinating web of technicalities governing the calculations of operations. All raids to Germany counted as one raid, but those on Belgium, Holland and France as far as 6⁰ longitude and mine-laying off those coasts counted as 1/3rd of a raid. Mining inside German waters and certain heavily defended French ports and harbours counted as one raid. Leaflet raids did not count, nor did an early return that did not involve dropping bombs on Germany. There were also different rules for different sections of Bomber Command. Mosquito squadrons' tours were set at 50 operations; Serrate and Intruder (see chapter five) 35 and Pathfinders 45.

For all Harris's innovations the early part of his tenure saw high losses and little chance of a man reaching the end of his tour. Some men cracked under the pressure and refused to fly. The Air Ministry and Bomber Command were hardly sympathetic to such cases and psychiatric treatment was often frowned upon. Men relieved of operational duties were classified as 'LMF' – 'Lacking Moral Fibre' – stripped of rank and put to work on ground duties. Such a response was grossly unsympathetic and old fashioned, for the Great War and the cases of shellshock had greatly advanced the study of psychological illnesses. Maurice Chick was on the receiving end of a stinging rebuke for cowardice even though he was only acting according to usual operational procedures:

> I was introduced to the new C.O.
> 'I've heard of you,' he said, 'I believe you weave.' [This refers to the gentle rolls a pilot conducted in order to minimise chances of being hit by staying too long on a steady course.]
> I said, 'Yes, sir, I do weave.'
> He replied, 'This will stop henceforth. Pilots on my squadron will give their gunners a steady platform and will fly straight and level.'
> I said, 'With due respect, sir, if you lay down this order you will lose most of your pilots.'
> He then accused pilots who did this of being yellow. I was upset about the accusation and wanted to vent my feelings by striking him, but my colleagues thought I was going to do something of the sort and I was whisked out of the Mess and told to go to bed.[36]

Air gunner J.M. Catford found his job and life in the RAF exciting.[37] But he admitted to feelings of intense fear over a heavily defended target, especially if there was a host of searchlights illuminating the sky. He sweated so much that he turned off his electrically heated suit and he felt his sweat soak his clothes. As soon as the aircraft was through the worst he immediately froze again and turned his suit back on. K.M. Pincott, a navigator, remembered briefings in which crews looked round and tried to identify those men thought to be near collapse.[38] Everybody thought it would never happen to them. But once Pincott's crew suffered a casualty fear entered his life and the next few raids were an ordeal. For Pincott, as for many others, there was no alternative other than to carry on: 'In spite of the fear you pressed on regardless – there was not any real alternative – and you lived each day with the expectation that it could be your last.' Another navigator, B. Bressloff, confirmed this feeling.[39] He survived an emergency landing in a badly damaged Lancaster. The bomber smashed through a line of saplings and caught fire. For a few moments Bressloff was trapped by the fire engulfing both the fuel and oxygen tanks. Using all his physical and mental energies he managed to get out of the escape hatch and sprinted away before the aircraft exploded. His skipper, Flight Lieutenant G.A. Thorne, was taken away to hospital. The crew then had the horrific experience of seeing the charred body of their wireless operator. The next morning a Lancaster from their own squadron came to pick up the remaining crew. For Bressloff it was an appalling moment for as he was about to clamber aboard he found himself paralysed by fear. He knew it was irrational. There was no danger. They were only going home and yet he could not move. He also realised that if he did not force himself onboard he would never fly again. Somehow he summoned up the resolution and did it. He went on to complete his tour of operations and did not experience such profound fear again.

Throughout the war about 200 cases a year were classified as LMF, or slightly less than 0.4 per cent of all bomber crews. This is an amazingly small number that is a tribute to the general spirit of the air crews, but belies the millions of battles men must have had with their imaginations and minds.

Men tried to stay in control by filling their leisure hours. Living under stress and the constant fear of death made their spare time riotous and manic. On their days off men tried to drown their memories. Maurice Chick recalled how many days he spent in the pub drinking solidly.[40] Rod Rodley felt there was little point in saving money when death was always so close.[41] Like Chick he spent a lot of it on drink. On occasions mess parties were thrown. They were usually explosive affairs. If a piano player could be found they would sing lustily. A particularly mad game involved stacking chairs in a pyramid. Then one person with soot-blackened feet climbed to the top and put his foot marks across the ceiling all the way to the chimney.

As a reward for facing death night after night bomber crews were given luxuries and treats unobtainable to the rest of the nation. Rationing was not applied to the diets of aircrews. They received extra milk, fruit juice, sugar and eggs. Breakfast always consisted of fat rashers of bacon and fresh eggs. Treats most British people tasted only in their dreams.

Before the preparations for a raid began in earnest, or if operations had been cancelled, men wedged in visits to the station library or film show. They played football and cricket or just sat around chatting. On nights when they weren't flying they would go into Lincoln, Cambridge, Nottingham or York for a good soak in the pub. It was a life of routines but such odd ones that they became completely detached from the civilian life that surrounded them.

During the quiet period of November 1941 to February 1942 losses stood at 2.5 per cent. From February to May 1942 it went to 3.7 per cent and then from May to August it went up to 4.3 per cent. Finally, from May to December it went up again to 4.6 per cent. It was already known that losses much over 4 per cent were unsustainable insofar as it would lead to insufficient crews to provide the leadership and experience necessary for keeping the new crews together and effective. Halifax squadrons were particularly badly affected thanks to the host of niggling problems this otherwise sound aircraft suffered from in its early models. From March to August 1942, 109 Halifaxes were lost from 1770 sorties, a casualty rate of 6.2 per cent. In the light of this the whole Halifax force had to be rested for nearly a month in order to recuperate and recover.

But the public did not get to know about this. Just before, Cologne Sydney Veale's *Warfare in the Air. The RAF at war since the Battle of Britain* was published. It was a semi-official publication, written by the Secretary of the Air League and the editor of *Air Review.* The book was generally an up-beat assessment of the role of the RAF and of Bomber Command in particular. Veale stressed the care with which the RAF delivered its bombs right on to legitimate targets and so was actually a little old fashioned. Most literature by this period was – consciously or not – implying a much wider spread of bombs. But it was yet another example of the high profile of the RAF and Bomber Command. With the continuation of the new campaign in the summer against targets such as Bremen, Duisberg and Düsseldorf, the public continued to be fed a diet of bomber glory. Few saw through the statistics, Cologne had vindicated and galvanised the image of the air offensive. The *Spectator* noted in July that bombing was still the 'best available offensive weapon towards beating the Germans', and a few weeks later followed this up with an urge to raid intensely and 'in quick succession to prevent repair of damage and shatter morale'.[42] A *Telegraph* leader of early August argued that bombing was reducing German industry to its knees and was particularly helpful in blunting the supply of submarines to the Battle of the Atlantic. The BBC broadcast from a bomber station in the winter, it was filled with a quiet, stoical heroism, but the atmosphere did seem to reflect the toll the campaign was taking:

> The men themselves do not speak to you of the hazards and dangers unless you ask them; and they do not talk thus among themselves. But men back from a raid have been known, when a loved flight commander or comrade has been hours overdue, to hang about, tired out, but just not going to bed, hoping against hope. Next day the phrase used is laconic: 'He didn't get back.' The word 'he' means half-a-dozen men and an aircraft. It could have been used over a thousand times of the bombing of Germany in the past twelve months.

> For, as our onslaught has grown to dimensions the world has never seen before, rising to the crescendo of thousand bomber raids, and inflicting heavier losses than we ourselves have suffered, our own job has got stiffer, more hazardous... I have spoken of these hazards of bombing because we had better know, I think, what this task of bombing Germany means to the men who do it and what they overcome.[43]

Sober indeed.

The continued erratic nature of bombing accuracy forced the same old question to the fore, how could concentrated bombing be achieved? The *Gee* navigational device could get, or give bombers a good start, to the target, but it could not be used to pinpoint the actual target area. For some time Bomber Command had been using 'raid leaders' in attempts to improve target finding and marking. The sensible answer was to gather together the best navigators and crews to form a 'target finding force', which would then mark the target for the rest of the force. This idea had been floating around for some time. Group Captain S.O. Bufton, Director of Bombing Operations at the Air Ministry, was the brain behind this scheme. Bufton, while flying with 10 Squadron had pioneered the technique of dropping coloured flares on the target and then firing a Very flare in order to attract other crews. Once at the Air Ministry he set about trying to convince others of the merits of this scheme.

Bufton soon had wide support from within the Ministry, but when he put it to Harris the response was not encouraging. Harris resented what he saw as Bufton's interference within his own realm. It was the start of a fractious relationship between the two men. Harris said such a move would create an elite formation within the Command and he did not like the idea. His preferred scheme was for more experienced men to remain with their original units passing on that experience. Harris's Group Commanders, anxious not to lose their best crews to some new formation, backed him in this.

A compromise was suggested by Bufton. Would Harris allow six ordinary squadrons to be gathered together and stationed in close proximity to one another, giving them the chance to exchange ideas, compare methods and develop target-finding tactics? Harris still refused. In reply he said that *Gee* and bombing cameras would improve matters across the board. Cameras revealing performance would ensure a tremendous sense of competition according to Harris. But lurking below the surface were two opposing concepts of the bombing war. Harris was on the side of the fence that believed in sheer weight of numbers to achieve an overwhelming area offensive. He believed Bufton's attempts to improve accuracy were a cover for returning the Command to precision bombing, a complete waste of time, machines, bombs and crews in his opinion.

The argument continued throughout the summer and it was eventually left to Portal to decide. He came down on that of his Staff Officers, a new unit was to be established, known as Pathfinder Force. Harris does appear to have made a mistake here. His reasons for not supporting the creation of the force do not appear as persuasive as those in favour. To Harris's credit, having received a direct order he was commendably quick in demanding a special badge for the new force and an immediate rise of one rank for all men seconded to it. This was designed to compensate for the slower promotion within this smaller unit and longer tours of duty. After some procrastination the Treasury agreed to the pay demands and on August 11 the force was born. It was Harris himself who suggested the title Pathfinders and he kept them under his control, for at this point they were not given Group status but led directly by orders from Bomber Command. Bufton had wanted Basil Embry to lead the force, but for some reason Fighter Command would not release the man who had an incredible flying record and had escaped from behind German lines earlier in the war. Instead his Senior

Air Staff Officer got the job, the Australian Wing Commander D.C.T. Bennett, a navigation expert and holder of several long-distance flying records. He established his headquarters at Wyton, later moving to Castle Hill House, Huntingdon.

Bennett was a tough character, not easily browbeaten. His appointment came not long after he had arrived back from neutral Sweden. It was a trip forced on him by the loss of his aircraft in an attack on the battleship *Tirpitz* moored in a Norwegian fjord. He set very high standards for his men and achieved them. This was largely due to his personal example. He visited his men regularly, flying between bases in his own aircraft. Occasionally he would slip out on raids to see conditions for himself. Having gained extra knowledge he immediately set about finding ways to implement it.

Harris never actually issued a firm order as to who was to form the new squadrons. Rather than the elite being asked to volunteer, as had been hoped by Bufton, Harris allowed each Group to designate a squadron to move over. Four 'ordinary' squadrons thus found themselves made into an elite force. Each Group was made responsible for supplying replacements for 'its' squadron within the new unit. This led to arguments between Bennett and the Group Commanders, for he sometimes suspected that they were dragging their heels over sending their best men. The only man to give him consistent support was Air Vice-Marshal Carr of 4 Group and it is interesting to note that both Bufton and Bennett had served under him.

No sooner had the Pathfinder Force been gathered on August 17 than Harris ordered them to be ready for operations immediately. (Incidentally, this was the day the United States Army Air Force carried out its first raid on the continent from England.) Only a day after the men transferred they took part in a raid on Flensburg. The Pathfinders had many problems to deal with. They had no standardised equipment, flying all the aircraft of the Command; they had no special flares or bombs for marking targets in a distinctive way. To get round this they were soon cobbling together their own special incendiaries, designed to burn very brightly, the so-called 'Pink Pansy'. They were also, like the rest of the force, just about to face the winter weather. The Germans were beginning to jam *Gee*, the flak defences were growing and German night-fighters were beginning to make it impossible to use the full moon period of the month. However, the 'Pink Pansy' soon proved to be a great success and it was clear that good and distinctive target marking was a great help to the attacking force.

The winter of 1942 was to prove influential on the course of the Bomber Offensive for reasons other than the purely operational. Much of the winter was taken up with preparations for the Casablanca Conference between the British and the Americans. The aim of the conference was to thrash out a combined strategy. British and American airmen decided to support each other in order to promote the cause of strategic bombing. American air forces had been building up slowly in England, but its leaders too had a grand vision of the capabilities of a strategic air offensive. In the case of the Americans the clamour may have been even more insistent, for at this point the air force was not a separate service but still a part of the army. General Ira Eaker, commander of the US 8th Air Force, was therefore determined to push his case and win greater independence for his force. In other respects Eaker faced similar problems to Harris. As fast as his aircraft arrived in England they were shipped off to the Middle East. With the British victory at El Alamein in November this became all the more acute, for the British and Americans then opened a second North African front with an invasion of Tunisia. In January 1943 Eaker only had about 80 bombers in England. Harris lent him great support, claiming that the deeds of the American bombers had produced excellent results and that Eaker should be given a chance to really prove himself and his force. Eaker, in turn, made loud pronouncements about the achievements of Bomber Command. It was all very cosy.

In private, each man doubted the strategy of the other. The Americans were convinced they could succeed where the British had failed, namely in daylight precision bombing. Eaker doubted whether Harris's area campaign could hit anything of real substance. Harris took exactly the contrary view, lacking fighter protection and a guarantee of clear weather he pointed to the British experience as definitive. The conditions would not allow for a successful daylight precision campaign. But both men believed passionately in the air offensive and both wanted to fight off the claims of their armies and navies for more resources.

Portal gave assistance to Harris and Eaker by submitting a paper on the future of the bomber offensive to the Chiefs of Staff in November. He wrote:

> I am convinced that an Anglo-American bomber force based in the United Kingdom and building up to a peak of 4000 to 6000 heavy bombers by 1944 would be capable of reducing the German war potential well below the level at which an Anglo-American invasion of the continent would become practicable.[44]

Portal predicted the loss of six million German homes, making twenty five million Germans homeless and a million German dead. Civilian casualties were expected and it does not appear as if there was any concern about that fact.

By this time the bomber offensive had been going on for three years and had not produced very much, apart from the odd spectacular raid. Other service chiefs, less susceptible to the line printed in the newspapers, were not sure whether such a backing of the bomber force was a good idea. Sir Alan Brooke, Chief of the Imperial General Staff, expressed his doubts openly. As might be expected the First Sea Lord, Sir Dudley Pound, was even more critical. The Admiralty was desperate for more long-range air power to help in the crucial battle being played out on the seas. In the end the Chiefs of Staff came to a compromise, they supported the idea of a force of 3000 bombers, to be operating from bases in Britain by the end of 1943.

Portal could now go to Casablanca with a fair amount of confidence. The key man was Churchill, if he could be persuaded the battle was won. In the event Churchill was persuaded that the bomber offensive should go ahead, but it was for reasons entirely different from Portal's, Bomber Command's and Eaker's. The nightmare that haunted Churchill was of being bounced into an invasion of northern Europe in 1943. He knew that Britain was in no position to launch a full-scale invasion of Europe, and that

America had neither collected enough men nor enough equipment in Britain for such an operation to have any chance of success. The raid on Dieppe, carried out in August 1942, had ended in bloody failure and had fully revealed just how tough German defences were. Churchill was intent on dissuading the enthusiastic and unblooded Americans from their schemes for invasion. To that end the bomber offensive was the perfect alternative. It could be argued that it was a European front in itself, and therefore deflect criticism from Stalin about the lack of a Western Front, and it was the vital prerequisite to any invasion of the continent. Military operations could be confined to the Mediterranean and more experience gathered by an invasion of Sicily and Italy. For these reasons Churchill was a supporter of the bomber offensive. The bombers at Casablanca were going to get their own way, not thanks to the power of their rhetoric, but due to the pragmatism of Churchill and his wider strategic grasp.

The airmen were jubilant, 1943 was really going to be their year. The western allies had now made it a part of their grand strategy. Harris and Eaker were out to prove that bombing alone could win the war. But Portal stuck more closely to the letter of the Casablanca agreement and the Trenchard doctrine, bombing was to reduce the enemy so much as to negate his ability to successfully resist invasion. A fresh directive was needed for the new Combined Air Offensive. A range of targets was drawn up to give as much assistance as possible to the eventual invasion. First priority was given to submarines and the Battle of the Atlantic. It was no good America mobilising vast armies and the huge potential of its industries if it could not get them across the Atlantic in safety. Ports and submarine component factories were to be hit. Next in line was the German air force, its factories and depots. In order to achieve a massive attrition of the German air force and on Germany's general ability to wage war, ball-bearings, synthetic rubber and synthetic oil plants were also identified as key targets, as well as military transport industries. The opening phrase of the directive covered all this *and* an attack on German morale:

> Your primary aim will be the progressive destruction and dislocation of the German military, industrial and economic system, and the undermining of the morale of the German people to a point where their capacity for armed resistance is fatally weakened.[45]

Harris and Eaker really had all the targets and freedom they wanted.

But much of the Casablanca directive was actually rather woolly. Eaker set about trying to transform it into something a little more solid. Eaker's Plan promised massive reductions in German submarine, fighter, bomber, ball-bearing and synthetic rubber production. Portal and Harris accepted much of the planning, but expressed some reservations about the need to hit French ports and the subsequent loss of French lives. They also had a very good military reason for this, the RAF's own experience had shown that German submarine pens were virtually impregnable and even the best aimed bomb did not do much more than scratch the surface.

When it came to co-ordinating the offensive both Harris and Eaker were prepared to accept Portal as their immediate boss. Portal was then to inform the governments and chiefs of staff of the progress of the combined bombing operations. For General Arnold, the American Chief of Staff in Washington, this was a bit too neat. He felt that it let the airmen off the leash and they would lose sight of the fact that they were actually preparing the way for invasion. Arnold suggested more formal administrative machinery for running the offensive. The airmen were once again lucky for their fear of being tied too tightly to alternative strategies was matched by Churchill's fear of Britain becoming dominated by Washington and the resurrection of the 'quick invasion' chimera. The pressure was resisted.

A final draft of instructions and directions was drawn up in the spring of 1943, the Pointblank Directive. Pointblank was actually just as woolly as the earlier drafts and suited both Eaker and Harris. Churchill's limited interest in the bomber campaign was becoming obvious. It was now a convenient tool for him in his wider strategy. He needed time, the bomber would buy it. When he went to Washington in May he showed his lack of interest by nodding through the bomber campaign without asking any detailed questions. The bomber offensive had staved off talk of an invasion for 1943, and that was that. The Pointblank Directive was then formally issued to Bomber Command on June 10.

Harris went straight back to his area offensive. He certainly did not intend to take too much notice of the instruction to reduce the German air force and was prepared to leave that to the Americans. Harris does not say much about Pointblank in his memoirs and this seems to show his interest in it. For him the directive was only about confirming the role of the bomber, nothing greater. However, he was ignoring an extremely important point. In identifying the German air force as a primary objective the directive was absolutely right. For not only did the invasion depend upon the reduction of the German air force, but the efficiency and effectiveness of the bombing campaign did as well.

Eaker went off equally determined to make his campaign succeed. An ironic situation had been achieved. In public both Harris and Eaker would always proclaim that they were stringently following a jointly agreed policy, which was carefully co-ordinated. In practice both fought their own wars according to their own concept of air power. Both were determined to reduce Germany to submission without invasion, and that was their real point of common interest. Pointblank had agreed on something rather less.

The strategic developments of the winter were matched by some developments in the 'nuts and bolts' of the offensive itself. Early in the autumn of 1942 another new navigational device appeared, *Oboe*. *Oboe* was a blind-bombing device. A screen in the navigator's 'office' showed how the system worked: two beams produced from ground stations guided the aircraft along the course of one beam and when it intersected with the beam of the second station it was on target. *Oboe* was very accurate and so was, at last, a way to see through cloud. But it suffered from some problems. Firstly, only six aircraft an hour could use it otherwise it would swamp the ground stations. Secondly, like *Gee*, it was a line of sight device and so was affected by the curvature of the earth.

It was therefore decided to use the equipment in Pathfinder aircraft in order to make maximum use of it. They would use the device to find and mark the target for the rest of the force. Results were phenomenally good, they soon proved that they could bomb to an error of less than 300 yards – an amazing feat. Of equal significance was the fact that the Germans never managed to jam *Oboe* effectively.

Hard on the heels of *Oboe* came *H2S*, an early airborne ground-scanning radar, which was not tied to any land station. *H2S* therefore promised complete freedom. Once again, however, there were problems. The sets were liable to break down, and it had problems defining anything other than very obvious landmarks and shapes. It worked best on things like coastlines, or large rivers or lakes, but to a force relying on dead-reckoning and *Gee* it was a great advance. Industry would take some time to produce these sets on a large scale and so, like *Oboe*, they were originally fitted to Pathfinders. Twenty-three aircraft of 35 Squadron were fitted with the first sets in January 1943. It took until early 1944 for the rest of the main force to receive *H2S* sets.

The first *Oboe* attack was in December 1942. In that month two electronic devices designed to interrupt German communications made their debuts, *Mandrel* and *Tinsel*. *Mandrel* was a ground device in England for jamming German radar and radio devices. *Tinsel* was a small microphone near one of the bomber's engines. The radio operator could then tune this to the frequency of any German transmissions he heard thus drowning them. These devices could only be a steady irritant, they could never decisively swing the battle.

After the slump in morale and the continued high losses, these devices provided the means of reducing casualties and reinvigorating the campaign. Bomber Command now no longer needed to use the full moon period of each month, sticking instead to the safer dark periods. The increasing size of the force also meant that there was more chance of overwhelming a few boxes of the Kammhuber Line.

Pathfinders were being feted at this particular period. Not only were they receiving all new equipment, but the target marking problem was also being addressed with much greater attention. The pre-war firework industry had been put to work on the task and they produced a standard 'target marker'. Essentially the target marker was a 250lb bomb packed with pyrotechnic candles, which could be ejected at various heights by a barometric fuse and cascade to the ground in a mass of colour – red, green and yellow were the standards. These were reliable and hard to miss, and not easily copied by the Germans, and were ready for use by January 1943.

At last, at long last, British industry was pouring out the bombers. In addition Coastal Command was creaming-off fewer and the Middle East commitment was less demanding. 1 Group was going over to Lancasters. 3 Group had Stirlings, and only one Wellington squadron was left. Three quarters of 4 Group was equipped with the better, newer mark Halifaxes that had overcome their earlier difficulties. 5 Group was entirely a Lancaster force and could deliver a greater tonnage of bombs in one night than the entire Command a year earlier. A sense of growing power was prevalent. John Gee, a pilot who had been off on a flying instructor's course, returned to his unit and found that a transformation had taken place in his absence. New navigational equipment had been delivered, the Pathfinders had come into being, the bomber stream developed: 'To fly in a stream of 500 aircraft out over Beachy Head with all the navigation lights on! Soon they were switched off, and you couldn't see any of them. But they were still there, a wonderful feeling of power.'[46]

A new group became operational on New Year's Day 1943, 6 Group, entirely paid for and manned by the Dominion of Canada. Its commander was a Canadian, Air Vice-Marshal G.E. Brooks, and his headquarters were at Allerton Castle Park, near Knaresborough in Yorkshire. The Pathfinders had achieved Group status on January 8, taking the number 8. Bennett was promoted to air commodore at Harris's insistence, retained above a list of higher rank officers recommended by the Air Ministry.

By the spring of 1943 Bomber Command had an average night raiding force of 450 aircraft, almost double the number of a year earlier when 250 bombers would have been regarded as a high profile effort. One ton of bombs had been the average dropped a year earlier, now the Command could drop two and a quarter tons.

In all this 2 Group was still languishing. It was only slowly re-equipping with the North American Mitchell day bomber, and had yet another new commander, Air Vice-Marshal J.H. D'Albiac, who took over from Lees. It was the fifth commander for 2 Group in the war. Harris was still not using the Group much and it felt itself to be very much a sidelined force.

Harris was later to describe 1942 as the 'preliminary phase' of his campaign. It was the period during which he achieved a couple of great successes in order to win approval, but then fought hard battles for new equipment and had to refine his tactics ready for the real offensive. Just as he prepared for this, just as Casablanca seemed to give him the chance he wanted, he was diverted by yet another maritime directive. On January 14 the Air Ministry directed Harris to come to the assistance of the Admiralty by attacking submarine pens on the west coast of France. Harris was reluctant to help the Navy in this way. He had a shrewd idea of the of the strength of the pens and was even more reluctant to allow any of his force to go to Coastal Command and take part in Atlantic sweeps. He argued that the best thing he could do was bomb plants and ports in Germany thus stopping submarines from reaching their theatre of operations at all. Six months earlier he had written to the war cabinet pointing out that:

> While it takes approximately some 7000 hours of flying to destroy one submarine at sea, that was approximately the amount of flying necessary to destroy one third of Cologne... The purely defensive use of air power is grossly wasteful. The naval employment of aircraft consists of picking at the fringes of enemy power, of waiting for opportunities that may never occur, and indeed probably never will occur, of looking for needles in a haystack...[47]

But Harris had his orders. French ports were bombed to dust, destroying everything but the pens. The RAF had actually missed the chance to cause significant damage to these installations. If they had been bombed while the very obvious construction work was under way significant results might have been produced. Bombing now was shutting the stable door after the horse had bolted. Only once Barnes Wallis had designed a special 'earthquake' bomb would these huge shelters succumb to allied bombing.

In the middle of the maritime campaign came the tenth anniversary of Nazi government of Germany. It was too good an opportunity to miss, and a daylight raid over Berlin was ordered. The air raid sirens sounded in Berlin in the middle of the celebrations. Back in Britain the comic vision of the Nazi leaders scuttling for cover was a jolly aside in the grim war. *The Times* caught the atmosphere: 'Besides sharing the nation's pleasure over this imaginative *coup*, they take justifiable pride in the distinction of having taken part in this historic attack on the heart of Nazism.'[48]

The maritime directive lasted for about a month and was generally a waste of time and costly in terms of French lives. With spring beginning to show Harris was given his chance.

The Ruhr had held a fascination for Bomber Command for a long time. It was the heart of German industry and offered a string of vital towns all of which virtually merged into one another. So far it had been attacked often but inconsistently and indifferently. Strong defences, and the problems of negotiating the haze produced by the thousands of chimneys, precluded effective bombing. But *Gee* and *Oboe* had overcome these difficulties. Being so close to England it was also the best area to aim at in the short spring and summer nights. The public wanted to see Bomber Command fulfil its potential. A *Spectator* article of March 1943 noted the general disappointment that there had not been more 1000 bomber raids.[49] Now Harris planned to give them what they wanted.

Harris realised that his campaign against the Ruhr needed diversions and dummies. If all his attacks went there it would allow the enemy the chance to concentrate defences and so raids to the Baltic, Czechoslovakia, Munich and Turin were included as part of the plan.

The Battle of the Ruhr opened on March 5/6 with a raid on Essen and continued until July 24. During this period Bomber Command flew 24,355 sorties, losing 1038 aircraft (4.3 per cent). It was a high loss rate, but it did lead to concentrated attacks on Essen, Mannheim, Dortmund, Duisberg, Wuppertal, Krefeld and Cologne.

Unlike Fighter Command's headquarters in a former girls' school at Bentley Priory, Buckinghamshire, Bomber Command's headquarters at High Wycombe were built expressly for the purpose. The buildings were gathered in a clearing surrounded by beech trees. It was a secluded spot deliberately chosen for security reasons. In fact, it was actually closer to the small village of Walter's Ash some five miles from High Wycombe, the town which provided the postal address. From these buildings in the heart of Metroland's 'beechy Bucks' RAF staff laboured to bring death and destruction to Germany.

The nerve-centre of the headquarters was the Operations Room. Huge maps of Europe, supplemented by reams of statistics and information about targets, weather and previous missions covered the walls. Desks filled the room with places for RAF staff and the various liaison officers. Army, navy and American officers had hotlines to their commanders. This gaggle of liaison officers passed on the target preferences of their own services and passed back information. There were tables with maps showing the position of German anti-aircraft measures and one carrying a mosaic of aerial photographs showing the Ruhr, the industrial heartland of the Reich. Harris presided over this court. Each morning there was a conference. Before the conference started a huge blackboard chalked up with the orders of the previous night's raid was completed by annotations in red giving the results. Sir Robert Saundby, the Senior Air Staff Officer, then provided a more detailed summary of the previous night's operations as a prelude to the main business. Once completed, the Meteorological Officer was called in to give his predictions. The main part of his job was to provide information about cloud cover over Germany and then over Britain at the estimated return time of the raiding force. Later in the day a Meteorological Flight would go out over Germany to check the forecast and bring back fresh information. After hearing this report Harris turned to his quarter inch scale map of Northern Europe. All large and important cities, towns and targets were marked with colour-coded pins. At this point he would have consulted his target files.

The target files had been started by the Air Ministry, but had been sent down to High Wycombe to be maintained by the Targets Selection Committee. There was a file for every city in Germany, each one having a fish code name given by Saundby. Some files contained an impressive array of information about population figures, nature of industries, lay out of the area, on searchlight concentrations and flak batteries. Others had little more than could be conned out of a tourist guide. These files also had a record of any previous Bomber Command attack. The staff of the committee often had a shrewd idea of the destination of the attack based on season and local weather. Like the main operations room, this office also contained a meteorological map amended hourly by reports from weather stations, ships at sea and the RAF meteorological flight. The staff selected a list of possible targets, based mainly on the weather prediction. The files were then sent to the morning conference.

As Harris mulled over potential targets he would have checked the figures of available aircraft. Peering through his spectacles, Harris's mind made many calculations. He was carrying a huge weight of responsibility, upon his decisions thousands of men's lives depended. He took his responsibilities seriously, which sometimes made him seem a gruff, unapproachable man. Barking out his decision he then set the forthcoming night's operations in train by ordering the completion of the form entitled 'C-in-C's Daily Allotment of Targets'. This form gave the name of the targets, strength of force to attack each target and type of bomb for each job. Included on each form was a main alternative and a list of diversionary operations. Having concluded the conference, Harris would stroll briskly from the room back to his office to continue with the mountains of paperwork his job entailed. Saundby then took over, starting the detailed planning and contacting the headquarters of each group.

Harris was rarely seen outside of his headquarter buildings. He never took a day off from the time he arrived at High Wycombe till the end of the war. Trawling through photographs of Harris it is hard to find one of him outside or at an airfield. The vast majority of them show him studying at his desk or poring over maps and photographs in his operations room. His prematurely white hair and close-cropped moustache, heavy cheeks and spectacles made him appear like a gruff old bank manager. In fact, there is something of the Captain Mainwaring about him. But this belied his tremendous energy and what he lacked in simple courtesy – he could be very intolerant of fools – he made up for in his dedication. Accused by some of being cold and unfeeling, partly based on the fact that he never inspired his men in person, he was in fact the opposite. He was very aware of the cost of the bomber campaign and that in turn made him all the more determined.

Not one man, not one aircraft, was going to be lost in vain. The enemy was to be smashed even harder, made to regret its decision to plunge the world into war. Harris, like Churchill, had no regard for German civilian lives. That is why the British people liked him. He was the man for the job of war leadership. In peace their consciences would react against him, just as they reacted against Churchill. But that should not blind us to the fact that at the time he was the man of the hour. In victory the British wanted to return to the values Shakespeare's Henry V had ascribed to the peacetime English: 'in peace there's nothing so becomes a man as modest stillness and humility.' That meant rejecting the fact that in war they had imitated the action of the tiger, stiffened the sinews and summoned up the blood, disguised fair nature with hard-favoured rage. Harris was just the man to express the hard-favoured rage of the British.

Swamped by work, Harris did not forget his crews. Though he rarely saw them personally he inspired by his ruthless confidence and straight-talking. His communications became legendary. On coming to high office he set the standard with that dead-pan delivery, which actually made his threats all the more chilling:

> There are a lot of people who say that bombing cannot win the war. My reply to that is that it has never been tried yet. We shall see… The Nazis entered this war under the rather childish illusion that they were going to bomb everybody else and nobody was going to bomb them. At Rotterdam, London, Warsaw and half a hundred other places they put that rather naive theory into operation. They sowed the wind and now they are going to reap the whirlwind.

Harris's orders to reap the whirlwind streamed out of High Wycombe day after day. Orders were transmitted to the groups via a secure teleprinter line. Group staff determined the correct mileage to target and then made fuel calculations. The commanding officer then met with his Operations Officer to discuss the attack. Like High Wycombe, each group had its own Meteorological Officer and he was always summoned to the conference. It was vital for each group commander to co-ordinate his attack and avoid clashes with the other groups.

Once the group conference finished the responsibility for the raid transferred to the Group Operations Room, where the staff worked on the detailed planning. The first job was to confirm the returns of available men and aircraft from each squadron within the group.

The Operations Officer wrote up Form B, the detailed instructions for each squadron, which was then checked by the Chief Operations Officer, signed and counter signed. The form was taken to the teleprinter room to be simultaneously transmitted to each squadron on secure lines.

At squadron level the day would start with a set of regular routines, regardless of whether a raid was on or not. Each aircraft, either in hangar or standing out on its pan, was normally covered with mechanics carrying out routine maintenance or repairing battle damage. The crews of mechanics were vital. Bomber Command would never have been able to operate without the skill and dedication of these men. Spending so much time with the machines made the ground crews fiercely protective of them. As far as they were concerned the aircrews borrowed them each evening only to treat the machine like rubbish. Aircrews put the machines through violent dives, steep banks and allowed them to get riddled with bullets. The next day the ground crews worked to restore such damage.

Unless the weather was very bad most squadrons worked on the assumption that there would be an attack. Therefore, before a raid was confirmed, the squadron was preparing. The pilot would meet the senior mechanic and have a chat about the aircraft. Both men would then sign a Daily Inspection Form confirming the technical details of this meeting. Around lunch time crews would board the aircraft for a brief air test, ensuring that all the vital equipment was working properly. German listening stations often picked up on the radio activity as hundreds of wireless sets were tested. This gave the enemy the first scent of the night's planned activities.

In the squadron offices the senior staff reacted to the sudden chatter of teleprinters. Once the orders had been received from group and the target confirmed the Senior Navigation Leader and Bombing Leader of each squadron met with the Squadron Leader and Meteorological Officer to plan for the crews' briefing. The senior navigation and bombing leaders were exactly that. Men with solid experience behind them who had proved themselves in numerous missions. They applied their joint experience to help the others.

Out on the airfield the preparations would move up a notch. The fuel tankers began their rounds. Each Lancaster had capacity for nearly 2,500 gallons of fuel in its wing tanks. Ground crews made shrewd guesses as to the target from the fuel figures. The more they had to put in, the longer the flight.

Away at the bomb dump, protected by its ring of blast walls, the tractor trolleys were loaded up. Each tractor pulled a string of trolleys. 500lb general purpose bombs were put on six at a time. The huge 4000lb 'cookie' was a blast bomb resembling a massive dustbin, capable of causing enormous damage thanks to the weight of its explosive and its thin casing, which allowed the blast to radiate outwards viciously. Other trolleys would have been loaded up with the bundles of incendiaries. They were clustered in small racks and looked like long firework rockets. A single Lancaster could carry a maximum of 12,500lb of ordinary bombs plus one 'cookie'. It was this weight lifting ability that made the Lancaster the supreme bombing aircraft of the Second World War. It was the result of years of experience – often bitter experience – and refinement which had created this machine dedicated to one purpose, the delivery of death and destruction to the enemy.

The tractors chugged across to the fusing hut. Fuses were set for different times. Most were set to explode on impact, others were set to explode hours, even days, after the raid was over. This was a clear example of the British commitment to demoralising the enemy. A delayed action fuse ensured that the enemy could never feel safe. Just as a city felt that it was staggering back to life a bomb might go off pushing people back into shock and resurrecting carefully suppressed memories. Each bomb was fitted with a small windmill that unwound during the drop thus finally charging the bomb. These windmills were temporarily taped-up for safety.

Each bomber stood on its dispersal pan awaiting its load. Armourers, having completed the checking of ammunition belts for the machine guns, stood ready to help once the tractor arrived. WAAFS were often tractor drivers, and they took a great deal of pride in driving more smoothly and efficiently than their male counterparts. The tractor swung under the wing and dragged the trail of trolleys under the bomb bay. 'Bombing-up' was hard physical work, despite the fact that they could use the bomber's winch. The 500lb bombs were fitted in pairs in special carrier racks. Armourers pushed, pulled and grunted to ensure the bombs fitted neatly into the racks. Carelessness or bad luck at this moment could lead to appalling accidents. On March 15 1943, at Scampton, a 'cookie' fell out of a Lancaster and blew-up killing several ground crew and writing-off six Lancasters.

During these preparations the navigators gathered for their own special 'pre-briefing'. Occasionally pilots and bomb-aimers would attend these in order to help in the preparation of charts and the making of flight plans. Most would get an inkling of the possible target at this meeting. At some point the other members of the crew would also get their own specialised meetings. The gunners would discuss tactics, the wireless operators would compare notes and fix frequencies.

After the operational meal of eggs and bacon, the crews would start arriving for the main briefing. Men arrived in trucks and on the ubiquitous RAF issue bicycles. In the main hall the men sat down. Strange little rituals took place. The young and novice crews sat near the front, anxious to pick up on every scrap of information. Older and more experienced men sat nearer the back. At the front of the hall was a large wall map. Sometimes this was curtained only to be drawn back at the last moment revealing the target as if the Squadron Leader were a magician completing a conjuring trick.

The senior officers came in together – the base, squadron and station commanders. Once it was silent the target for tonight was announced. The map would have been marked by ribbons showing outward and homeward routes. If the target was a nasty one – such as one in the Ruhr – there was often a muffled groan. First up was the Meteorological Officer. The navigators, pilots and flight engineers all made careful note of his predicted wind speeds and icing level. Witticisms were often chucked out during the prediction since meteorology, despite many advances, still appeared a very crude and random science to many airmen. Next came the Flying Control Officer with his take-off plan. It was vital each crew knew its place in the sequence, for the whole thing was carried out in radio silence. Every aircraft had to be in the right place, at the right time, to allow the squadron to get away according to schedule. Then came the Intelligence Officer with details of the route, enemy strength, nature of target, attack height, homeward flight and all counter-measures. As at every briefing it was drummed into the men to aim for the red flares, aim for the centre of the red flares. Don't just aim for the nearest big fire, it might be a diversion started by the Germans. The Squadron Commander would then reinforce that message. Then came the Station Commander with a welter of general advice. He urged navigators to keep to the flight plans and pilots to keep to time. With watches then synchronised the briefing was dismissed with messages of good luck and any communications from Harris himself.

The meeting then broke up with the crews chatting about the mission. The crews wandered over to the stores to sign for parachutes and 'Mae West' lifejackets. Pilots wore seat parachutes, which were strapped to their bottoms, other crew wore chest harnesses. As parachutes were always a clumsy nuisance they were stored once in the aircraft and were only clipped on in the event of an emergency. Keys were drawn for the lockers. Each crewman had his own locker containing flying kit. Each locker also bore the melancholy scars of scratches from being forcibly broken open to empty it of a dead man's effects. Flying gear was piecemeal and customised for personal use, but most men were all too aware of the need to fight cold with -40°c common over Europe in winter.

WAAFs provided each crew with ration packs. These consisted of flasks of tea and coffee, sandwiches, barley sugar, gum and chocolate. Rations were usually avoided on the outward journey. No man wanted to be forced to answer a call of nature over enemy territory. The Elsan chemical lavatory onboard was hardly welcoming and, of course, it was freezing! It was also considered tempting fate to eat before the bombs had been dropped.

Lorries took the crews to their aircraft. Each pilot met his senior mechanic again to sign the Form 700 that confirmed that the aircraft was airworthy. The aircraft was now the pilot's possession. The Flight Commander drove round to wish each crew good luck. Before climbing in to the cold aircraft the crews completed common rituals. The most usual one was to collectively urinate on the tail wheel for luck. In this modern scientific war men still clung to animal-like rituals to appease the gods of battle. Once aboard the escape hatch was tested, though the awkward upright tubular main spar in a Lancaster stopped many men from bailing out in an emergency.

On the tarmac the ground crews had not quite finished their tasks. The protective covers over the tyres were removed and a trolley accumulator was moved into place to help fire the engines. Starboard inner was started first. Then the pilot and engineer checked all dials, gauges and equipment. Having done this the aircraft was ready to taxi along the perimeter track to the main runway. Taxiing was a tricky business as it was done by rudder and brakes alone. If a bomber strayed from the taxi-way it could sink in the soil making a dangerous obstacle for following aircraft.

Out on the main runway a mobile control station kept the take-off procedure in order. The controller switched his red Aldis signalling lamp to green and the bomber started its run. As it moved along the track the crew inside saw the groups of WAAFs, mechanics and other ground staff who gathered winter and summer, in fair weather and foul, to wave good luck to the departing force.

Each Lancaster used the full 1390 horsepower of its Rolls Royce Merlin engines to get into the sky. As it rose the ground controllers chalked its take off time onto a blackboard. Once all aircraft were away the squadron plot commenced with the information repeated to group. A Lancaster took about forty minutes to climb to its ceiling of 20,000 feet. For every 1000 feet they rose the temperature dropped 2.5°c. At 8000 feet the crew needed oxygen.

A maximum effort raid on Germany, say the attack on Dortmund on May 23/24 1943, which involved a total of 826 aircraft, represented a massive commitment on behalf of the British state. A Lancaster required the manufacturing capacity needed for forty basic motor cars. The man-hours spent building a Lancaster would have completed a mile of motorway. The radar and radio equipment was the equivalent of a million domestic wireless sets. A total of 5000 tons of hard aluminium was required for a heavy bomber or eleven million saucepans. In 1943 prices, with profits reduced to an absolute minimum, each Lancaster cost £42,000. To train the crew it cost £10,000 each, more than enough to keep them all at university for three years. Add a conservative estimate of £13,000 for bombs, fuel, servicing and ground crew training and it meant that the night of May 23/24 cost the British tax-payer well over £100,000. Night after night the national treasure in terms of money, blood and brains was sent out to chastise Germany. It was more than a strategy, it was a national obsession.

On that night of May 23/24 Tom Wingham, bomb-aimer of a Mark II Halifax, was on his 20th operation.[50] It was a clear evening and the weather forecast was accurate. One aircraft had taken a new wind speed reading and broadcasted it back to base. This correct signal was then sent out to the force. Over Holland few bombers were lost. The German box system was overwhelmed by the bomber stream and only stragglers fell victim. But, as ever, the game changed as the Ruhr, 'Happy Valley' in ironic Bomber Command parlance, approached. The flak barrage increased, but without accurate radar prediction because of the difficulty of getting a fix on the thick stream of bombers, it became a hail of rather random, though nonetheless scary, fire.

The Pathfinders went in first, spearheaded by thirteen *Oboe*-marking Mosquitoes. The Mosquitoes were in charge of primary marking. They dropped a shower of target indicators. Target indicators were detonated by barometric pressure at 1000 feet, which then threw out benzol, rubber and phosphorus to make a huge splash of red. The lower-level heavies of the rest of the Pathfinders then dropped their secondary markers. Bundles of green markers and pyrotechnic candles on parachutes filled the air. They looked like bunches of grapes, or Christmas trees, depending on whether air temperature and pressure made them top or bottom heavy.

As Wingham and his comrades approached the target they suddenly saw the red of the *Oboe*-guided primary markers. This was a relief, for they could aim at the real target and were relieved of the dangerous task of making a circuit looking for the markers. Wingham, as bomb-aimer, now took over the aircraft, for he fed instructions to the pilot. Staring through his bomb-sight, adjusted for local wind speeds, he needed the aircraft to be kept level and steady. For this reason the bomb-run was the most nerve-wracking moment of a flight. It was the moment when searchlights had a stable target and the flak batteries could make best use of their radar directed fire. The bomb doors opened and they moved in. 'Left… left… steady… steady.' Tom pressed the release trigger, universally known as 'the tit'. 'Bombs gone.' As usual the bomber would have leapt upwards having shed so much weight. At the same moment the million candle-power photoflash was dropped from its chute, and the bomber flew on straight and level for another ten seconds to release all of the incendiaries as well. Then the camera took its photo illuminated by the special flash. With bomb doors closed the Halifax turned out of the storm of fire, colour and smoke and returned to the reassuring pattern of weaving.

Just as the crew believed they were leaving the main danger area a huge crash hit the aircraft. The pilot realised that the Halifax had lost a great deal of power and did not believe it had long to live and he ordered the crew to prepare to bail out. Wingham did not fancy bailing out over the Ruhr, for fear of being lynched by the locals. The Halifax lost height and fell to 7000 feet, well within the range of every German gun. Suddenly a miracle occurred, for the engines began to splutter back into life and the pilot stabilised the aircraft. By good luck and good flying the Halifax gained a little height and limped home. This was why men urinated on tail wheels. Survival often appeared to hinge on something more than human skill.

Back in the squadron plotting room, WAAFS waited for the first radar blips showing the return of the force. They would then begin plotting on the table each returning aircraft. There was little point in maintaining radio silence once a raid had started. Once the enemy coast had been reached by the bombers VHF radio was used by aircraft needing emergency landing fields. Many bombers suffering from loss of fuel, failing engines or very badly wounded crew, needed permission to land at the nearest airfield. Yellow discs on the squadron blackboard marked planes landed at other airfields, green discs marked each safe return at the home base.

Once a bomber landed there would be the usual sigh of relief. The pilot supervised the shut-down checks. Unless a bomber was in serious danger of fire or other disaster the fixed routine held firm. Men clambered out of the bombers stiff and cold, pounding joints to restore vitality. Cigarettes were lit and they wandered over to the interrogation room, via the parachute and lifejacket store, with the roar of the engines still humming in their ears. It was a sensation that took several hours to wear off.

At the interrogation room men were offered cups of rum-laced tea or cocoa as they waited their turn to move from table to table. The station padre often played the role of waiter, delivering fresh cigarettes as well. It was vital to keep the crew together and to question them while the memories were fresh. Crews were asked questions by the various specialist teams. 'What was the flak like?'; 'Was the bombing concentrated?'; 'How accurate was the weather forecast?'; 'How did the guns/radio/radar/engines perform?' Men added other scraps of information, confirming the loss of an aircraft or a spotting of a missing aircraft.

The Station Commander, his team and the interrogation staff, waited until the last aircraft had arrived back at base before retiring, Station Commanders and many others praying that the missing aircraft would turn up at some point later in the day. Their prayers often went unanswered. For the aircrews the final routine was the eggs and bacon breakfast. After many hours in the air, with its intense mental effort, men felt drained and hungry and so the luxury of a cooked breakfast was appreciated. Then it was off to bed. The next night they would probably go through it all again. And so the bomber boys' war ground on with its own pattern.

With the Battle of the Ruhr raging Harris could certainly claim to be razing large areas of Germany. After the big Dortmund raid of May 23/24, the *Daily Mirror* carried Harris's message of congratulation to his men:

> In 1939 Goering promised that not a single enemy bomb would reach the Ruhr. Congratulations on having delivered the first 100,000 tons of bombs on Germany to refute him. The next 100,000 tons, if he waits for them, will be even bigger and better bombs, delivered even more accurately and in a shorter time.[51]

The leader then announced that Winston Churchill had said 'that the attempt to knock out Germany by bombing alone was "well worth trying"'. In addition, Harris's Command was gathering in strength the whole time. When the battle started he had 600 aircraft available, by May it was 800, four fifths of which were four engined bombers. He was therefore achieving an accuracy and concentration that was unheard of – but not undreamed of – in the early days of the war. By June, the *Daily Express* could proclaim in its headlines: 'Ruhr Bomb Onslaught Reaching Climax'[52] and went on to add: 'The great Battle of the Ruhr was officially stated in London last night to be approaching its climax. In a last minute bid to save this vital area from complete destruction the Germans have massed there every gun, every fighter and every searchlight they can spare.' In August HMV put out a recording made in a Lancaster during a raid over Essen in the Battle of the Ruhr. The listener must have been struck by the diversity of regional accents and social classes of the crew. It was also clear that Essen was heavily defended, for a crew member stated 'I can read my watch in the searchlights, 21.54.'[53] The conversations revealed the stresses of war in a most understated way, the pilot muttered, 'Come on "T for Tommy" get cracking.' When a flak shell exploded nearby a laconic 'My God' was heard, and then 'You could light your fag on one of those.' After a further vicious crack, one crew member exclaimed, 'Wow, that was close,' which was met by the reply, 'I think we've been hit personally.' Then, as the aircraft circled away and the men were looking down on the scene, 'By God I've never seen anything like this before,' and the almost stereotypical RAF reaction, 'Yes, not a bad prang.' Such recordings no doubt helped the public to understand exactly what the bomber boys were like and how they actually carried out their job.

The greater bombing concentration was very much helped by the Mosquitoes proving themselves vital members of the team. Flying much higher and much faster than the bomber stream, their *Oboe*-directed target marking actually paved the way for the Pathfinders, who then carried out the secondary marking. Alongside this, the Pathfinders were further helped by the creation of 1409 Meteorological Flight directly under their control. Weather and windspeeds were now predicted with much greater accuracy. Bomber Command was achieving success, but was it having a significant effect on German war production?

The most glorious achievement of the Battle of the Ruhr was the raid on the Möhne, Eder and Sorpe dams on May 16/17. Indeed, the action of 617 Squadron earned it a reputation which has echoed down the years. It is one of the enduring images of the Second World War.

An attack on German hydroelectric production was not new in 1943. Since at least 1937 the British planning staff had shown an interest in the dams of the Ruhr tributaries of the Möhne and Sorpe. There was also knowledge of the significance of the Eder dam. The three dams held back nearly 500 million tons of water. But any attack had to overcome two problems. Firstly, the dams were impervious to ordinary bombs. The Möhne was 25 feet thick at the top and 112 feet thick at the bottom. The Sorpe was slightly different, being of earth, rather than concrete construction, faced with stone and resting on a 30 feet concrete core.

The resurrection of the idea was the result of Dr Barnes Wallis's efforts. Wallis was an engineer with the Vickers Company, the man who had already designed the excellent Wellington bomber. Few men have looked less like a great engineer. When you look at a photograph of Isambard Kingdom Brunel you see the swagger in him. His cigar, his very tall hat, his fingers in his waistcoat pockets, the pose in front of a huge spindle of hawser chains, all leave the viewer with the sensation of looking at cocky, unbridled genius and confidence incarnate. Look at a photograph of Barnes Wallis and you will see a clergyman straight from the pages of Trollope. The thick grey hair and hornrimmed spectacles, complemented by a placid expression, were actually a bluff. Wallis was a determined and stubborn man. Once he began work on a problem he stuck at it until the answer was revealed. He applied his mind to the question of the Nazi economy. He reached a simple solution: rather than trying to knock out the factories, why not sever their arteries of power? If a way of destroying the Ruhr's electricity supply could be found then German industry could be hit a mighty blow. Wallis realised that the elimination of the hydroelectrical supply would be the most effective action. For a man like Wallis the problem of the dams was a personal and professional obsession. What an engineer had built another engineer should be able to destroy. It was an obsession that revealed perversity as well as genius.

The sort of bomb capable of destroying a dam was not in existence. Further, the means of delivering it posed profound problems. Torpedoes were impossible, for the dams were protected by nets moored to the bottom of the lakes. His initial idea was for a 10 ton bomb, to be delivered by a six-engined aircraft. He discounted this, realising that any sort of bomb dropped from above would not produce the right sort of blast. If a dam was going to be breached it needed to be hit at its base. How was it to be done? Wallis devised a bouncing bomb. He further deduced that if the bomb was rotated backwards before being dropped it would skip on impact with the water and bounce its way along the lake to the dam. This was the easy part of Wallis's labours. The hard part was to convince the authorities of the validity of the scheme.

In his memoirs, Harris told the story of the dambusters raid in a fairly matter of fact way. On his part there was certainly no real hint of any resistance to the raid, he did not state that he had been highly sceptical at the time. But, given the amount of fantastic schemes dangled before Harris, and every other commander of consequence, this should not be read as a serious criticism. Nonetheless tests went ahead at Chesil Beach, Dorset in December 1942. Portal was enthused by the idea and he lent it his weight, ordering the building of specially modified Lancasters on March 8 1943. If the raid was going to achieve maximum impact it needed to take place before the end of May when the water levels dropped as the winter and spring rains died away. A rush job was suddenly put into operation.

Harris finally agreed to co-operate and a new squadron was formed for the mission under the twenty-four year old Wing Commander Guy Gibson. Gibson had already completed 170 operations and was a man straining under the weight of his own achievements and responsibilities. He was a man who demanded success and efficiency and he achieved it in a number of ways. Filled with an obsessive crusading zeal he infected others. Never asking his men to do anything he would not do himself, he gained respect. But, aside from a few close friends, he did not inspire affection. He could be cutting, arrogant and cold. He could be insufferably snobbish, refusing to acknowledge ground staff and even N.C.O. aircrew on occasions. Whatever faults he might have had as a man, his skill as a leader and his ability to train and cajole the best out of others cannot be doubted.

He put 617 squadron through intensive training for Operation CHASTISE. A collective total of 2000 flying hours was accumulated in six weeks. Gibson took the crews on hundreds of passes over lakes and reservoirs. They practised flying low and maintaining a set height, for the bombs, codenamed upkeep, had to be dropped with precision. A fresh set of tests then took place at Reculver, on the Kent coast. Wallis realised that the bombs needed to be cylindrical and set the release height at 60 feet. This was a tough task, for most altimeters were not absolutely accurate. Fortunately Ben Lockspeiser, Director of Scientific Research at the Ministry of Aircraft Production, came up with an extremely simple and effective solution. He fixed a spotlight to each of the Lancaster's wings. When the two beams converged the aircraft was at exactly 60 feet. Accurate distance from the dam was fixed by an equally simple method. A handheld wooden frame was devised in the shape of a y. At the end of the arms were two small, upright markers. When these lined up with the towers on the rim of the dam the Lancaster was at the right distance.

So great was the strain of this operation on Gibson that on the day itself the Medical Officer at Scampton wanted to ground him. Run down and irritable, the M.O. thought he was not in a fit condition to lead a major operation. It is a tribute to Gibson's endurance and sense of duty that he overrode all such advice and led his men into action.

Only 19 Lancasters took part in the raid on May 16/17. Gibson led the first wave of nine Lancasters. They flew at low level across the North Sea, Holland and Germany, so as to avoid radar and night-fighters. One Lancaster was lost to flak on the way. Gibson led the assault on the Möhne only to miss. Flight Lieutenant Harold Martin then went in and missed too. Both men then set themselves up as decoys to draw flak, while the other aircraft moved in for the attack. The third and fourth aircraft scored hits, the fifth moved in and scored a success. Then the impassive dam began to crack and crumble. It gave way with an awful shudder and groan, releasing 130 million tons of water. Gibson and his crew let out a tremendous scream. Harris, Wallis and other top brass listening to the raid back in High Wycombe thought it signalled disaster. Only once the codeword 'Nigger' – after Gibson's black labrador dog – came bellowing out did they realise they had a success.

Gibson flew on with Squadron Leader H.M. Young to the Eder with three Lancasters still carrying their mines. The first aircraft to attack scored either a near miss or a hit. Those watching were unsure whether the huge splash actually signified a hit on the base of the dam. The second certainly did hit the dam, but the aircraft was lost probably because of the blast from its own mine. The third Lancaster scored a perfect hit, right in the centre of the dam. A thirty feet breach opened up. The six surviving aircraft turned for home, but Squadron Leader Young was lost on the way back. The last wave of five Lancasters tried to attack the Sorpe. One turned back earlier due to flak damage, two more were hit later on in the flight and they too turned back. Another lost its mine by flying too low over the North Sea. Only the American, Flight Lieutenant J.C. McCarthy, who had taken off late and separately, got to the Sorpe and bombed. Without support one bomb was not enough and the dam held despite showing a distinct dent.

Big trouble came the way of the five reserve Lancasters, for the German defences were wide awake by this time. Two were shot down before they reached the target area. Flight Sergeant Brown received orders to bomb the Sorpe, which he did without causing much more damage than McCarthy. Of the two remaining Lancasters one returned damaged and the other attacked the Ennope dam without effect.

Of the 19 Lancasters involved, 11 found the targets and bombed and eight failed to return. One hundred and thirty three men set out, 53 were killed and three became prisoners. In the rush of congratulations that followed no fewer than 24 awards were distributed. Gibson topped the list with the Victoria Cross. Additionally there were five Distinguished Service Orders awarded, four bars to the Distinguished Flying Cross, ten new D.F.Cs and 11 men were awarded the Distinguished Flying Medal. The men decorated reflected the cosmopolitan nature of the Command, for they included an American, six Canadians, eight Australians and a New Zealander, alongside their British colleagues.

In Germany there was profound shock. One thousand, two hundred and ninety four people were drowned and 1000 homes destroyed. Eleven factories were completely gutted and a further 114 damaged. Two thousand, eight hundred and twenty two hectares of farmland were ruined and 6316 cattle and pigs killed. Twenty five road bridges were washed away and ten damaged. A vast array of power and sanitation plants were damaged with their capacities severely reduced. But was it really worth it? Was it worth the lives of eight of the best crews in the entire service? Debate has raged ever since. The real problem was the choice and ranking of targets. The really important dam was the Sorpe, as the Ministry of Economic Warfare knew. However, Wallis's weapons were not suitable for the different design principle of the Sorpe, and in any case most of the force sent to attack it was lost. A vast collection of talent and energy and commitment was frittered away. It was a gross example of the failure to understand exactly what needed destroying in Germany. On the plus side, the Germans diverted 20,000 workers from their labours on the coastal defences of France and Belgium to repair the damage. Security around surviving dams was stepped up and more defensive measures taken. This at least was a diversion from other war work.

Debates over the effect of CHASTISE were confined to the key strategists of the time, and to historians since. What the public knew was that the Germans had suffered a stunning blow. For the evil perpetrators of war the floods had come. There was a definite sense of Old Testament judgement in the air, and it unleashed another bonanza of publicity for Bomber Command and 617 Squadron with its young leader, Guy Gibson. The leader of *The Times* certainly took up the element of Chastise: 'Only now are the German people beginning to pay the penalty of their own leaders' crimes – the bombs rained on Warsaw in 1939 without so much as the warning of a declaration of war, and in 1940 on the open and defenceless city of Rotterdam.'[54] 'Huns get a flood blitz/Torrent rages along Ruhr'[55], was the headline in the *Daily Mirror*; 'Floods roar down Ruhr valley'[56] proclaimed the *Daily Express*. News of the raid also made a big splash in the States. The *New York Times* ran the headlines: 'RAF Blasts 2 Big Dams in Reich; Ruhr Power Cut, Traffic Halted As Floods Cause Death and Ruin.'[57] Movietone treated its British viewers to a full history of the development of the raid, including footage of the training runs showing the dropping of test mines, Germans rustling through their ruined houses looking for belongings, and flooded streets. Others took a slightly less triumphant line. The *Spectator* noted that: 'The effects of these bombing attacks on the war as a whole cannot be seen immediately. They are cumulative, and will play their decisive part in straining Germany's fighting power to breaking point.' While the *Sketch* sought to distance itself from cheap gloating, the leader praised the cool determination and courage of the airmen involved. Urging its readers to reflect on the events it reminded them that the floods were a 'terrible but unavoidable necessity'.[58]

In fact, the *Sketch* was probably identifying a sensitivity Gibson did not have. When he attended the Sheffield Wings for Victory celebrations soon after the raid, he addressed the dignitaries of the town in the City Hall. His speech does not seem to show too much sense of a 'terrible but unavoidable necessity':

> I had the displeasure of watching from the air your city burn during the air raids of 1940. I knew there would come a time when we should do the same to the enemy. It is said that the British can take it. We can also give it and we are engaged in blasting the middle out of Germany.[59]

Gibson was a hero. The King and Queen visited his station at Scampton in order to meet him and his crews. The dams had already gained a legendary status, a status

Gibson was to help buttress by his tour of the United States and Canada later in the year and his book, *Enemy Coast Ahead*, which was published posthumously in 1946, for he was killed in September 1944 aged only 26. Gibson has remained a hero ever since. He lives on in the form of Richard Todd's portrayal in the film, *The Dam Busters*. For the general public the raid remains high on the list of Britain's triumphs. Operation Chastise is regarded as a national parable. Vast, seemingly impregnable objectives destroyed by small teams of dedicated men. It is a reassuring message of human skill in a cold, brutal war. Attempts to strip those men of their glory have been lost in a sea of public indifference. Harris fits the other side of the coin, for he along with the entire British bombing war, has a particular popular image. Like Gibson's it has proved peculiarly impervious to the investigations and writings of academics and well-informed critics. This is often the result of the way in which the war was presented at the time.

The Battle of the Ruhr restored morale in Bomber Command and there is no doubt that when given a job in which there was a fair chance of success the crews pushed on hard, determined to bomb in the right place regardless of obstacles. The problem was with targets beyond *Oboe* range, for success against such targets remained as elusive as ever. Few of these raids achieved anything like the concentration of those within *Oboe* range. 2 Group also continued to pose problems, the USAAF was doing the real day bombing by this point, and so a raison d'être seemed to be missing. In May the group was transferred to Fighter Command, and then went on to become the core of the RAF's Second Tactical Air Force, which played such a vital role in protecting British forces in Normandy and Germany in 1944 and 1945. Just before they went Harris pulled out 105 and 139 Squadrons – their Mosquitoes were vital – moving them into the Pathfinders.

With these realignments completed, and with Harris's men riding high, he turned to a new job, Hamburg, Germany's second largest city. He told his Group Commanders to prepare for a major operation against Hamburg on May 27. Though Hamburg was beyond the effective range of *Oboe*, he knew that the distinctive shape of the River Elbe and the many dock basins should show up well on the *H2S* sets. By this stage Harris was also well aware of the problems of 'creep back'. 'Creep back' was caused by bomb-aimers releasing their bombs too early. When this happened on a large enough scale the bombs tended to fall further and further short of the actual aiming point. To get round this Harris deliberately ordered target indicators to be placed just beyond his actual aiming point. This meant that even with 'creep back' he would hit his target. Harris knew that the 'creep back' would place the main weight of his attack directly on to the working class areas of Hamburg. He was not centring his attack on the important industrial heart of the city, he was placing it on the workers' houses. But, if the raid went well, it would probably cause massive damage to the port area and the submarine yards, all of which were his preferred way of helping the Battle of the Atlantic. Interestingly, the Hamburg raid was one of the few occasions when the Combined Bomber Offensive revealed itself, for the USAAF was invited to take part with follow-up daylight raids. They agreed but found the smoke caused by the RAF raids too much of a nuisance, which deterred them from accepting future invitations.

Harris directed four major raids in ten nights against Hamburg, starting on July 24/25, dropping 10,000 tons of bombs in the process. The results were phenomenal. Thanks to the hot, dry, still, conditions an incredible, terrifying firestorm was created. It has often been claimed that Bomber Command dropped an unusually high number of incendiaries, but this is not true, it was the weather conditions that created the firestorm. In these freak conditions the fires sucked greedily at all available oxygen, creating a whirlwind in the process. Trees were uprooted by the power of the suction, people were snatched up and tossed into the air, the temperature soared to 1000° centigrade. One pilot called it the daddy of all RAF raids, most were stunned at what they had achieved:

> I was amazed at the awe-inspiring sight of the target area. It seemed as though the whole of Hamburg was on fire from one end to the other and a huge column of smoke was towering well above us – and we were on 20,000 feet! It all seemed almost incredible and, when I realised that I was looking at a city with a population of two millions, or about that, it became almost frightening to think of what must be going on down there in Hamburg.[60]

Operation THUNDERCLAP had succeeded beyond all expectations. Germany had reaped the whirlwind, and felt the searing power of the RAF's pillar of fire.

The Germans were stunned. Forty thousand people had been killed and as many again injured. Six thousand, two hundred acres of the city were razed and the four great shipbuilding yards were severely damaged. Speer, the Minister of War Production, thought that six more attacks like Hamburg would end the war. Hamburg, however, was a freak. It could not be easily repeated. Success was due in no small measure to that most fickle of variables, the weather. The RAF had also unleashed a secret weapon: *Window. Window* was small strips of aluminium foil which, when dropped in large enough numbers, completely threw the German ground-based radar, Wurzburg, and the airborne Lichtenstein sets. *Window* had actually been developed back in April 1942, but had not been used for fear of the Germans copying it and using it against Britain. It was a bad decision. The German air force was heavily engaged in Russia and could not use it effectively against Britain: in the embargo period the RAF lost 2,200 aircraft. But *Window* then proved to be a remarkably short-lived advantage, for the Germans rapidly re-thought their entire night defences and displayed a great flexibility of mind.

Back in Britain the news of Hamburg was greeted with a mixture of joy and awe. To a certain extent it did not cause the same effect as Cologne or the dams, but this was due to the fact that Mussolini had been sacked by King Victor Emmanuel and the newspapers were feasting on that story. But Hamburg was by no means ignored, and there was a definite sense of the effect it had had in Germany. *The Times* believed that the fate of Hamburg had become known throughout Germany.[61] It told of renewed and frantic efforts to evacuate other German cities for fear of their suffering a similar fate. The report concluded by mentioning the dramatic reversal of fortune for the Germans.

In the first year of war the Germans had dished out such punishment indiscriminately. By the fourth year it was rebounding back on to them. A similar note was struck by the *Daily Sketch*: 'the bombing battle which has raged over Hamburg since Sunday night is renewed evidence of the terrible power of the air… Hamburg, however, has further repercussions on the German military machine… What has happened to one town may happen to another'.[62] The *Mirror* headline crowed simply and stridently: '50 German Cities Will Be Hamburged.'[63] The newsreels also waded in: Paramount showed official Air Ministry footage of the devastation, as did Universal;[64] Gaumont announced that 'Bomber Command smashes Germany's second city.' But the most striking line came from Movietone which stated: 'The second largest city of the Reich, is being *liquidated* in a series of record attacks by the RAF.'[65] [emphasis added] A more measured approach was taken by the *Express*, in fact there was clearly a feeling that something rather awful had happened, something which perhaps needed some defending. Basil Cardew visited a bomber station and wrote of the men involved in the raid:

> They have no views on the civilian side of the devastation. They take no pleasure in attacking other than military personnel. The rest of the population should have cleared out on Mr Churchill's advice, they say. Now they must accept the consequences… Never has Bomber Command's morale been higher. The men know they are winning a great strategic battle. They know the losses among them are lower than ever before. They know they are attacking the Germans just twice as hard as only seven or eight months ago.[66]

But, just what sort of effect was all this bombing having on German morale? This was a question many were asking. The *New Statesman* expressed doubts as to whether German morale would crack. It found the whole argument spurious. It asked why German morale should crack in the face of bombing when that of the British hadn't. The article sneered at the prospect and called it 'one of those mystical illusions which beset otherwise sane people in time of war'.[67] But, this did not mean that the bombing campaign was not effective. The British bombing campaign was said to be performing the same function as a naval blockade, slowly but surely strangling the German war effort. The diplomatic correspondent of *The Times* was in agreement with these sentiments: 'evidence goes to prove how baseless are any lingering hopes in allied countries that air raids will cause a political crack in Germany. The effects of the raids are to be assessed in terms not of mind or spirit but of sheer physical stamina and material resources.'[68]

Such sentiments were very much the preserve of the 'high brow' press. In the popular imagination Bomber Command was still the most effective weapon the British had and the pride in their achievements was immense. A year earlier Harris had announced on Movietone news that 'no part of the Reich is safe', in 1943 that was looking more and more true.[69] In the spring of 1943 London had played host to a 'Wings for Victory' week designed to encourage people to buy RAF war bonds. Trafalgar Square was dominated by two Lancasters, and a Stirling was placed in St Paul's churchyard. The response of the public was stunning. Over a million people flooded through Trafalgar Square and then blocked the Strand as they made their way towards St Paul's Cathedral. The *Express* announced 'the Biggest Crowd since the Coronation'.[70] Such was the size of the crowd that the organisers were overwhelmed, stopping many people from investing. It fully reveals the commitment of the British people to the RAF and Bomber Command. When the *Daily Mirror* recounted the deeds of the RAF soon after the Hamburg raid a sense of pure pride infused the writing. Readers were told of the widespread, intensive and well-planned operations of the RAF. The RAF was portrayed as the paragon of air services, capable of delivering more bombs to more places than any rival or ally. 'We therefore salute its gallant members of all branches and thank them, in the name of their countrymen, for the splendid work they are doing.'[71] In the public mind Bomber Command was the sharp end of the RAF. It was Bomber Command which would bring Germany to account. The *Daily Sketch*, writing a week later than the *Mirror*, added: 'With every day that passes the writing on the wall is standing out in bolder and bolder letters. And the writing declares that the day of reckoning for Germany is drawing closer and that the advance guard of Nemesis are the dauntless crews of the bombing aeroplanes'.[72]

As the Americans brought more and more of their men, material and ideas to the war Britain was left behind. By this stage of the war America was showing that it was the dominant western power and was taking the upper hand. Bomber Command was Britain's last, effective, entirely independent contribution to the war effort. Each Lancaster represented the pride of British industry, the best of British technical know-how, best of British and Commonwealth blood and the bulk of its treasure. Each raid rubbed the Union Jack in the faces of the enemy. The little island that had suffered so much was not going to rein in the giant it had created. The giant was brutal, it was indiscriminate, but it was British. During the war the press hinted at Bomber Command's awesome powers of mass destruction. But the obsession with walking the tightrope of moral superiority meant that it shied away from too much overt gloating. Unable to keep out all elements of this, the British press simmered with a fearful subtext: the British people were colluding in the deaths of thousands of German civilians. Some, most probably the majority, believed it was the by-product of a strategy aimed at paralysing German industry. A few guessed that the strategy was aimed at destroying the property, will and lives of the Germans themselves. After the war they all pretended they never knew a thing and exorcised themselves by blaming the men who had carried out the national will. It was shameful to blame the few when so many had been part of it. It was pathetic to forget that it was a policy devised to destroy the appalling evil of Nazism. It was remarkable to have forgotten so quickly that in the dark days of 1941 and 1942 the cupboard was bare. Unable to pierce the fearsome hide of the German beast the British had turned to a bludgeon to strike that beast repeatedly until it was either punch drunk or dead.

Harris had turned Bomber Command around. He had infused the force with a new pride and energy. It had not been simple. The early days of his command were marked by continuing technical difficulties. There were too few aircraft, the bombing was not concentrated enough, the German defences were not overwhelmed often enough. But Harris had worked on all these problems and had simplified them by adopting a clear, crude policy. He told his crews they could bomb Germany and they would bomb Germany. He gave them new pride. They would do it by rigorously sticking to the previously agreed policy of the area assault.

The British public continued to live on a diet of truths, half-truths and outright lies. Germany was going to be ruined from top to bottom. They knew this was the promise of Bomber Command. Germany was going to have the guts ripped out of it. They knew this too. But some managed to convince themselves that it was going to be done by bombing factories alone. Most did not manage this trick and silently accepted the implications of the policy, probably even rejoiced in it. Some, a very few, yelled out loud against it.

For Harris the way ahead was clear. He had the machines, men and technical support in place for the big job. The big job was to attack the 'big city', Berlin. He planned to reduce the capital of Nazism to rubble and win the war. It was a grand task, but he had a weapon of massive power.

. . . .

CHAPTER FIVE

Berlin, 'the Big City'

On August 23 1943 Flight Sergeant F.R. Stuart, a young Australian air gunner, found out he was going to Berlin that night.[1] Though he had quite a few operations under his belt he had never been to Berlin. The briefing stuck in his mind, the memory diminished little over the years: 'I'll never forget that briefing, when the curtain covering the map of Europe was swept aside and – there – the tapes ran to that great, evil looking, blood-red blob – Berlin – the Big City!' He broke out into a cold sweat. The knowledge that he was a good air gunner suddenly seemed insignificant. Berlin was different. Berlin was the enemy heart and as such the enemy would fight furiously for it. That night he gave his turret an extra polish. He was sure he would need perfectly visibility to survive the defences of Berlin.

For much of August Harris pressed home the advantage of *Window*, attacking German and then Italian cities. Bombing undoubtedly played a role in encouraging Italy to make its exit from the war on September 8. The moon period at the end of August saw the force reined-in, apart from the major attack on the special weapons research unit at Peenemünde. As the raid was shrouded in secrecy press reports describing the target referred to it as some sort of electronics and radar research centre. There was certainly no mention of rockets or pilotless flying bombs.

Expectation grew in Britain that Berlin was next on the list. As early as August 4 the *Daily Express* was claiming that Berlin would face Hamburg style raids within the next two-three weeks.[2] Their intelligence was very good, for Harris opened his campaign on August 23/24. This initial phase lasted until September 4, but it was not a particularly effective set of raids. Berlin was not a good *H2S* site and the Germans were already recovering from the effects of *Window*. Harris therefore drew back, waiting for the new improved *H2S* sets to come into operation and for another new navigational aid, the Ground Position Indicator. As an alternative he put the force to work against Hanover. This was also a poor *H2S* site and bombing was disappointing.

Whatever the actual results of the raids on Berlin, the press sensed an important new chapter opening. The *Daily Mirror* declared dramatically 'Battle of Berlin Opened' on August 25;[3] while the *Daily Express* referred to the first raid of the battle as 'a feat of war the glory of which nothing can dim'.[4] The leader of the *Daily Telegraph* mused on the significance of Berlin. Referring to Berlin as the single most important objective in

Germany, it urged the destruction of Germany's military, political and communications centre.[5] According to the article an attack on Berlin was worthwhile for the blow it would strike against those 'German people who still retain any faith in the assurances of the leaders that the Allies cannot find men and machines to carry the offensive [they] will soon by disillusioned'. It is hard not to read this as anything other than a coded incitement to bomb Berliners.

In this preliminary phase to the main battle of Berlin the long-serving, much-loved Wellington finally disappeared from the front line, but would remain on such duties as minelaying until well into 1944. Though the main swell of expansion was over 3 and 6 Groups were phasing out Stirlings and Halifaxes for Mark II Lancasters. But the need to replace the lost and worn-out Lancasters in their existing squadrons prevented this from forging ahead too rapidly.

One of the most dramatic pieces of reportage about Berlin came from the BBC. On September 4 Wynford Vaughan Thomas accompanied the crew of Lancaster ED586 'F for Freddie', of 207 Squadron, piloted by Flight Lieutenant Letford. The recording revealed the 'matter-of-factness' of the crews, and their dedicated determination shone through. Vaughan Thomas stressed the fury of fire, defensive and offensive that covered Berlin: 'That's the city itself. And there in the heart of the glow there goes a red flash – the biggest we've yet seen… it's pretty obvious as we're coming in now through the searchlight cones that it's going to be hell over the city itself.'[6] All the time the drone of the Lancaster engines shuddered in the background and the odd dull thud. The conversation of the crew itself is remarkable. The audience heard the 'steady… steady…. steady' of the bomb-aimer as they made their bomb run. Then came a sudden rattle of machine guns and the shouts of 'down, down… he's come down.' A fighter had clearly been hit and was crashing downwards. The Australian navigator asked 'Did you shoot him down?' and the reply 'Yes, he's got him boy right in the middle bloody good show' and then loud cheering. The skipper brought them all back to their jobs with understatement, 'OK don't shout at once… keep quiet it's ok.' The bomber then made its 600 mile return to Britain and Vaughan Thomas's heartfelt gratitude at seeing home is heard. The crew was obviously relieved too, for one of them exclaimed: 'It's good to see old England again.' Vaughan Thomas then concluded:

> The crew of 'F for Freddie' and thousands of others like them will be preparing to set out again tonight. Well I can only say that the next time we both of us [he was referring to his recording engineer] hear this roar of English bombers over the countryside we'll feel a new and a very deep respect for the crews who man them.

The BBC conducted a survey of listeners to the 'Cutting the Skipper' programme. They found that the listening figures were 'exceptionally large for an isolated feature programme'. The appreciation index was 92, which had only been equalled once before by a programme about the Battle of Britain. Listeners were asked whether the live material was worth it considering its technical shortcomings. '95% gave an emphatic affirmative… 80% considered that the additional material made the programme much more interesting.'

The most commonly expressed feeling was of admiration for the crew and, not far short of it, admiration for the BBC men who took part. It is clear from the report that people were thrilled by the realism and felt they had learned something about the dangers involved in bombing. Many expressed the deep impression the stoic, quiet heroism of the crew had made on them. It was noted that very few objected to the recording of a bombing mission. Fewer still expressed sympathy with the Berliners. 'Others expressed great satisfaction to have participated in the sensation of dropping a bomb on Berlin.' 'Retired' called it 'a magnificent programme'; 'Secretary' considered it 'the finest broadcast to date' and 'Civil Servant' said 'a most exciting broadcast and one that would stand repeating'.[7]

Earlier in the year Richard Dimbleby had accompanied a Lancaster crew to Berlin, in order to see for himself 'the wonderful work of the men of the Royal Air Force'. While over the city he had been fascinated by the thought 'that down there only a few thousand feet from us Hitler, Goebbels, Goering and Ribbentrop might be hiding in their shelters.' Dimbleby, like Vaughan Thomas, gained an even deeper respect for the men of Bomber Command by the experience:

> For me this attack on Berlin was an unforgettable experience but to the crew of 'W for William' this was routine for they are out on bombing operations day after day, week after week, they are carrying the war right into the heart of Nazi Germany... I understand the hardships now and I am proud to have seen the stars with them.[8]

Listening to these recordings now it is hard not to be profoundly moved. One is thrilled, sobered, shocked, amazed. The immediacy is striking, they are recordings of men in the middle of battle. If they have this effect now, after more than 50 years, then one can only imagine the power they had at the time.

All German cities were given fish codenames. Whitebait was the incongruous name for Berlin. But, to the men of Bomber Command it was simply, and rather ominously, known as 'the Big City'. That was the way both Harris and his men often referred to it, and it was against 'the big city' that Bomber Command was to concentrate its greatest effort. With that flair for the dramatic and theatrical that he possessed Harris told his men in one signal: 'Tonight you go to the big city. You have the opportunity to light a fire in the belly of the enemy which will burn his black heart out.'

Harris felt that he would end the war by burning the black heart out of Germany. He would wreck Berlin from end to end and that would cause Germany's surrender. It was a bit of a strange hope. After all London had not collapsed. Admittedly, it had not faced anything like the bombing potential the RAF now had. But, why should an attack on a capital city result in surrender? Especially if it was a city which did not contain some absolutely vital industry not found anywhere in Germany or its empire? He must have assumed that most of Germany was close to ruin. That his bombers had done as much damage as an invading army and that with an equally heavy attack on the capital it would appear as if Berlin had been surrounded and invaded just as successfully and as completely as any land force could.

During this period, as with much of the year so far, Harris was unchecked by any other orders. He was free to concentrate on his own strategic aim. He mounted thirty-two major raids against Berlin. For his crews it meant long flights in winter weather and reliance on Pathfinders and their *H2S* sets. Within a week of the offensive opening the Stirlings had to be withdrawn. Their ceiling was just too low and they took disproportionate punishment. Though Lancasters and Halifaxes were ordered to come lower to share the dangers and divide the fire, they went for height once the night-fighters appeared. Between August and November 109 Stirlings were lost over Berlin, 6.4 per cent. 3 Group was withdrawn from the battle and Stirlings never flew over Germany again. The Group began a slow conversion to Lancasters. The Stirling was a sad aircraft. Bedevilled by the problem of its poor ceiling, it was never the impressive bombing platform it had promised to be. It also handled badly on the ground and landing and taking off proved heavy going. Despite this, some had affection for it. Flight Engineer W. Westcomb loved its agility in the air.[9] He recalled its tight turning circle, giving it the performance of a fighter. It partly made up for its inability to climb to the highest altitudes by its solid build, Westcomb referred to its 'battleship' strength. The Stirling could also fly on one engine and handled much better than some of the other heavies when lacking power. The bombing war had thrown up an irony. Technical sophistication was proved only by meeting two crude tests – height and weight-lifting ability. Handling and performance in the air almost ran second best to these overriding considerations. The withdrawal of the Stirlings only had the effect of placing 4 and 6 Groups in the firing line with their Mark II and Mark V versions of the Halifax. In the 11 week period from the beginning of December to mid-February 9.8 per cent of Halifaxes despatched to Germany were lost. 434 Squadron suffered a massive 24.2 per cent loss rate and others were not far behind. Harris was forced to withdraw the Halifaxes from the battle. These two depletions lost him 250 aircraft. On the plus side the Mark III Halifaxes were proving to be very good aircraft and their numbers were increasing, as were Lancasters, but they were mainly devoted to replacing losses.

It was not all depletions and losses. A new blind-bombing device was introduced called *G-H*, and was tested by Mosquitoes in October. It was found to be successful, but was then withdrawn until more of them could be made available. *Corona*, the technique of broadcasting German instructions from England, was introduced in order to confuse German night-fighter pilots. Similarly German-speaking aircrew members were also put to work on jamming devices in 101 Squadron, 1 Group, in special aircraft known as *A.B.C.*s (Airborne Cigar). As well as performing the various interdiction and distraction duties, these aircraft also took part in bombing in the normal way. Measure and counter-measure were being thrown into the bombing war at a much greater pace.

The Kammhuber Line and the box system had been made redundant by *Window.* This forced the German defence to become far more mobile, responding to trouble, and so the need to conceal the ultimate destination of the bombers was vital. Mosquitoes were now also used on diversions. They would fly over a town or city and drop target indicators, hoping to confuse the defenders into believing that it was the real target of the raid, thus forcing fighters and defences towards it. This could be a major nuisance to the Germans only when they were actually followed up by small, but nonetheless genuine, raids. Otherwise it quickly became clear that it was not the target and the night-fighters were free to return to the genuine battle. Diversionary raids had the effect, however, of weakening the concentration over the main target. And concentration of bombing was the key to Harris's formula.

The introduction of *Window* therefore revolutionised the German defences. By making the boxes redundant more fighters were free to enter the battle and so-called 'Wild Boar' tactics soon developed. This was the use of fighters as freelance operators, patrolling around cities and bomber streams hoping to get in among them and cause damage. 'Wild Boar' aircraft, however, had few navigational and radar aids and so were assisted into the bomber stream. Because these fighters had to be assisted towards the bomber stream they did not always catch it before it reached the target. 'Wild Boar' aircraft intercepted when and where they could attacking the stream either on its way in or out from the target. Over 400 were in action before the Battle of Berlin was over. This gave all crews the chance to get a slice of the action and improve their techniques.

The German defence began before a raid even started, for they monitored British radio traffic. Before a raid all equipment was tested, including radio and so the increased transmissions usually gave a warning. German radar then looked out for *Window* clouds. German fighters took off and were guided by radio beacons, which often held fighters if it was felt that the bombers would pass close by. Special Junkers 88s would look for the stream and, if they found them, would climb to drop flares thus drawing attention to the stream. All the time a continuous running commentary on the strength and direction of the raid was broadcast: hence the British *Corona* and *A.B.C.* techniques.

Bomber Command responded with the dropping of massive *Window* clouds during its North Sea mining operations in attempts to confuse the Germans as to the actual direction of the attack. Sometimes training flights would come into German radar range, but would then fly home. This was a move also designed to fool the Germans into moving fighters in that direction. Large diversions were put into approaches and routes were often changed. Swedish neutrality was often violated in this way, as the bombers flew across its airspace. The duration over the target was shortened again: 800 bombers passing over Berlin in 20 minutes, with the stream reduced to 70 miles (in 1942 it had been over 300 miles long). Fighter Command was asked to put on more intruder raids, which entailed sweeping over German night-fighter stations and generally causing a nuisance. A new group was formed, 100 (Bomber Support) under Air Commodore E.B. Addison, to co-ordinate intruder and serrate (airborne radar designed to home in on enemy airborne radar) operations and radio counter-measures. This rolling list of measure and counter-measure, innovation and response, gives some impression of the cat and mouse game played over this huge, grinding battle against Berlin. Night after night the crews went out into the freezing winter weather. They flew half way across the continent and back again, against an increasing and vicious German defence.

The Battle of Berlin cost 384 aircraft, lost in 7,403 sorties. Just as the battle was being wound up Bomber Command conducted a disastrous operation against Nuremberg. That dreadful night of March 30/31 saw the Command lose 95 aircraft of the 795 dispatched, 11.9 per cent. It was the biggest Bomber Command disaster of the war. Fortunately for the Command it was also a freak night. The weather was clear all the way into southern Germany and so gave the bombers no cloud-cover in which to hide. The German controllers also ignored all the diversions and sent all fighters against the main stream. The biggest losses occurred during the outward flight, with 82 aircraft shot down. Navigational failures compounded the disaster, for after gallantly fighting their way deep into Germany the bombing was random and scattered. Bombs fell in the outskirts of the nearby town of Schweinfurt and a ten-mile creep back occurred over Nuremberg itself. As successive aircraft tried to avoid the fury of the centre of the battle they dropped their loads short and early, causing the concentration to weaken over the heart of the target. This gave rise to the phenomenon known as 'creep back'. The press reported the raid in a remarkably calm and matter of fact manner. Recalling Peirse's debacle over Berlin in the winter of 1941, much of the blame was put on the weather. Though undoubtedly a freak night for the Command, the Nuremberg raid, like the Battle of Berlin, revealed the power of the German night defences which became formidable when combined with bad weather.

Damage to Berlin was erratic, though it caused more damage than Bomber Command assumed at that time. Berlin could not be destroyed like Hamburg. For a start the weather conditions were never going to approximate those of July. Secondly, Berlin was essentially a nineteenth and twentieth century city, made up of broad boulevards and avenues. It was therefore extremely difficult to create a massive, all-consuming fire. As a large city, it was also very hard to concentrate the bombing. Sergeant Hannah of 9 Squadron flew his first mission over Berlin; he remembered the intensity of the defences, but 'most of all the immensity of the city and our excruciatingly slow progress across it. Doubtless this is how it came by its nickname "The Big City".'[10] By April 1944 Berlin was nowhere near the state of devastation Harris had predicted.

Such a vicious battle was a severe test of morale and the resilience of the crews. Some Halifax squadrons had a consistently higher early return rate than other squadrons, reflecting the growing sense of vulnerability within these crews. The mood was not lightened by attempts to increase tonnage of bombs. 1 Group tried this on a wider scale than any other Group, but its Lancasters were the ones that most often jettisoned them over the North Sea in order to improve manoeuvrability. Strikingly, however, these incidents were the exception. Bomber Command's crews, as a whole, pressed on with remarkable fortitude and bravery. But for those involved survival could not be guaranteed by skill and common sense measures alone. Rituals and superstitions were important. Harry le Marchant always took a Victorian penny, given to him by a WAAF, on missions.[11] He also recalled that many men had lucky scarves or teddy bears and similar items, all of which were ritually worn or placed in the aircraft before a raid. After a raid men did their best to unwind. Most could not sleep directly after a raid, even though they had been up many hours. 'You were just so highly strung. You tried to calm down, but you had to let off steam to calm down… You would have a number of beers and get yourself into the state where you could go to sleep. That was how you got over it. You were just glad to have got back and survived,'[12] recalled John Gee, a Lancaster pilot.

Men turned to any comforts at hand. All Ranks dances gave men the chance to meet the WAAFs at closer quarters. In 1943 a report condemned these dances and noted that Bomber Command had the highest rate of venereal disease in the RAF.[13] The very worst levels in the service were found in the Canadian 6 Group. Further away from home and less class and discipline conscious than their British comrades, the Canadian boys lived for the moment regardless of consequences. Air Ministry snobbery meant that such findings confirmed prejudices about other ranks and colonials. But those who flew a desk – as the Air Staff was contemptuously referred to by aircrew – did not have the first inclination of what a raid over Germany could be like. They did not know the strain it caused on men's minds and bodies.

The Air Staff might have known the technical details of the German defences. If they checked one of their reference works or files they could probably find that a Junkers 88 night-fighter mounted three 20mm cannons. They might have known that each shell was explosive and armour piercing, with a reinforced incendiary tip that burned at a temperature between 2,000 and 3,000 degrees centigrade for nearly a second. They might have known that each cannon could fire 520 rounds per minute. But they probably did not know – and would never know as the men at the sharp end did – that the shell could decapitate a man in a bomber. That a mere 20 shells could destroy a bomber. They probably could not imagine men feeling their bladders and bowels relax in the extremity of fear. Not even when they stretched their imaginations to the full did they realise that a cannon shell into the stomach of an airman would atomise his abdomen spraying a bloody foam around the fuselage. While writing scathing reports about V.D. cases they probably did not pause to consider that men were sometimes sucked out of gaping holes in aircraft opened by the sudden slam of cannon shells. These men fell without their parachutes, for they had been stored earlier. From about 16,000 feet a man fell at 120 mph and would take about 90 seconds to reach the ground. On hitting the ground the body split open like a bloated water balloon, having suffered a deceleration equivalent to 450 times the force of gravity. Death was at least instant, but what about those 90 seconds before death?

Incredibly morale did not drop so much as efficiency, caused by men and machines flying in atrocious winter conditions at the limit of their endurance. As in all military matters, new crews were the ones to suffer most. Lack of experience decreased the chances of survival. It was the old vicious circle, for you could not gain experience unless you survived. Berlin was a defeat for the Command, but it was not for want of trying on the part of its crews.

In his memoirs Harris stressed the devastation wrought on Berlin, but avoided any final judgement. When interviewed by Thames Television for its series *The World at War*, in the early seventies, Harris stuck to his line: 'I am not saying the Battle of Berlin was a defeat or anything like a defeat. I think it was a major contribution towards the defeat of Germany.' The views of those who carried out the task are mixed. For C.J. Gray it was a defeat: 'The city was not destroyed, nor the German will. Far from it. It was the weapon itself, our Bomber Command, that was blunted and brought close to destruction.'[14] T.R. Lister puts a slightly different interpretation on it: 'I always think that we never quite sorted Berlin out. Perhaps it was too far; bomb loads were smaller, defences were very considerable, but we did paste it. Perhaps we could call it a draw.'[15] For H. Hudson the need to break Germany by any means was paramount: 'It was a battle, no question. My own impression was that we were engaged in a tremendous effort to smash Germany and nothing else mattered.'[16] Harris set out to smash Berlin and win the war without the need for invasion. He did not do that. Berlin was a defeat. Berlin was a city too far.

For the public the battle was presented as the ultimate clash. The *Daily Mirror* implied the spirit of an end-game on November 20, running the headline, 'RAF Went Out Again: Knock-Out Assault Starts', and went on to record the opening of a new chapter in the strategic air campaign.[17] Readers were told of the blackout of European radio stations as British bombers caused disruption to German power supplies and communications networks. It was the fulfilment of the earlier promises made by Churchill and Harris. The report was filled with a sense of wonder at the strength and ability of Bomber Command. The choice of words also reflected an atavistic pleasure in hitting the city of Berlin. It was reported that Berlin was on Harris's list of German 'arsenals and war-making centres' marked for 'emasculation' and that 'they will be razed, often two a night or perhaps more.'

Reporting on the successive raids, the *Mirror* implied that ordinary daily life in Berlin was grinding to a halt, phone communications down, no newspapers and streets blocked off to traffic.[18] The *Express* was keen to report that the key Nazi buildings had been hit, including the Chancellery, Hitler's official apartments, the Foreign Office, the War Office and the homes of Ribbentrop and Goebbels.[19] The leader struck an attitude of judgement. It asked Berliners to judge for themselves how their leader's war was progressing. 'He who took up the sword will perish by the sword. And the flames in which he swore he would convulse the world in his fall will be the flames of Berlin and the cities of Germany'. A promise rang out from the leader. Readers were told that the campaign would not stop until Berlin had been reduced to the same heap of smouldering ashes as Hamburg. The feigning of ignorance about bombing policy by British people after the war seems more and more of a confidence trick.

The sheer tonnage of bombs dropped and aircraft involved was a further source of interest to the newspapers. Constant comparisons were made between the tonnage dropped on London and that Berlin was now receiving. The *Mirror* noted that 'in about thirty minutes a load nearly six times as big as the heaviest tonnage ever dropped on London in a night was unleashed.'[20] And in March 1944 it trumpeted a new record of tonnage dropped in one night. Berlin was 'the most bombed city in the world', according to the *Sketch*.[21] A few weeks later it referred to 'the elimination of the capital of Nazism', and a few weeks later still it succinctly stated that Berlin had suffered 'an obliteration attack. Just that'.[22] Just as it was said that Germany was unable to save the

Ruhr, the same was true of Berlin. The *Daily Telegraph* said: 'All Germany must soon realise that Hitler and the generals cannot defend the capital and that it has been irrevocably lost... Now the Battle of Berlin has become the Battle of Germany.'[23]

Occasionally the press felt it had to explain the bombing policy, and defend it from any charges of being pointless or merely a retribution (even though that element did bubble under the surface throughout):

> There is nothing hypocritical in asserting that we regret the necessity of delivering these terrible blows on Germany, for it is the literal truth [a leader in the *Daily Sketch* said]. But the necessity is inescapable if the war is not to be unduly prolonged.
>
> Totalitarian war – a German invention – is one and indivisible, and the economic structure of the enemy is as fully a military target as an army in the field, a squadron of aeroplanes in the sky, or a fleet of ships at sea. So much so that Bomber Command does not select its own targets, but, as Mr Dingle told a Manchester audience yesterday, has them chosen for it by the Ministry of Economic Warfare.[24]

In fact, the Ministry of Economic Warfare waged a constant battle with Harris over the right to choose targets. Harris never agreed with the so-called panacea or bottleneck theory, and ruthlessly pursued the area strategy. The only reason why he was allowed to defy a government department was down to the War Cabinet itself. Harris was never stopped because the War Cabinet was in agreement with him.

The *Spectator* noted that the civilian casualties inflicted on Berlin were 'not intended as an act of revenge for the bombing of London in 1940 and 1941'.[25] It went on to regret the loss of civilian life in Germany, 'but it is a consequence which the Germans have made inevitable by compelling us to strike at the centres of their strength as they have struck at ours.' The tone of all such pieces seems to be 'sorry: but they started it.' Movietone caught this tone perfectly. One of its stories on the battle reported that 'Berlin is getting a real taste of total war.'[26] The Hun was reeling according to the commentary. Not only reeling, but regretful. 'How he must regret the ruthless attacks he made on Warsaw, Rotterdam, Belgrade, London, Coventry and the rest. The day and night of reckoning is definitely near.'

An extremely interesting leader appeared in the *Daily Mail* in November. It claimed Britain was not out to smash German morale, but was involved in a new strategy of war, an attempt to break the enemy by destroying its sinews.[27] All Goebbels' claims that the RAF was involved in a terror mission were laughed off. But this reveals a split in opinions, for many in Britain were convinced it was an attack on morale, and that Bomber Command had been carrying out such a policy for a long time. The decision to go for morale was indeed made by the Air Ministry a long time previous, but the British people were never told this clearly and unambiguously. The public debate about bombing and the debate carried out by the various newspapers and newsreels was grounded in the facts presented to them by the Air Ministry and Bomber Command, aided by a great deal of reading between the lines. By following this procedure the British people must have had a knowledge of what British bombing policy actually entailed. But deductions made from such varied and contradictory sources make it much less surprising that the popular image of the bombing war, and its memory since has become shot through with contradictions, myths and legends.

Berlin, as the culmination of the campaign, also brought it with the culmination of much of the debates about the nature and value of British bombing. 'Can the war be won by bombing alone?' This question was asked more and more as the bombing campaign moved towards its crescendo. There were certainly very few doubts that bombing was seriously affecting German industry. In April 1944 the *National Review* ran an article detailing the losses of German industrial capacity.[28] It produced a list of cities hit and the industries they contained. Others doubted not the effect of bombing, but the nature of the policy. Hugh Quigley, writing in the *Fortnightly Review* in August 1942, believed that bombing cities such as Lubeck was a complete waste of time. For Quigley these targets were not of enough industrial significance and he added 'it is quite clear that, as far as industrial objectives are concerned, our bombing policy requires drastic revision.'[29]

Many were coming to the conclusion that bombing was a very important part of the war, but it would not end the war in itself. Squadron Leader John Strachey, a man who would later play a significant role in Harris's life, wrote in the *Listener* that 'bombing is *one* of the ways by which Germany will be brought to her knees. One of the ways. Of course we are not trying to "win the war by bombing alone". How could bombing alone win the war?'[30] A similar stance was taken by *The Times*, though stressing the importance of the bombing offensive, it was noted that it 'offers no assurance that [it]... would in time bring the enemy to his knees. All the other fighting resources at the disposal of the allies will be demanded.'[31] There were very few who believed that the bomber offensive was having no effect. One of the apostates, writing under the title 'XYZ', thought that the 'current programmes are pushing the development of our strategic bombing force too far' and was concerned that a further £615 million had been allocated to it.[32] As far as he was concerned there were just too many variables involved to be reasonably confident of any success coming from bombing.

A potent argument in favour of bombing was the two-pronged one that it would prepare the way for invasion – the actual justification of the campaign in the Point-blank Directive – and that it would reduce British casualties. Lord Trenchard took up this line when he wrote to *The Times*, urging still more resources be poured into the bomber programme:

> The bomber is the spearhead of the vital offensive that dominates the war. This is proved by Bomber Command – that force which is so much smaller than many of us who believe in the power of the bomber consider absolutely necessary. Yet what an effect that force is having on Germany. It is not too much to say that our bombing of Germany is causing much more alarm and anxiety to the Nazi chiefs than anything else at present [this, of course, rather ignores the titanic struggle on the eastern front]... An attack by armies on Germany can only be successful, as in the last war, with appalling casualties, unless, through previous bombing, the whole organisation behind the armies is demoralised and destroyed, as it is steadily in Germany... [The raids] are battles comparable to the effect on the outcome of the war to the Somme of the last war... This is

the way the war will be shortened and lives will be saved, provided we double or treble our bomber offensive. Nothing must stand in the way of this.[33]

The omnipresent shadow of the Great War is clear in this piece. The air offensive was the way of avoiding the slaughter of the Western Front between 1914 and 1918. It was a spirit succinctly caught by the *Daily Express* when it announced that air power 'means no more Passchendaeles'.[34] But that is exactly what the campaign had become. Between September 1942 and September 1944 Bomber Command lost nearly 30,000 men. Germany was being reduced to rubble, but the cost in British lives was enormous. The supposedly clean, surgical campaign of the air had become a brutal slugging match as prolonged, vicious and frustrating as any battle of the Western Front had been.

For Strachey the value of the bomber lay in its ability to reduce Germany to such a degree that invasion would become a guaranteed success. He urged every man and woman to support the bomber offensive in the winter of 1943, for by it 'the lives of hundreds of thousands of our men may be saved when the last great battle comes.'[35] The *Daily Telegraph* added that bombing by itself might not make the Reich collapse, but 'it would certainly smooth the invasion and therefore it is the most effectual means of shortening the war.'[36]

The *Spectator* managed to make the increasing bomber losses in the tough fight against Berlin almost a moment of triumph by the use of a subtle, but valuable argument. It noted that the losses proved German industry had moved over to the defensive and that all its fighters were now employed on defending the Reich rather than offensively fighting for it.[37] The bomber offensive was therefore working. Albert Speer's testimony lent weight to this assertion. After the war Speer maintained that the air offensive was a second front from 1943, for it forced a massive diversion of resources from the hard pressed eastern front. Of particular importance was the commitment of much of the production of the 8.8 cm gun to anti-aircraft duties within Germany, rather than their deployment on the Russian front. Speer recalled, 'I think the damage you did by bombing was very heavy, but the damage you did by weakening the German Army was much more.'[38] However, the use of such an argument seems a little disingenuous for it appears that the true success of the bombing came from an almost accidental by-product.

As the bombing campaign struck at more and more targets and caused more and more destruction, the debate over its morality intensified. 1943 and the Battle of Berlin merely served to heighten an already established public debate. J.M. Spaight, contributing a further article to the *Spectator*, argued that in modern war the distinction between combatant and non-combatant was blurred, for the civilian working in a war factory was as much a combatant as a soldier at the front. British bombing, according to his argument, was also essentially defensive and therefore justifiable, for the British were destroying in order to save millions of others. His thesis was given much greater credibility by his reference to the reality of the situation in 1943: 'There would, in fact, be no case against bombing if as great a degree of precision were possible as was thought at one time to be practicable.'[39] For many people bombing in itself was not wrong, but they were unsure whether it was the technical problems of bombing or whether it was by deliberate policy that British bombing had an indiscriminate nature.

Having no definite knowledge of Air Ministry and Bomber Command policy, the press and public were always in a state of some confusion. Certainly the BBC had indulged in much thought as to the best way to cover the bomber offensive. The BBC archives include a memo in which various approaches were discussed. First on the memo was the 'so-called rational point of view'.[40] According to this argument, it was the job of the Corporation to explain that heavy bombing had to be accepted because it would shorten the war. The second point considered whether it was correct to off-set any pity for the Germans by reminders of German aerial atrocities such as the raid on Rotterdam. Inserted into this point was a note on the danger of such reminders fanning the spirit of revenge. According to the final recommendations the best attitude for the BBC to adopt was one in which it was stressed that: 'the war must be short-ened, if necessary by the most dramatic methods, because Jews are being tortured and children dying of hunger. Rotterdam is over and done with. Its inhabitants can no doubt be revenged if that is what we want, but French children can be saved – that is a matter for the future.'

In treading this delicate path the BBC occasionally ran into trouble. Portal was most upset to receive complaints about the BBC's coverage of the raid on Leipzig on October 20/21 1943. Portal wrote to his Deputy Chief of Staff, to Sinclair, Secretary of State for Air, and his Director of Publicity:

> I understand that a complaint has been made to you that the account apologised for our bombing offensive and attempted to defensively justify what we were doing by reference to marshalling yards of which the public were tired... In order to make the matter clearer I have for some time been expounding that the whole of an industrial city is in itself a military objective. Only last Thursday, as a result of special guidance given in regard to the purpose of area bombing, the prin-cipal newspapers were full of the damage done to 17 of Germany's major cities including a direct comparison with the damage suffered at Coventry.[41]

Portal was moving towards a more open explanation of what British bombing entailed, but it was not enough for Harris. Portal's letter provoked Harris into action. He demanded a full statement about British bombing. He demanded a clear admission that civilians were being killed *as a matter of policy*:

> The aim of the Combined Bomber Offensive [he wrote to Portal and Sinclair on October 25] and the part which Bomber Command is required by agreed British-US strategy to play in it, should be unambiguously and publicly stated. That aim is the destruction of German cities, the killing of German workers and the disruption of civilised community life throughout Germany.
>
> It should be emphasised that the destruction of houses, public utilities, transport and lives, the creation of a refugee problem on an unprecedented scale, and the breakdown of morale both at home and at the battle fronts by fear of extended and intensified bombing, are accepted and intended aims of our bombing policy. They are not by-products of attempts to hit factories.
>
> The successes gained should publicly be assessed in terms of the extent to which they realise

this policy. It should be made clear that the destruction of factory installations is only a part and by no means the most important part of the plan. Acreages of housing devastation are infinitely more important.[42]

Harris had given his understanding of British policy and how he was implementing it. Whether one believes it was militarily or morally justifiable, it is hard not to have a grudging admiration for Harris's forthright and honest attitude. But it was not an attitude he could expect the Air Ministry or government to share. After many drafts the Air Council drew up a reply to Harris. The Council accepted that the Pointblank Directive had referred to an attack on German morale 'but your directive neither requires nor enjoins direct attack on German civilians as such'.[43] They concluded that 'the emphasis [in all official communiqués] is such as to bring out what to the Air Council is an obvious truth i.e. that the widespread devastation is not an end in itself but the inevitable accompaniment of an all-out attack on the enemy's means and capacity to wage war.' Harris was not satisfied and went back on the offensive: 'I repeat that the cities of Germany including their working population, houses and public utilities are literally the heart of Germany's "war potential". That is why they are deliberately attacked.'[44]

Harris was never to get his unequivocal statement and the lack of it has led to much misunderstanding, argument and mythmaking. The Secretary of State for Air, Sir Archibald Sinclair, never made a clear statement in the Commons. Sinclair was not the man to rock the boat. In his high wing collar, with his chiselled face and thick grey hair, he had the look of middle aged actor specialising in cerebral detectives. His moment of principled action came and went in the early 1930s. As a Liberal committed to the cause of free trade he resigned over the issue of protectionism. His war years were marked by a willingness to do whatever Churchill and the Air Ministry wanted. Bland, empty statements were Sinclair's tools. It was a policy committed to obfuscation and outright dissimulation. In the long run it did Bomber Command, Harris and the British people no good whatsoever. The public, lacking this clear knowledge, continued to argue out the pros and cons of British bombing. J.B. Davy replied to Trenchard's letter to *The Times*, for him it was obvious 'that the human destruction is now much in the categories hitherto regarded as non-combatant – including women and children – and not exclusively in those of combatant man-power.'[45] This was an acceptance of the need to kill civilian workers engaged in war industries. But it revealed qualms about the deaths of women and children. It was perhaps this more intense and brutal prosecution of the war that provoked Leo Chiozza Money MP to write to the *New Statesman* complaining of public gloating at the success of allied bombing.[46]

Morality and military expediency were clashing more intently than ever before. Bishop George Bell had entered the debate early on. In 1943 the Archbishop of York, Dr Cyril Garbett, expressed his views. He published a diocesan letter, which then appeared in *The Times*. Garbett understood that civilians were being killed by British bombing, but he did not think they were being deliberately targeted.[47] He then explained that life often involved choices which were not clear cut and often involved the acceptance of a degree of wrong in order to prevent an even greater evil. He accepted that the RAF aimed at military objectives with the aim of breaking down the enemy. While pursuing this policy civilians were killed. But, he argued, if the bombing succeeded it would shorten the war and would save thousands of lives. Those who demanded the suspension of the British bombing campaign were probably condemning thousands more British soldiers to death. 'Often in life,' he concluded, 'there is no clear choice between absolute right and wrong.' Finally he added: 'frequently the choice has to be made of the lesser of two evils, and it is a lesser evil to bomb a war-loving Germany than to sacrifice the lives of thousands of our own countrymen who long for peace and to delay delivering millions now held in slavery.'

The concept of a war-loving Germany could be used as an excuse for the area bombing of Germany. It was felt that the accidental deaths of ordinary German civilians might help to chastise a people who had twice in one century unleashed the dogs of war. Even those who doubted whether bombing was having any great effect on the outcome of the war thought this 'punishment element' might be worthwhile. According to 'XYZ''s article in the *National Review*, the Germans were suffering the realities of war for the first time for over a century.[48] 'All the other wars of aggression which the Germans have waged during the nineteenth and early twentieth centuries have devastated other nations… Now the Germans are having a lesson they have long needed.'

Richard Stokes MP, reiterated his earlier doubts over the efficiency of the strategic air offensive. Unlike 'XYZ', however, he believed that the entire area offensive was misconceived and its punishment element was only likely to sow more bitterness in Germany. In December 1943, at just the moment Harris was urging the Air Ministry to make a clear policy statement, Stokes asked Sinclair in the Commons whether the government wasn't simply afraid of admitting that it was carrying out an indiscriminate area offensive. Sinclair repeated the official line that civilians were killed as an unpleasant side-effect of the air campaign against German industry. Stokes' opposition was hard to deal with, for he was a man with real experience of war. A man whose opinions were based on something other than home front philosophising. Stokes was also a passionate believer in the tactical use of air power and a shrewd thinker on military matters. Sinclair was often forced to waffling replies and repetition of official phraseology. He certainly did not want to get into a detailed argument with Stokes. Two more famous military thinkers, and fellow veterans of the Great War, Basil Liddle Hart and J.F.C. Fuller, were in agreement with Stokes' questioning of the military value of the offensive. Fuller argued that the RAF was now so powerful as to dictate strategy to the government. An Air Staff official wrote to Sinclair reminding him that Fuller was entirely wrong, for the RAF was carrying out government policy, a policy 'adopted after due consideration by successive governments, after weighing the advice of the Service reports'.[49]

Still no one asked the bomber crews themselves what they thought about the campaign. They continued with their routine. Detached, dedicated and rarely aware of either the criticism of their countrymen or the experiences of the Germans down below. The crews did their jobs. They bombed on the target indicators and stoked up the fires. They had their orders and they carried them out. The Germans could surrender if they did not like it. For aircrew critics were a bunch who lived in safe surroundings, armchair strategists who could afford to make pronouncements. They did not take kindly to those who said their protest was as much to spare British lives as Germans. It all seemed too patronising. It often looked as if British lives were mentioned only as an after thought. The real point of concern was the suffering of the Germans. Most aircrews, like their boss, simply did not care about the Germans one way or another.

The most famous of Bomber Command's critics, Bishop George Bell, brought the debate to a head in February 1944, when the Battle of Berlin was still raging. Bell had been urging the Church, and the Archbishop of Canterbury, Dr William Temple, in particular, to take a stronger line. In July 1943 he had asked Temple to raise the issue of the nature of area bombing in the Lords and force a clear response from Bomber Command. Temple had dismissed the whole idea and remained silent, but the Archbishop of York was prepared to make a public statement though not of the sort Bell wanted. Frustrated by Temple and Garbett, Bell took matters into his own hands. In February he stood up in the Lords and attacked Bomber Command's policy as one which shamed the British cause and threatened a wholesale collapse of morality and civilised society. As in his earlier protests he was at pains to point out he was not against all bombing and he understood that civilians would be killed, but he believed the current strategy of area bombing was too horrifically random to be accepted. 'I fully realise that in attacks on centres of war industry and transport the killing of civilians when it is the result of bona fide military activity is inevitable,' he said. 'But there must be a fair balance between the means employed and the purpose achieved. To obliterate a whole town because certain portions contain military and industrial establishments is to reject the balance.'[50]

Bell's protest has been taken as the cry of decent British people everywhere when they began to realise the implications of British bombing policy. But this was, and is, a myth. Sure enough the 'quality' newspapers remarked upon it. The *Daily Telegraph* in particular, but the popular dailies did not seem to have been that interested in Bell. The *Telegraph* took on Bell and found his argument wanting. For its leader writer Bell's attitude was naive, he was placed in the same category as the guilty men who had got Britain into the mess of war. The shadow of appeasement was resurrected by reminding Bell that those who had tried to reason with the Nazis had got nowhere. At the same time it denied British bombing policy was dedicated to revenge and pointless destruction. 'It is an indispensable prelude to a peace which shall be more than a mere armistice.'[51] The piece went on to state that to stop bombing might imperil civilisation thus inverting Bell's argument.

A few days after Bell aired his reasoned concerns, Lady Macassey wrote to the *Telegraph* pointing out her admiration for his moral courage and asking why the other bishops had remained silent, expressing no view one way or the other (she seems to have forgotten about Garbett and Woodward).[52] A.P. Austin, who pointed out the fact that he was an atheist, also expressed respect for Bell's decision to speak out.[53]

However, one correspondent said German industry had to be crushed and the Germans should have evacuated women and children from their cities. Another said he worked in a factory and understood the risks involved in that. If he knew and accepted he might be bombed then the German workers knew and accepted it too. The Reverend (denomination unstated) James Reid declared that the RAF's best method 'is to smash the wasp's nest'.[54] One of the most forthright condemnations of the critics of British bombing came in the spring of 1943. It was a response to Stokes' questions in the House. The *Sunday Dispatch* thundered out a message of retribution and punishment, claiming it had the support of the public:

> those MPs who appear to regard the German civilians as their own constituents can be assured that the British public is not shedding any crocodile tears over the bombing of German cities.
>
> … Hundreds of German civilians who exulted in the sufferings of Rotterdam, London, and the English provinces exult no more. They are dead in the ruins of those cities from which their flamboyant columns set out to enslave the peoples of the world.
>
> The bombs which we aim at Germany's armaments and communications have a secondary target, and let us make no bones about it.
>
> We are in a position, after years of humiliation and suffering, to blast an understanding of the war into the real German mind. That is not a matter for which we should apologise. It is a service to the rest of mankind.[55]

Did the British public really believe this? Bell's criticisms inspired the *New Statesman* to publish Mass Observation's latest survey of opinions on British bombing. It found that in London six out of ten people gave unqualified verbal approval to the raids.[56] Two said they were necessary, but expressed major qualms about their effects on the civilian population of Germany. Only one in ten felt they were too awful to be approved in any way, 'though few go so far as wanting them stopped'. It was found that very few expressed gloating or vengeful sentiments. Only one in six felt that bombing would end the war, but considerably more believed that it would shorten it 'and this is the most usual reason for approval of our raids'. The survey was obviously carried out in the knowledge that British bombing was aimed at civilians, for it was noted that 'an interesting reflection of the depth of guilt felt about bombing *people* is afforded by the extent to which men and women still manage to believe that we are only bombing military targets.' To imply that people were not interested in retribution is wrong, however, for the survey also found that most people wanted Germany dismembered and comprehensive war crimes trials. Whatever ambiguities surround the public knowledge of, and debate about, British bombing the overwhelming conclusion is that most people wanted it to continue and believed that it was proving effective in some way.

British strategic bombing reached its crescendo during the period 1942–spring 1944. During this period came such incredible feats as the first 1000 bomber raid, the mining of the Möhne and the Eder dams, the razing of Hamburg and the unleashing of a sustained campaign against the German capital. It was a period in which the bomber dominated British strategic thinking and in which there was agreement between government, Air Ministry and Bomber Command as to the policy. The points of disagreement were more to do with nuances of understanding and presentation than fundamental differences. British bombers set out to smash German cities into submission by killing Germans, destroying their houses and ruining their industries. Harris knew it, Portal knew it and Churchill knew it, the crews probably guessed it, but they were, in that rather hackneyed, but in this case nonetheless true phrase, only carrying out orders. The only difference was that Harris was prepared to admit it to all and sundry.

The British public was presented with many different interpretations of the aerial war, but deep down there probably was a sense of what the bombing policy actually meant. By 1942 the war was very obviously one of national survival. Nazi forces were rampant on the Atlantic. They were preparing to swallow even more chunks of the Soviet Union. They were driving towards the Suez Canal and had pushed their ships through the English Channel under the eyes of the impotent British. In the Far East Japan had taken Hong Kong, Singapore had fallen, Mandalay was abandoned, Darwin was bombed. It was not a moment for delicate stomachs. Britain needed to win, or else, in Churchill's words, it 'would slip into the abyss of a new dark age', and in that moment of supreme national emergency a force was created which would unleash a terrifying level of violence against the enemy. In 1943 that force was allowed its chance to win the war alone. It did not do so, but the spring of 1944 was to bring Bomber Command a new mission, a mission on which the real point of allied strategy as formularised by the Pointblank Directive depended.

1. Sir Richard Peirse, Commander-in-Chief Bomber Command 1940-1941, with Sir Robert Saundby, Senior Air Staff Officer, at Bomber Command Headquarters, High Wycombe.

2. Sir Arthur 'Bomber' Harris, Commander-in-Chief Bomber Command, 1942-1945, at his desk at High Wycombe. Harris rarely left High Wycombe thanks to his enormous workload.

3. ABOVE. Armstrong Whitworth Whitleys under construction. Britain made a huge industrial commitment to the bomber war.

4. BELOW. 'Wings for Victory Week', Trafalgar Square, March 1943. London witnessed its biggest crowd since the coronation of George VI for the fund-raising week, revealing the enthusiasm of the British people for the RAF.

5. ABOVE. A Vickers Wellington of 214 Squadron undergoing repairs in the hangar in late 1941. Without the tireless work of the ground crews Bomber Command would never have maintained its offensive.

6. BELOW. Bomber Command flew in all seasons and the weather rarely grounded the force completely.

7. ABOVE. 'Bombing up' a Lancaster and fusing a 400lb 'cookie'.

8. BELOW. 'Bombing up' a Whitley, 1940. Note the difference in bomb size and load compared with the Lancaster.

9. ABOVE. 'And your target for tonight is Nuremburg'. Crews at a briefing.

10. BELOW. An intelligence officer questioning a crew after a raid on Berlin.

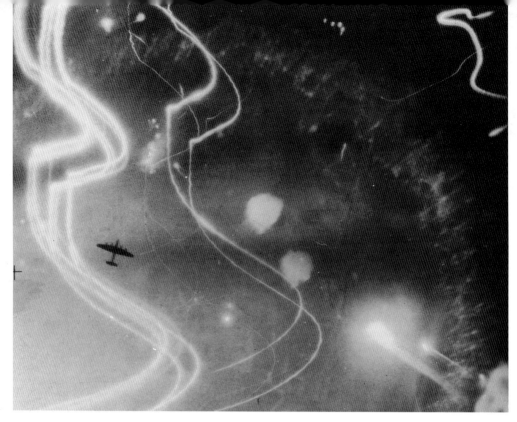

11. ABOVE. A Halifax caught in the light of a photoflash over St Ghislain, Belgium, May 1/2 1944.

12. BELOW. Halifaxes over Pforzheim, 1943. Note the target indicators tumbling down.

13. ABOVE. Halifax over Wanne-Eickel in a daylight raid, October 1944.

14. BELOW. Hamburg, 1945. The vast majority of the destruction was caused in July 1943.

15. ABOVE. Berliners awaiting burial, Christmas 1943.

16. BELOW. The Bielefeld railway viaduct after 617 Squadron's 'Grand Slam' attack, March 1945.

. . . .

CHAPTER SIX

Achieving Victory, Spring 1944–May 1945

Bielefeld railway viaduct was a huge and impressive structure. Brick spans arched up and supported the main Hanover-Hamm railway line. It was a major cog in the German transport machine. It allowed the Germans to move troops towards the western front quickly and efficiently. On March 14 1945 28 Lancasters of 5 Group supported by *Oboe*-marking Mosquitoes attacked the viaduct in broad daylight. A smaller group of aircraft attacked the Arnsberg viaduct. The Lancasters dropped Barnes Wallis's new 22,000lb bomb, the *Grand Slam* and his *Tallboy*. *Grand Slam* was a good name, for the bomb had the power to cause a mini-earthquake. It literally shook the viaduct to the ground. A significant blow to the German transport system had been struck.

All the newspapers announced the debut of this weapon and considerable pride was taken in the fact that it was a British design. The *Sketch* called it 'our new volcano weapon'.[1] Universal, Paramount and Movietone newsreels all showed the twisted ruins of tracks, the great craters and rubble of the brickwork.[2]

On November 12 1944 31 Lancasters had used Wallis's *Tallboy* on the last great vessel of the Germany navy, the *Tirpitz*. Moored in a Norwegian fjord, the *Tirpitz* had been a constant worry to the Royal Navy. Attacking it in 1944 was actually a waste of time, for her hour had long since come and gone. But Churchill, the romantic, loved the idea of sinking the 'glittering prize' of the German fleet. The Lancasters attacked and their crews watched in awe as the mighty ship was lost in a fountain of water and then smoke and steam. When it cleared they saw that the *Tirpitz* had capsized. One thousand of the 1,900 men on board had been killed or injured. The blow had little strategic significance, but it was yet another example of the terrific power of Bomber Command.

The RAF was out in broad daylight, conducting a precision bombing campaign. After five years of war the force was acting according to the plans made for it in the thirties. What had happened since the Battle of Berlin to alter the situation so radically?

The failure to destroy Berlin, and end the war, was not as big a blow to the prestige of Bomber Command as might have been expected. The preparations for the invasion of Europe, which increased with such rapidity in the spring of 1944, was such an enormous job that it completely precluded any deep enquiry into the Berlin campaign. Undoubtedly some felt depressed. E.J. Densley recalled the Berlin raids: 'I really do think that it was felt that we really were striking a blow against the Nazis that would be devastating, and I always felt surprised and disappointed that the war lasted for over a year after I finished my tour.'[3] The public was told that Berlin had been wrecked and this was a great service to the allies. Now the bomber force was to help the allies in a different way, it was to become a heavy, tactical bombing instrument designed to smooth the path of invasion.

The invasion of the continent required Bomber Command to hit a wide range of targets, large and small, precisely and effectively. It was therefore a very different type of bombing to that Harris's crews were used to and well versed in. The official date for the start of this new tactical campaign was April 14. But Harris had made a start on bombing some of the targets in March. Given Harris's commitment to strategic bombing and his brusque treatment of other strategies he should be given credit for his wholehearted co-operation in this enterprise.

The main part of the air plan for Operation OVERLORD (the codename for the Normandy landings) was an interdiction programme drawn up by the scientist, Solly Zuckerman. He planned to cut off Normandy from the rest of the Reich by bombing main railway junctions and viaducts. There were also raids on ammunition dumps, military camps and armaments factories in Belgium and France. Then, immediately prior to the landings, there was to be a pounding of gun emplacements, radar and radio stations. A massive deception plan had been built into this whereby bombs were also rained down on the Pas de Calais area so as to fool the Germans into believing the invasion would take place in this region. Along with the USAAF Bomber Command dropped nearly two bombs for every one dropped in Normandy, thus making it even harder for the enemy to predict the actual invasion spot.

Bomber Command had developed the tactic of the Master Bomber to direct raids. The Master Bomber arrived over a target and acted as an on-the-spot conductor, observing the fall of indicators and bombs and provided a commentary giving advice as to which fires and indicators to aim at. Master Bombers did much to achieve even greater concentration and helped to ensure that fires caused by stray bombs did not divert too many raiders from the precise target. These tactics were now used more widely against the invasion targets. Bomber crews showed great determination and skill in placing their bombs on the exact spot. It has been suggested that such work inspired the crews more, for here was no abstract way to help victory but a direct blow in support of a definite plan. Further, it was a lot easier attacking targets in France and Belgium than in the fiercely defended skies of Germany even though these raids ran the risk of killing friendly civilians.

A significant tactical innovation came about when 5 Group gained some squadrons from Bennett's 8 Group Pathfinder Force. 83, 97 and 627 (Mosquito) squadrons, like all of Bennett's force had a strong sense of *esprit de corps*. They, like Bennett, did not take kindly to the order to transfer to Sir Ralph Cochrane's 5 Group. Cochrane had turned 5 Group into an elite force to rival Bennett's. 5 Group gained its thoroughly well deserved reputation as the cutting edge of the Command thanks to Cochrane's drive and energy. He shared much in common with Bennett, for he too led by personal example. He visited his men regularly and took to the skies regularly too. This meant he always had a firsthand knowledge of each twist and turn of the air war.

Leonard Cheshire, who taken Guy Gibson's place as commander of 617 Squadron, and Cochrane became convinced that low-level marking was possible which would improve bombing accuracy still further. Cheshire also believed the speed of the Mosquito would allow him to safely remain over the target directing operations, correcting and adjusting the bombing by live commentary. Bennett believed it was impossible to map-read accurately at low level but Cochrane persisted.

Harris was a convert to Cochrane's ideas and he ordered Bennett to transfer some squadrons. But the men were to retain their Pathfinder badges, ranks and pay. Bennett was furious and argued fiercely with Harris. Harris being immovable he eventually, reluctantly, conceded. It was a fascinating clash for Bomber Command had produced men capable of passionate, intelligent debate informed by genuine experience.

5 Group went to work. The mixture of low-level marking and the new Stabilised Automatic Bomb Sight achieved excellent results. On April 5/6 the new tactic was given its debut, when Leonard Cheshire of 617 Squadron acted as Master Bomber in a Mosquito during a low-level raid on an aircraft factory at Toulouse. Though he flew over the target three times at low level he was not hit due to the speed of the Mosquito. This advantage allowed him to place his back-up flares in exactly the right place thus allowing perfect concentration. In May Cochrane added another element to help achieve accuracy, the 'offset' marking technique. Target indicators were dropped deliberately away from the target itself. The rest of the force then adjusted their bombsights according to instructions from the Master Bomber. In turn this allowed for accurate bombing without smoke or flames obscuring the vital orientation device of the target indicator itself. 5 Group could now carry out its own operations using its own marking techniques. In effect it had become an independent air force. The only problem with the technique was its reliance on relatively good weather conditions and it could sometimes delay an attack as the Mosquitoes patiently sought out the right spot. But the improvement in accuracy was absolutely vital when attacking very small targets.

The Mosquito force with 8 Group continued to grow, but more modest expansion of this invaluable aircraft took place in other groups. 3 Group was only slowly phasing out its battle-scarred Stirlings, but it had replaced all its early, inferior Halifaxes, with the far superior Mark III's. All of 4 Group and part of 6 would also use Mark III Halifaxes until the end of the war in Europe. Bomber Command was then supplemented by the arrival of the first Free French squadrons, 346 and 347, both of which were formed in 4 Group just before the invasion.

At exactly the same moment the casualty rates began to drop away. The Luftwaffe night-fighter force was still powerful, but it did not have the range to intervene in the battle for French and Belgian industry and transport. A further reason for the decrease in casualties was the arrival of the long-range fighter, in the form of the new Spitfires and the American Mustangs. The new Mustang in particular proved to be a superb machine, matching a bomber's endurance with a fighter's performance. American daylight raids now went out surrounded by Mustangs. These aircraft then inflicted a terrible attrition rate on the German defenders. Bombing could now become more effective and the aerial superiority needed for invasion could now be assured. However, the conditions of the Pointblank Directive of 1943 ordering the allied bomber forces to reduce the German air force had been met in only an indirect way. According to Point-blank and the bomber commanders the Luftwaffe was to be crippled before it even reached the air by bombing its factories. In reality the Luftwaffe was defeated not by bombing but by combat in the air with other fighters.

In the run-up to invasion Bomber Command and the USAAF staged a massive and vital preliminary operation. On April 12 the *Daily Mirror* reported on a 'massive night raid in which 900 of our bombers dropped a record of 3,000 tons of bombs on targets in France, Belgium and Germany.'[4] The *Daily Telegraph* also remarked on this record, and openly stated that it was part of the invasion preparations. 'RAF Bomber Command broke all bombing records on Monday night... They dropped well over 3,600 tons of bombs, the heaviest load yet delivered in one operation anywhere in the world, and most of it fell on five great invasion traffic centres in the railway systems of France and Belgium.'[5] In preparing for the invasion the government decided there was no point denying that such an operation was planned. All Britain, but especially the south coast, was full of encampments and dumps of ammunition, equipment and rations. It was impossible to miss – but they did want to keep the enemy guessing as to where and when. A month later the *Daily Telegraph* reported on the continued attack on enemy communications. 'In what the Air Ministry announced last night as the war's biggest attack of its kind, about 1,500 planes from Britain yesterday blasted the Nazis' strained and battered system of rail, road, river and canal communications throughout Northern Germany, France, Belgium and Holland.'[6]

On May 3/4 Bomber Command launched a large, and thanks to a failure of communications costly, raid on a German military camp at Mailly-le-Camp. Three hundred and forty six Lancasters and 14 Mosquitoes of 1 and 5 Groups supported by two Pathfinder Mosquitoes set out to bomb the camp. Cheshire planted his indicators accurately and they were well backed-up by the supporting markers. But the Main Force leader Wing Commander L.C. Deane could not transmit the signal to attack to the waiting force. His wireless was tuned to the wrong frequency and he found himself drowned out by an American forces broadcast. The Main Force was left loitering without intent. The delay gave the Germans the chance to co-ordinate their attack. Forty-two Lancasters were lost, 11.6 per cent. The bombing started only once the Deputy Leader Squadron Leader E.N.M. Sparks, took over. The raid then unfolded with great accuracy. One hundred and fourteen barrack buildings, 47 transport sheds, 102 vehicles and some ammunition stores were destroyed. On the way back Sparks' aircraft was shot down, but he evaded capture and soon returned to England. The losses were not reported next day, but the fact that it was an invasion target was. The *Daily Mirror* stated that 'Bomber Command has now opened a direct attack on the German anti-invasion army.'[7] The *Telegraph* head-line read: 'RAF Bombers make "Invasion Raid."'[8] The *Sketch* headline stated: 'RAF

Smash Tank Lair in France'[9], and then went on to add, 'strong forces were out in several areas, one of which blew to pieces a secret depot of massed tanks which the Germans had accumulated for some time past in the French town of Mailly.'

This was obviously a change of tack in the way the bombing war was reported, reflecting the changed role of Bomber Command itself. However, it did not mean that strategic bombing had been forgotten. A leader in the *Daily Mail* in April argued that tactical bombing for the invasion was both the partner and result of the strategic campaign.[10] The enemy was being 'softened-up' for the invasion of the west, just as Italy had been. But the invasion was a possibility thanks to the attrition of Germany caused by the relentless allied strategic air campaign. The strategic campaign was also kept in mind by the publication of a spate of books and pamphlets. Soon after the end of the battle of Berlin J.M. Spaight's *Bombing Vindicated* appeared. Spaight sought to achieve a delicate balancing act. He wanted to show that the bombing of civilians was only a by-product of bombing policy and not deliberately conceived. While at the same time claiming that there was no distinction between civilian and combatant in modern war. He therefore argued that dehousing was justified as a way of dislocating industry. This revelation revealed that the British public did know, and accepted, 'deep down', that bombing was aimed at the civilian population. He then added that 'the old clear distinction between soldiers and civilians has been obscured... Today the weapons of war are made by millions of workers... They are in no proper sense of the word non-combatants.'[11] However, he refuted suggestions that the bombing policy actually set out to kill women and children. Quoting Balfour, Under Secretary for Air, he wrote, 'if in pursuit of our objective the German civilian population have to suffer, it is not our fault.'

According to Spaight, bombing had saved civilisation by destroying the unspeakable enemy. The shadow of the Great War was then used once again, for bombing had caused the enemy grievous damage at a much lower cost than that exacted by the Western Front:

> We have at least escaped the holocausts of 1915-17. We have come without having to endure them to a stage in the conflict corresponding to that we had reached in the summer of 1918. By our air raids and our blockade we have hurt Germany at least as much as we had then. We have done so at a cost in British lives almost negligible in comparison with that which we had to pay before we entered on the final round in 1918.[12]

The ultimate sanction for bombing came in the old argument of 'original sin'. The Germans had started the bombing war and so had no right of appeal against it. Hitler was responsible for the bombing of towns and cities. Hitler had no right to speak of international treaties and conventions when he had ignored them all. For Spaight, as with Harris, Portal and Churchill, the deaths of German civilians meant nothing because they were the original aggressors.

Around the same time Vera Brittain's pamphlet *Seeds of Chaos: What mass bombing really means*, was published for the Bombing Restriction Campaign. Her pamphlet carefully dissected the claims of Bomber Command, the government and the Air Ministry. She claimed that if bombing was achieving its objectives it might be justified, but it was not. It was therefore not a wickedness accepted in order to prevent a further wickedness, but an unjustifiable, because ineffective, wickedness in itself. She berated the press for taking such a glib and bloodthirsty attitude to the whole campaign and claimed it was making people tolerant of all kinds of appalling transgressions. She concluded by speculating on the wealth of further problems the campaign might be stoking up, such as post-war resentment in Germany. This was just the latest in the campaign's series of pamphlets which included such titles as *Night Bombing, Stop Bombing Civilians, Bomb, Burn and Ruthlessly Destroy, What Happened in Hamburg, Sear, Scar and Blacken, Obliteration Bombing, Stop Massacre Bombing, The Chimneys of Leipzig, When Will it Stop?* and *Terror Bombing*.[13] However, just how many people ever came across such titles is a debatable point. They certainly did not provoke much comment from the popular press or on the newsreels.

The Duke of Bedford had lined up with the critics of bombing and his pamphlet *Wholesale Bombing*, also published in the spring of 1944, seemed to imply that the Germans would never have bombed Britain had not the British bombed Germany in the early days of the war. He felt it was difficult to 'avoid the conclusion that the British government had the chief share of responsiblity for starting the grim contest in night bombing, …[and they] have been mainly responsible for re-starting it in the spring of 1942.'[14] Like Brittain, he condemned the press for making 'a sporting affair of cold-blooded massacres' and wondered whether it was possible to get sense from 'the thick skulls and torpid imaginations of our politicians.'[15] However, the Duke of Bedford was hardly an impartial observer, for he was a friend of the British Union of Fascist's leader Oswald Mosley, had been a Nazi sympathiser and had come close to internment earlier in the war.

The Times Literary Supplement found *Bombing Vindicated* to be an interesting and convincing study, calling it a 'logical, well-reasoned account'.[16] The review of *Seeds of Chaos*, on the other hand, condemned Brittain for never suggesting a credible alternative strategy. She was also accused of leaving 'out of the account the fact that the Germans began it and inflicted terrible suffering on us without trying to avoid the massacre of civilians', this was 'hardly the way to win recruits for Miss Brittain's "rebellion"'.[17]

It is therefore clear that even with the suspension of the strategic bombing campaign interest in it and its implications remained high even though it was still an interest based upon incomplete knowledge and misleading information.

On the night of June 5/6, the eve of D-Day, Bomber Command flew in continual support of the landing forces. A rain of bombs fell on German coastal defences and emplacements. 617 Squadron flew a massive *Window* raid across the Straits of Dover, designed to fool German radar into thinking an invasion fleet was sailing for Calais.

At 22.30 hours on June 5 Flying Officer Gerry McMahon joined his skipper and crew in their Stirling E-Easy.[18] The aircraft was full with a complement of paratroopers. They crossed the French coast and found exactly the right location of the dropping zone. The paratroopers then jumped in perfect conditions. Back at base McMahon found it impossible to sleep thanks to the excitement of taking part in the invasion.

On the afternoon of D-Day he set out again. The sky resembled an aerial regatta, for it was full of aircraft. Bombers and transport aircraft were making their way across to France. The sea below them was equally busy with ships plying to and from the Normandy beaches. McMahon and his crew were acting as a tug for a glider and released it near Caen. Just after the glider was released the Stirling was hit by a stream of accurate gunfire coming out of a wood below.

The petrol tank in the port wing exploded destroying most of the wing in the process. Without warning the Stirling rolled over onto its back pinning the crew down. By an incredible stroke of luck the aircraft righted itself and the pilot was able to make a perfect belly-landing in a ploughed field. By an equally incredible stroke of luck the entire crew escaped without a scratch.

After a discussion they decided to wait until nightfall before trying to contact the invading allied soldiers. At this point their luck ran out, for they walked straight into a bunch of German soldiers who promptly took them prisoner. Instead of finding safety with the invaders, they found themselves falling back with twitchy, irritable Germans. After much wandering they were locked in a barn in the grounds of a chateau. The chateau did not last long as it was attacked by RAF rocket-firing Hawker Typhoons. Probably sensing that the game was up the German soldiers decided to surrender to McMahon and his mates!

They started to march towards the allied lines, picking up German stragglers on the way. Eventually they ran into a Canadian patrol that took the party of prisoners from them leaving them with a receipt for one German officer and sixty-one other ranks.

When McMahon finally returned to his home base, he learned that his parents had been sent a letter saying 'missing, believed killed'. He headed home for a week's leave. As he reached his garden gate he saw his family returning from his requiem mass. His mother took one look at him and promptly fainted. In the excitement and confusion McMahon had forgotten to inform his family of his safe return. The story is reminiscent of the classical myths. Its fateful twists and turns provide the reason why men urinated on their tail wheels. Survival was as much mystical as technical.

In the weeks following the invasion Bomber Command acted as a tactical force bombing targets at the request of the land forces. Alongside this tactical campaign was an effort to reduce German synthetic oil production in order to cripple enemy aircraft and vehicles. Bombing of these plants had started in May and was to continue. It meant attacking the Ruhr, which was still a tough spot.

But these uses of airpower were then deflected by the need to bomb German v-weapons sites. The V-1 flying bomb came first, falling on London and the South East from June 12. Later in the summer came the V-2 rockets. Bomber Command flew against the launch sites and sent two Mosquito squadrons to Britain to assist the home defence forces against the raids.

Even when there were no major raids against Germany, from June to August the men of Bomber Command were constantly engaged. On June 14 came the massive step of bombing by daylight. Le Havre was attacked in the first such raid since the departure of 2 Group in 1943. Harris's fears about the safety of his crews proved unfounded provided the fighter cover was adequate and within range of those available. Daylight raiding revealed that Bomber Command was more than capable, in good visibility, of hitting even the smallest targets and its success rate was extremely impressive. New tactics, especially designed for daylight activity, were used by which the aircraft dropped their bombs simultaneously with either an *Oboe*-leader or *G-H*-leader. *Oboe*-leading was more accurate, but *G-H* was more flexible for there was no limit to the number of aircraft which could use this device. Bomber Command was also given a formidable new tool. On June 8/9 617 Squadron used Barnes Wallis's 12,000 lb *Tallboy* bomb for the first time. The squadron attacked a railway tunnel at Saumur and achieved great accuracy, with Wallis's bombs causing the stoutly built tunnel to cave in. These bombs were then used against submarine pens and v-weapon sites. *Tallboys* were used in the daylight raid against Le Havre on June 14. The *Daily Mirror*'s headlines gleefully announced: 'Tidal wave sweeps Hun e-boat nests as RAF and Navy hit Le Havre/ Lancasters carrying 12,000 lb bombs did the damage flying their first daylight raid since 1942'.[19] So busy was Bomber Command during this period the average number of sorties in one week was 5000, or the equivalent of the number flown in the first nine months of the war.

On July 1 the *Mirror* bannered 'RAF Heavies Smash Hun Tanks'[20] and the *Daily Telegraph* stated 'Great RAF blow at Panzers'[21] in response to the raid on Villers Bocage. The attacks on flying bomb sites were also covered, on June 20 the *Mirror* noted that 'the battle against the flying bomb is on at full blast... Heavies batter flying bomb launching bases in France'.[22]

The invasion brought about a marked reduction in Bomber Command's press coverage. With hindsight it can be said it was the beginning of the eclipse of Bomber Command as the nation's favourite topic of conversation. This was only natural for the press now had a plethora of stories to cover. Between Dunkirk and D-Day Bomber Command was the only offensive weapon capable of striking Germany available to the British, and so it not only swallowed a huge slice of the nation's resources it also had a great deal of print and celluloid devoted to it. Operations in the desert, the Mediterranean and Far East occasionally overshadowed it but not for long. Bomber Command was always given good coverage, for it was fighting the Germans night in, night out, for three years. Now the Navy and army were competing for column inches as never before. Harris was always conscious of the need for publicity and reacted to these developments quickly. He wrote to Portal on July 1, claiming that Bomber Command had not received its fair share of publicity for the success of Overlord. On July 4 the Vice Chief of Air Staff wrote a memo on Harris's note, claiming it was an important matter for it might affect 'the future of the RAF post-war'.[23]

When the allies finally broke out of their bridgehead the advance was spectacular. Paris was quickly liberated and the allies drove on to Belgium and the Dutch frontier. But the supply line was becoming elongated and under ever greater pressure to sustain the momentum. The failure of Operation Market Garden at Arnhem ended the attempt to turn Germany's flank by 'bouncing the Rhine' in Holland. Instead, the allies would have to 'batter on the front door' and attack the Siegfried Line.

In mid-September Harris was released from Eisenhower's direct command and reverted to Air Ministry control. Eisenhower clearly appreciated the support Harris had given him and later wrote him a fulsome letter of thanks.

> My gratitude to you is a small token for the magnificent service which you have rendered, and my simple expression of thanks sounds totally inadequate. Time and opportunity prohibit the chance I should like to shake you and your men by the hand, and thank each one of you personally for all you have done. I can do nothing more than assure you of my lasting appreciation, which I would ask you to convey to all those under your command for their exemplary devotion to duty and for the most magnificent loyalty which has been shown to a commander.[24]

The question was, which role should Bomber Command now adopt given the massive change in the nature of the war? Bomber Command was to continue to lend all possible assistance to the ground forces, but what other aims should it set itself?

The two main schools of thought favoured a continuation of the precision air campaign against either the synthetic oil plants or the German transportation system. The oil policy, which would ground the Luftwaffe and bring German transport grinding to a halt, was favoured by Portal. Air Marshal Tedder, Eisenhower's British deputy, favoured a continuation of a transport interdiction campaign, citing the success achieved in Normandy. A third, much smaller group, which included Harris, favoured the re-start of the general area attack against German cities. Portal, and the allied governments and chiefs of staff, considered the situation and ordered the attack on oil, to be followed by transport and the area attack only when the weather precluded other sorts of attack. This was a perfectly rational and sensible plan, it took full consideration of the fact that Bomber Command was now a multi-roled force, capable of precision destruction by day and night and large scale destruction where necessary. Harris had been surprised by the success of his crews against precise targets and seemed to lack conviction in the continuation of such a policy, hence his desire to return to the area attack. For once Harris appears to have done his crews a severe disservice in doubting their skills. Harris was convinced the area attack would crush Germany without the need for a costly invasion from the west. It was the old argument in new form. Relations between Portal and Harris took a sharp downward turn. This was the first time there was a major, and continuing, division of opinion between them and it has caused controversy as historians have sought to understand the true significance of the clash.

When Portal ordered Harris into the offensive against oil he was attempting to face down a fierce contrary argument from Harris. Not all of Harris's points can be dismissed as those of a man unwilling to let go of his tried and tested methods. However, he was certainly very obstructive and seemed unable to grasp the significance of the transformation effected by beating the Luftwaffe day force and overrunning some of the ground control stations of the night force. Harris appears to have shown that bulldog tenacity he was famous for. It was an asset when things looked bleak, but it was a hindrance when it stopped him from appreciating the new situation.

Harris received his orders on September 25, which were expanded upon on October 13. Clearly, Harris remained unconvinced for his reply on November 1 pointed out his objection to attacking specific industrial targets when he felt more chances of success lay in a general attack, particularly in the Ruhr. Portal, the opposite of Harris in so many ways, tried all his calm, persuasive tact. On January 19 1945 the Air Ministry reminded Harris of his orders once again. Rather than leap at Harris it was a way of nudging him in the right direction. But it also reveals that Harris was not, according to Portal's understanding, following his original instructions.

If Portal felt Harris was ignoring orders he had every right to replace him. No subordinate commander has the right to contradict a superior. Portal may have considered this option, but it would have been very hard to replace a commander with such a high profile and reputation. When Harris threatened to resign if Portal insisted he was not doing his job properly Portal caved-in. Instead of calling Harris's bluff Portal decided to leave it up to history to judge who was right. He wrote: 'I am very sorry that you do not believe in it [the plan to attack oil, then transport, then the area attack in that order] but it is no use my craving for what is evidently unattainable. We must wait until the end of the war before we can know for certain who was right...'[25] In not coming to a definite conclusion on what to do with an insubordinate commander Portal may have been responsible for prolonging the war. Portal should surely have been decisive. When men's lives were at stake it was no time to be making philosophical statements about the judgement of history. Portal had been instrumental in sacking Peirse for not being able to make up his mind. Portal should have sacked Harris for he was showing no interest in prosecuting the orders he had been given and was subverting them in order to pursue his own strategy. If Portal was looking for statistics to back him up they were there. The campaign against fuel had seen German production of aviation fuel fall from 156,000 tons in May to 10,000 tons in September. Thus a vigorous and continued assault on the oil industry had the potential to literally bring the German war machine grinding to a halt.

Harris and Portal largely fudged this matter in their post-war writings. Harris did not refer to a clash with Portal in his memoirs. He did say that he launched an offensive against oil, but his triumph was 'largely the result of our general attack on German industry'.[26]

Two personalities had clashed. One dedicated, clever and bullish. The other dedicated, clever and diplomatic. The bull won. All nations need bulls in times of emergency, but they also need to be kept on a tight rein.

The numbers of front line aircraft rose by 50 per cent in the second half of 1944, with Lancasters providing the bulk of new bombers. Expansions took place in all groups. 1 and 5 Groups, fully equipped with Lancasters, could drop more bombs in one night than the whole Command two years earlier. 6 Group was mixed with Lancasters and Halifaxes, gaining the new Mark IVs in the process. 3 Group finally re-emerged gaining

G-H equipped Lancasters to replace its Stirlings. This allowed 3 Group to act independently, like 5 Group. The main bombing force was therefore made up of 1,4,6 and 8 Groups. 8 Group received improved *H2S* sets and an increase in Mosquitoes to supplement its Light Night Striking Force. Finally 100 Group was also increasing in strength and improving in technique giving it greater ability to fox the Germans.

German defences were crumbling and Bomber Command casualties were dropping. At the end of August major daylight raiding against Germany was resumed. The attack on Homburg on August 27 was the first major daylight raid since August 1941. Targets deeper into Germany were hit and a second battle of the Ruhr took place as old targets were revisited. As Harris was pursuing a continued area campaign, with nods in the direction of the oil and transport campaign, he was forced to attack smaller towns, having already hit the biggest cities in Germany. During this period such towns as Darmstadt, Bremerhaven, Bonn, Freiburg, Heilbron and Ulm were attacked. Amazingly, approximately 46 per cent of the total tonnage dropped during the war was in the final nine months.

As winter settled in the weather turned, hampering large-scale air activity. It also provided Hitler with perfect cover for his last desperate gamble in the west. The battle of the Ardennes, designed to drive a wedge between the British and American armies. However, once the weather improved the offensive was soon contained as air power gave the allies superiority and the allied armies rolled on. But the argument as to the best way to use the bombing force was still rumbling on. A flurry of activity against factories producing the new Nazi jet fighters and 'schnorkel' submarines was ordered in January 1945. But the Air Ministry continued to push Harris towards an oil and transport campaign. Harris gave these targets more attention than is sometimes assumed, but the winter weather often stopped him.[27]

The differences of opinion obviously did not reach the British people at the time. But the newspapers tried to make sense of the strategies and sought to understand how the bomber force was being used. There was certainly a sense of a new chapter opening on September 14, when the *Daily Mail* announced that Bomber Command had switched back to German targets with a vengeance. 'Many hundreds of RAF Bomber Command's Lancasters showered 600,000 incendiaries on two German cities – 400,000 on Frankfurt, 90 miles from the advancing Allies, and 200,000 on Stuttgart, 60 miles from the front.'[28] This was actually the follow-up to two earlier raids on Stuttgart, reported by the *Daily Sketch* in July: 'For the second night in succession Stuttgart, centre of precision engineering, was the target for Air Chief Marshal Harris's renewed and mightier-than-ever onslaught on industrial Germany.'[29] This was the sort of reportage the public was used to. The nature of the area assault and its standard newspaper coverage was back on the main pages. On November 6 the *Daily Telegraph* reported on the 'shattering blows at Germany's war industries and communications… It was one of the greatest air onslaughts of the war and signifies the complete failure of the Luftwaffe to interfere seriously with the Allies' strategical bombing programme.'[30] The *Sketch* had stressed the technological superiority of the RAF in this new phase of bombing, for it noted that Brunswick suffered a '15 minute "scientific assault" through ten-tenths cloud,' which 'struck another crippling blow at Germany's much battered aircraft industry'.[31] By January 1945 the *Sketch* could report that the new bombing campaign was reaching a crescendo: 'Germany is being pounded by a great hour-by-hour blitz in which thousands of British and American planes are being used day and night.'[32] A month later it added, 'Germany is reeling under a merciless hail of high explosive and fire-bombs rained down by waves of Allied bombers day and night.'[33] When Berlin was attacked yet again, the *Mirror* rejoiced in the fact that 'The RAF stokes up blazing Berlin'.[34] As the end approached for Germany the newsreel cameras got the chance to see the effect of the British area campaign. On February 22 Universal carried a story on the day and night assault, showing ruins across Germany.[35] A month later Movietone showed Churchill in the ruins of Cologne.[36]

The newspapers were aware that there was another strand to the latest phase of the bombing war, noting attacks on transport and communications. Just as the allies were breaking out of Normandy, a leader in the *Daily Sketch* praised the brilliance of the transport interdiction plan which had done so much to ensure the success of the landings.[37] Then in the autumn came the equally brilliant operation to destroy a vital section of the Dortmund-Ems canal. On November 4/5 174 Lancasters and two Mosquitoes of 5 Group attacked the canal. The results were extremely impressive. The loss of water from the canal stopped coke getting to three important Ruhr steelworks. Stocks of coal in the Ruhr rose from 415,000 tons in August 1944 to 2,217,000 tons in February 1945. Yet, during the same period coal production in the Ruhr fell from 10,417,000 tons to 4,778,000 tons in February. RAF bombing had not only drastically reduced the amount of coal mined it had also, thanks to the severing of the canal, ensured that it piled up unable to reach its destination. The *Mirror* called it the severing of 'Hitler's life-line waterway'[38] while the *Express* headline announced 'Dam Busters Cut Ruhr Lifeline/Five-Ton Bombs Run Great Canal Dry'.[39] By the spring of 1945 the press picked up on how the transport campaign was gaining in momentum. In February the *Mirror* ran the headline, 'Mighty Blow At Hun Rail Routes' and then added:

> Bombers from Britain, bombers from France, bombers from Belgium, bombers from Holland, bombers from Italy – in all more than 6,000 British and American heavies, fighter bombers and fighter escorts – struck a colossal blow at Hitler's road, rail and canal system from a cloudless sky in daylight yesterday.[40]

In March the *Sketch* told its readers that the allied 'air offensive... is pulverising German road and rail links'.[41]

Dresden is now indelibly associated with Harris and Bomber Command. The bombing of Dresden has achieved the status of a modern legend and is regarded as the awful stain on the escutcheon of British Second World War glory. Now it is almost totally forgotten that the raid took place with the aid of the United States bomber force and was part of a grand allied-agreed plan. It is not remembered like that. It is remembered as the moment when Harris, desperate to rub out all the grand towns and cities of Germany, got his last great chance to stage a demonstration, a demonstration, which it is alleged, served no military purpose. In other words a piece of British terrorism, a crime against humanity. Crucially, it is felt that this raid finally turned the British people against Bomber Command and its leader. Dresden was the raid that finally opened their eyes and forced them to confront the realities behind the official terminology and media coverage. And yet this is all very much a post-war perspective.

Towards the end of January 1945 the British Joint Intelligence Committee considered ways in which to help the Russians in their advance into eastern Germany. The Air Ministry was also very keen to make its willingness to help the Russians known. On January 29-30 there was a flurry of activity at the Ministry planning an announcement of assistance. An assistant to Portal wanted the BBC to make a statement and noted in a memo:

> We are very anxious to stress the point that one of the principal objectives of the present heavy attacks on transportation targets in the West is to hold up the movement of German formations over to the Eastern Front and thus help the Russians in their great offensive.[42]

He added that the *Herald, The Times,* the *Express* and the *Telegraph* had already been informed of this.

The decision to help the Russian forces by launching a huge attack on one of the bottlenecks of the east such as Dresden, Leipzig and Chemnitz was put to the Russians at the Yalta Conference. Churchill also seems to have been keen to give the Russians a demonstration of the power of the forces of the western allies. The Russians were in broad agreement and so Harris was ordered to put on the raid. Harris certainly had Dresden on his list of cities due for Bomber Command attention, but this was a job he was ordered to do. Dresden was chosen to be the recipient of Operation THUNDER-CLAP for a number of reasons. Firstly, the city contained an important railway line which could be used to transfer troops from one front to the other. Secondly, it was just in front of the Russian advance and thirdly, it was packed full of refugees. Dresden was bulging at the seams with displaced people and wounded soldiers. The allies felt that a blow against Dresden would cause unbelievable chaos and terror in an already tottering Germany.

A force of 796 Lancasters and nine Mosquitoes were despatched on the night of February 13/14. The force carried 1,478 tons of high explosive and 1,182 tons of incendiaries. For the RAF it was the most effective fire-raising raid since Hamburg. A vast swathe of the city was completely gutted and cost somewhere in the region of 40,000-50,000 lives. A bomber aimer of 635 Squadron noted that: 'It was the only time I ever felt sorry for the Germans. But my sorrow lasted only for a few seconds; the job was to hit the enemy and to hit him very hard.' It shocked and excited even hardened bomber boys: 'It was my practice never to leave my seat, but my skipper called me on this particular occasion to come and have a look. The sight was indeed fantastic. From some 20,000 feet, Dresden was a city with every street etched in fire.' For another it truly was the moment of biblical reckoning for the Germans: 'My immediate reaction was a stunned reflection on the comparison between the holocaust below and the warnings of the evangelists in Gospel meetings before the war.'[43] The next day 311 American B-17s dropped 771 tons of bombs on the still burning city, returning again on February 15 and March 2. Ironically, the fact that the raid went absolutely according to plan and achieved everything it was designed to, did more to darken the record and role of Harris and his Command than any other raid or operation.

Historians have been obsessed by the high level arguments this raid sparked. Churchill probably realised the incredible violence of the raid and sensed the overall military significance of Dresden to the German defence of the eastern front had been overstated. He therefore sought to distance himself from the affair. Further, he tried to imply that he was shocked by it and was somehow unaware of what the RAF could do given the right conditions. On March 28 Churchill composed his infamous memo:

> It seems to me that the moment has come when the question of bombing German cities simply for the sake of increasing the terror, though under other pretexts, should be reviewed. Otherwise we shall come into control of an utterly ruined land. We shall not, for instance, be able to get housing materials out of Germany for our own needs because some temporary provision would have to be made for the Germans themselves. The destruction of Dresden remains a serious query against the Allied bombing. I am of the opinion that military objectives must henceforward be more strictly studied in our own interests rather than that of the enemy.
>
> The Foreign Secretary has spoken to me on this subject, and I feel the need for more precise concentration upon military objectives, such as oil and communications behind the immediate battle-zone rather than mere acts of terror and wanton destruction, however impressive.[44]

Unsurprisingly, Portal was dismayed and outraged and he persuaded Churchill to withdraw the paper and substitute it with a slightly more measured piece.

But why had Churchill reacted like this? Partly, it seems to have been a reaction to the anxieties which had arisen from the report of an Associated Press correspondent based at the Supreme Headquarters Allied Expeditionary Force. The correspondent had referred to the attack as 'a deliberate terror bombing of German population centres as a ruthless expedient to hasten doom' and stated that it was launched 'for the avowed purpose of heaping more confusion on Nazi road and rail traffic, and to sap German morale.'[45] This despatch was suppressed by the censor in London, but distributed in the States where it caused a controversy. Echoes from the States certainly reached Britain, but whether it really made an impact on the ordinary man or woman is extremely debatable. The arrival of the newsreel cameras in German cities gave the public a good insight into the power of the airforces, but it is doubtful whether this made more protestors. The real significance of Dresden was that it caused dismay in high places. Dresden brought home to the War Cabinet the meanings of their decisions. The invasion of Germany and the liberation of occupied territories had revealed the horrors of the concentration camps. No allied leader wanted to be accused of similar atrocities. The government therefore started a campaign of forgetting. In the years after the war the British people would join them. The demonisation of Harris and his Command started with Dresden. But it started not thanks to a popular outcry, rather it was due to sudden squeamishness in influential circles.

When the British popular newspapers and newsreels are examined it becomes clear that few people realised Dresden was anything other than a highly successful RAF raid. Of course, this is exactly what it was. Its legend was a retrospective invention of history. The *Daily Express* told its readers that according to sources in neutral Sweden the attack on Dresden had 'brought confusion to southern Germany comparable only with that in the north after the last big raid on Berlin... Now the Dresden artery is severed, temporarily at least. Railway stations and yards have been demolished, bridges and viaducts blown up, and factories laid in ruins.'[46] The *Sketch* noted that: 'Dresden, capital of Saxony and key control centre in Germany's defence against Koniev's land forces, less than 70 miles away, was the principal target of two great blows by the RAF on Tuesday night, and by American airmen yesterday.'[47] Readers of the *Daily Telegraph* were met by the headline: 'Non-Stop Air Blows Aid Both Fronts/ 650,000 RAF Fire Bombs on Dresden/ Biggest Day in the West Since Falaise/ Air Fleets Sweep Reich by Day and Night'.[48] The report mentioned German claims that a terror attack had taken place. But this was part of a well-oiled routine, and it countered with the fact that 'Dresden is desperately needed as a concentration area for troops and to administrative services evacuated from elsewhere in the Reich'.[49] On March 5 the *Daily Mail* reported that: 'Dresden was completely wiped out by the massive Allied air blows on February 14 and 16, said the German Overseas News Agency last night... "Today we can only speak of what once was Dresden in the past tense."'[50] But there was hardly any remorse in the rest of the report. On February 22 the Movietone newsreel announced the 'elimination of Dresden' without a trace of regret.[51] It was Bomber Command reportage as normal. Dresden was used as a verb by the *Daily Express* on February 17 when its headline read 'West Wall "Dresdened" by Lancaster Fleet'.[52] A week after this, as if to rub-in the fact that there was no great moral debate going on in Britain, the *Express* carried the latest photographs of Julich, a city razed by Bomber Command the previous November.

Not long after the raid Flight Lieutenant Herbert's work *L for Lucy* appeared. The author served with a Polish squadron and provided a fascinating look at the work of the airmen of the occupied countries. As one might expect there is little in the way of moral hand wringing about the bombing campaign. The Poles had a ferocious desire to fight the enemy which had invaded and raped their homeland. He wrote of the Berlin raids:

> ...leaving all Berlin in fire and smoke behind us. Berlin, beaten, torn, crippled, maimed, with bloody streets into which the burning buildings collapsed. Berlin screaming with fright, hysterical, furious and powerless, shooting in blind despair and panic from her thousand guns, but incapable of effective defence. Proud, overbearing Berlin where men, women and children had laughed when the Luftwaffe martyred Warsaw.[53]

Popular feelings of guilt would grow only once the war was firmly in the past.

Bomber Command continued to rumble on, hitting more and more targets, right across Germany. The strategic campaign, however, was largely at an end by March and April and the role of the Command was now almost entirely tactical, supporting the armies.

Some command reshuffles took place, designed to give new men experience before the war ended. Air Vice Marshals Rice of 1 Group, Carr of 4 Group, Cochrane of 5 Group were all replaced. Bennett of Pathfinders was one of the few not rested, continuing to serve until the end of the war.

On April 8/9 Hamburg was subjected to its last major raid. On April 14/15 Potsdam was raided, it was the last major raid of the war against a German city. On April 16 Swinemünde was attacked and the pocket battleship *Lutzow* was sunk. Berlin was hit for the last time on April 20/21. Then, on April 25, came Berchtesgaden. Hitler's chalet was subjected to the full weight of Bomber Command. Three hundred and seventy five aircraft attacked. 617 squadron Lancasters carried *Tallboys* for the last time. The intervening mountains interfered with the *Oboe* signals, when combined with the awful weather it made for a tough job. Finally, on May 2/3 Bomber Command flew its last offensive operation of the war, flying against Kiel after a six day lay off. After five years and 389,809 sorties the last Bomber Command attack of the war was against Kiel on the northern side of the canal. On September 4 1939 Bomber Command had flown against Brunsbüttel at the other end of the canal. But Bomber Command had come much further than the width of the Schleswig-Holstein peninsula.

CHAPTER SEVEN

Remembering and Misremembering, 1945–1999

The 1990s saw the fiftieth anniversary cycle of the Second World War. Despite the passage of years the British bombing campaign revealed it had lost none of its power to stir up controversy. Two events were of key significance: the decision of the Bomber Command Association to erect a statue of Harris in the spring of 1992 and the fiftieth anniversary of Dresden in February 1995.

The Harris statue caused a furore, and revealed just how little the public actually knows about the bombing war. All the legends and myths came bubbling up, despite the writings of historians and commentators since 1945. The original snubbings of Harris and the deliberate campaign to mislead the British public had taken on a huge significance in the 1960s and their 'authenticity' seems to have become absolute in the 1990s.

As the unveiling date of the statue approached, the press began to take notice of its critics. Veteran peace campaigners Lord Soper and Bruce Kent planned a rival peace meeting, to coincide with the unveiling outside the RAF church of St Clement Danes on the Strand. Lord Soper told *The Times* that: 'The Harris statue makes me sick. Ours is in honour of the victims of mass civilian bombing on both sides during the war.'[1] The leader of the *Sunday Telegraph* reacted to this news with forthright indignation: 'On any historical appraisal the 50,000 who died in Bomber Command achieved far more for lasting peace in Europe than all the posturings of CND, and they deserve their memorial.'[2] A significant point had been raised, for the statue was designed not just as a tribute to Harris, but also as a memorial to all Bomber Command personnel who had died in the strategic air war. It was an act designed to rectify what one former Bomber Command crew member has called 'the Great Ingratitude'.[3] This was a fact often lost in the fierce debate.

Robert Harris (no relation) entered the fray in an attempt to put the record straight.[4] He quite rightly pointed out that those who argued for the removal of the statue should also campaign for the removal of the Portal and Churchill statues as well, for they were equally responsible for area bombing. Andrew Roberts also attempted to put the case for Harris. Writing in the *Spectator*, he argued that when Dresden was bombed the war was far from over and no one could tell whether the war would be over within a couple of months. He then went on to make a point far more significant for modern Europe:

If a German can convince himself that Dresden was a crime every bit as foul as Auschwitz – hence the concentration on the innocence of the women and children and the repetition of the ludicrous half million figure [of casualties] – he is well on the way to absolving his forefathers and nation. Shorn of the moral dimension, it will all boil down to statistics. Only then can a German clear his conscience... In combating this historical whitewashing 'Bomber' Harris may posthumously be fighting his most important battle yet.[5]

On the day of the unveiling a service was held in Cologne. The *Daily Telegraph*'s correspondent at the service expressed much the same sentiment as Roberts: 'Germany took advantage of the unveiling of the Bomber Harris statue yesterday to push some of its war guilt on to British shoulders.'[6] It can therefore be seen that Harris and the bombing war are now becoming part of a new political and social debate. With a new Europe looming to what extent should Germany be allowed to forget her past? But, with fears of a nascent neo-Nazi backlash in Germany and across Europe generally, should Germany be allowed to make any sort of statement designed to slough off her own war guilt or imply any sort of equality of guilt? Harris had once been a part of the Cold War. Now he is becoming part of the debate about the future of Europe

As patron of the Bomber Command Association, it fell to the Queen Mother to unveil the statue. Most of the newspapers, especially the tabloids, led with the fact that she faced a hostile reception from a crowd of protestors. Shouts of 'mass murderer' and comparisons with Eichmann were made. None of the press was much inclined to give these outbursts any sympathy. A *Sunday Telegraph* poll found that 56 per cent of the population supported the Harris statue and seven out of ten felt that the Germans had no right to criticise.[7] The *Daily Mail* called them 'peace idiots'[8], and mentioned the look of disgust on the face of Mrs Thatcher. The paper carried the story on a double-page spread under the headline: 'They would have died for him. 55,000 of them did. Now they come to honour their leader. Our mission accomplished.' A former gunner, when asked to comment on German objections, said 'Sod them.' Another former aircrew member reckoned the Nazis bombed civilians on purpose, whereas the RAF never had. The *Mail* then took the chance to swipe at all those who sneer or debunk British heroes and achievements:

> One of the ugliest aftermaths of war is the picking-over of the battlefields by monstrous regiments of hindsight heroes, using words as spiteful as swords as they seek warriors to debunk, victories to reclassify.
>
> To them the Battle of Britain was won not by courage but by 'home advantage'. Dunkirk happened because Germany permitted it, Arnhem and Anzio were mere farce, and Arctic convoys were lost mainly by Royal Navy incompetence or cowardice. To such sceptics as these, the hell of Dresden was heaven sent.[9]

Harris had become synonymous with Dresden, even to those who defend him.

The fierceness of the reaction to the statue in both Britain and Germany overshadowed an announcement by the German government. Plans for a national space museum were finalised. The new museum was to be based in the old workshops at

Peenemünde. Peenemünde may have been where modern space research began, but it was also where Germany had created its v-weapons designed to bring mass destruction to British cities. In order to make the v-weapons the Nazis used slave labour. Those condemned to construct these weapons were worked to death and treated like animals. But it is doubtful whether many people noticed the announcement or got as excited about it as they did over Harris.

Over the course of the next few weeks the press were bombarded with correspondence concerning the statue and the role of Harris and Bomber Command. Those opposed to the statue all seemed to work under the idea that Harris alone had shaped and executed British policy. Those who defended him seem to have forgotten what was known in the war, that British bombing killed civilians.

But the erection of the statue was not the culmination of the controversy. Three years later the anniversary of Dresden brought up exactly the same divisions of opinion. A week before the anniversary Simon Jenkins wrote in the *Spectator* that Britain should apologise for Dresden.[10] On the day of the anniversary *The Times* referred to those who believed that Dresden was 'the greatest single night's slaughter in the history of Europe'.[11] Interestingly, the German people seemed to have become aware of the Harris legend. The *Mail's* correspondent in Dresden said most Germans directed no bitterness towards the British and 'there is no evidence of any wish to spread blame beyond "Bomber" Harris'.[12] Harris was the scapegoat for the British government. He has now become the architect of suffering for the German people too. It is a cosy solution. The British government does not have to enter into controversy for as long as Harris is popularly held responsible.

A point of great contention arose when the bombing was compared with Auschwitz, for this implied a deliberate act of genocide and policy of terror. When the statue had been unveiled *The Times* had worried about 'the extreme hatred engendered by carpet bombing [which] survives to this day in the ability of many Germans, even now, to make a clear moral distinction between Auschwitz and Dresden.'[13] But, on the day of the commemoration service in Dresden, young German protestors disrupted proceedings with the cry that the Jews were the true victims of the Second World War, not the Germans. Attending the service was the Duke of Kent, he laid wreaths and expressed his regrets, but he did not apologise. In this way a distinction was made between the war the British fought and the war the Nazis fought. The British can express regrets for deaths, but the righteousness of the cause means that the British do not, and should not, apologise, such was the meaning of the Duke's comments. In this moment there were hopes for a new spirit of Anglo-German reconciliation. But a new knowledge of the war did not come about. In the spring of 1996 the Bomber Command Association told *The Times* of its dismay at the public ignorance of the true facts about Harris and Dresden.[14] Bomber Command Association found that most people still thought the city was bombed on Harris's order alone and were still convinced that everyone knew the end of the war was in sight in February 1945.

Harris has continued to suffer from a dire public image. Modern popular opinion holds it as a truth that Harris devised and carried out the bombing war according to his own ruthless desires, without reference to the British government or people. Television, the great disseminator of history, shows little sign of revising its opinion. Documentaries such as *Death by Moonlight* have peddled the idea of Harris as an unfeeling monster, happy to condemn thousands of his own men to death. It caused such a stir among former bomber crews that a legal action was instigated. The veterans pointed out reams of historical inaccuracies and generalisations. They eventually lost the case, but the action revealed the continuing depth of passions. As I write a new series is about to start on Channel 4, *Great Military Blunders*. The *Sunday Telegraph* of February 20 2000 noted the programme on Bomber Command will show how inaccurate most British bombing was. 'The result was that Winston Churchill and Arthur "Bomber" Harris… agreed to switch from precision bombing of military and industrial targets to area bombing, a tactic which cost the lives of 500,000 German civilians.' Both the series and the article are based on a mixture of truth and myth. The most potent myth being that Harris devised the area campaign. There are now Harris websites arguing out the morality and nature of his campaign. Better balanced pieces have been produced, such as *Bomber Command, Reaping the Whirlwind* shown on Channel 4, and a Radio 4 adaptation of Len Deighton's novel, *Bomber*. But the popular image is very hard to shift.

It is an image born in the truths, half-truths and collective deceptions forged during the war. The British people lacked the whole story then. They lack it today. They shied away from what they had taken part in then. Today they deny they ever suspected the truth. Harris still provides the most convenient figure to carry the burden of guilt. It can be claimed that during the war the full truth was never known. But it was guessed at. And if it was guessed at why was there not greater protest? Probably because most people were secretly content to let it go ahead. After the war the government confirmed the inner qualms about the campaign. By ignoring Harris and his men, the state ensured a diminished role for Bomber Command in the share of victory. This shunning did not lessen over the years, strengthening the inner guilt of the British people. But rather than admit the anxieties collectively or attempt to explain their wartime actions within their context many went along with the easy option of blaming Harris. Ironically, when newspapers like the *Daily Mail* complain of the debunking of British heroes, the blame lies not with dilettante intellectuals or the 'loony left', but with the State itself. The British State found it politic to blame Harris and eventually took the British people with it.

May 8 1945, Victory in Europe brought the war to an end for Bomber Command, even if the war itself was not quite over. The campaign of forgetting started at exactly the same time. On May 13 Churchill made a victory broadcast summing up the struggles and achievements of the five years of the European war. He did not mention Bomber Command. As if to force Bomber Command back onto the agenda, two days later the *Daily Telegraph* published a large article by retired Air Commodore E.L. Howard Williams under the statement 'Without Air Mastery There Could Have Been No Victory'. He wrote:

> Our bomber policy has paid a handsome dividend. My recent 800 mile low-level flight over the Ruhr confirmed all I had read or heard of the devastation. In that slough of despond the German

war machine has been gutted for all to see. Krupps of Essen is a staggering sight – two square miles of a huge modern arsenal rubbed out, not a man or a movement to be seen. Düsseldorf is a fantastic panorama of 'Lebensraum'. Elberfeld exists no more, and so on. My guess is that Bomber Command alone brought the entire German output to below 30 per cent of its peak potential.[15]

A day later the *Telegraph* called for a massive air review to salute victory.[16] Today we are used to Battle of Britain Sunday and fighters providing the dash and glory of British aerial achievement. For the *Telegraph* it was a completely different case, they argued that Bomber Command should be given pride of place and Harris should take the salute.

Criticisms of Churchill's broadcast had an effect, for he then sent a message of congratulation to Harris. The message was reproduced in the press and thanked Harris and his crews for all their efforts. Churchill concluded: 'I believe that the massive achievements of Bomber Command will long be remembered as an example of duty nobly done.'[17] But an insult was to come the way of Bomber Command almost instantaneously. The government decided against a special campaign medal. Instead they were given the Home Defence medal, of which Harris said 'only a Home Defence medal whilst every clerk, butcher, baker and candlestick-maker, serving miles behind the fighting fronts on the Continent, in Egypt and the East, were to get a campaign medal.'[18] This was not quite true, for a 1939-1945 Air Crew Europe clasp was issued, to be worn on the France and Germany 1944-45 Star, but it was a long way from the full campaign medals struck for Italy, North Africa, Burma and France and Germany. It was a long way considering the fact that Bomber Command alone had shouldered the great burden of the direct attack on Germany for so long. In the immediate flush of victory, the excitement of the General Election campaign, and the need to end the war in the Far East the British public did not have the chance to notice the exclusion of Bomber Command from its rightful place.

Why did the government take this line? Dresden clearly played a large role. The hideous mess of Dresden both scarred and scared them. While German cities had been a long way from the eyes of newsreel cameras it was easy to order their annihilation, but the politicians were made uncomfortable by the direct sight. The Russians had also started making capital out of the raids, claiming that bombing was part of a capitalist plot against the poor, oppressed German people.

Prime Minister Attlee ignored Harris in the 1946 New Year's Honours List. Other commanders such as Montgomery, Brooke and Alexander were raised to the peerage. It cannot be construed as anything other than a deliberate slight, and a hypocritical one at that. Not only had most of Attlee's government been members of the wartime cabinet and government, the Labour Government, which had swept to victory in July 1945, was the one that had agreed with the decision to drop atomic bombs on Japan.

The *Daily Mirror* announced its surprise, on January 1 1946, at 'the absence, in a list crowded with soldiers, sailors and airmen, of the names of one distinguished "architect of victory", Sir Arthur "Bomber" Harris'.[19] The following day the leader of the *Mirror* speculated as to the reason why Harris had been excluded. The conclusion reached was that he was just too much of a firebrand, a man who had told blunt truths; just the sort of man which was required in war but likely to be shunned in peace:

> As we emphasised in our news columns yesterday the name of Sir Arthur 'Bomber' Harris did not appear in the Honours List. This is a grave omission. Not only is it a slight upon Harris himself, but its effect is that Bomber Command as a whole is deprived of the recognition due to that splendid arm. Has it so soon been forgotten what a great job the bombers did at a period in the war when there was no other way in which we could strike back at the enemy? Have the incalculable results of the strategic bombing in the destruction of German war industries already become a faded memory? Harris may have been, in the personal sense, 'difficult'. Possibly he made himself as awkward to the Brass Hats as he did the Germans. Was that a reason for refusing him a mark of distinction. On the contrary.[20]

Harris's official biographer has suggested that exclusion was partly the result of a conspiracy campaign conducted by Squadron Leader John Strachey, Under Secretary of State for Air. Strachey, according to Saward, had a set of long standing grudges to settle against Harris and he used his influence to gain his revenge.[21] While this may be true, it is hard to believe that a relatively junior member of the government could have engineered such a plot and achieved its success. To blame one man lets the government off the hook. As a whole it turned its back on Harris.

In March 1946 Strachey gave an assessment of the bombing campaign to the House. He confirmed that the strategic bombing campaign was Britain's single biggest contribution to the war. He said that until the Air Ministry concluded its survey it was premature to make any final statement as to its effect. But he did seem to damn the area offensive, claiming that bombing was at its most effective at the end of the war when equipment and expertise made a precision campaign possible.

In drawing a veil over the campaign the coalition and its successor decided that the bombing survey should be only a token gesture. The Americans sent in a team over a thousand strong to investigate the results of bombing. The British, by contrast, sent about a dozen. The reports of the survey were then filed away and not published until nearly 50 years later. Another document which was not to see the light of day for 50 years was Harris's final Despatch. Unlike other commanders, he was denied the right to have his final assessment published. Such actions must be seen as a deliberate attempt to sideline the campaign and consign it to history. It was a history already becoming murky and far more susceptible to myth and legend thanks to exactly these kinds of suppressions.

Harris did manage to make a statement about the campaign, however. In 1947 *Bomber Offensive* was published. It was one of the earliest of the memoirs of the great commanders. Harris was clearly trying to establish a record of the campaign, before it became tainted any further by the official agenda of forgetting and altering. The work is a straightforward, blow by blow account of Harris's career and time in charge of Bomber Command. Where the account fails is in its treatment of his dispute with Portal in the winter of 1944-45, and in his curious assertion that he was never interested in attacking enemy morale. Perhaps he thought this was a point on which the government might be provoked even more. He may have considered the possible repercussions on the men formerly under his command. Interestingly, like many others living in the immediate aftermath of Hiroshima and Nagasaki, he believed the atomic age had consigned the strategic bomber to history.

The review in *The Times Literary Supplement* was generally favourable. However, there was a misunderstanding of Harris's ideas, or a coded criticism of them, for the reviewer praised him for his oil offensive and for using Bomber Command like 'a broom... [sweeping] away the bulk of a nation's industrial power, so that resistance in the long run was inadequate to meet invasion'.[22] There was also a misunderstanding of the Trenchard doctrine and Harris's interpretation of it. He believed Trenchard had never advocated the bomber as a weapon to attack morale. Instead, Trenchard's dictum of the bomber having a morale effect twenty times greater than its material, was passed off as a tool to gain greater government co-operation for his expansion plans. The reviewer found it curious that Harris said nothing on the gestation of the Dresden raid and kept to himself his reactions to such events as the drowning of thousands of civilians after the dams raid.

J.M. Spaight reviewed the work in the *Spectator*. He suspected Harris had had many arguments with other influential wartime figures. The avoidance of detail on such points was the proof as far as he was concerned. Curiously, he stated: 'It is evident from Sir Arthur Harris's own account that he expected less from moral effect than is here suggested.'[23] But, 'he did believe profoundly in the offensive against industrial centres. That view of his chimed with the popular demand of the time. He seemed to give us just what we wanted.' Spaight was one of Harris's great supporters and he had applauded what Harris had delivered. But he was beginning to recant some of his earlier beliefs. 'There is a hint, indeed of resurgent, unrepentant Bourbonism here and there in these pages... One cannot imagine another great airman, Tedder, betraying such a single-track mentality: which probably explains why Tedder is where he is and Harris is not.'

It has been claimed Harris was further snubbed by never receiving an invitation to take another state post. The position he coveted was the governorship of Bermuda, for which he was not considered. But he was offered the post of Chief Commissioner of the Metropolitan Police, which he turned down. Harris took up a job with a shipping line in South Africa, leaving Britain in 1946. He did not return until the fifties when Churchill returned to power and finally made up for his earlier ingratitude by awarding the title of baronet. It was a minor offer given by Churchill only once the dust had settled.

The fifties saw Bomber Command slip into the shadows. The government's campaign to marginalise the strategic air war was paying off, for it was a decade in which Britain relived the Second World War, recounting its glories and revelling in them. Cinema was the main instigator and reflector of this trend. Most of the films unswervingly buttressed the idea of plucky little Britain taking on two evil empires, eventually coming out on top thanks to the skill, common-sense and good humour of its people. Such movies have become standard Sunday matinee fare: *Odette* (1950); *Angels One Five* (1952); *The Malta Story* (1953); *Reach for the Sky* (1956); *Ill Met by Moonlight* (1956); *The Battle of the River Plate* (1956); *Carve Her Name With Pride* (1958); *Dunkirk* (1958). In all this outflowing RAF Bomber Command did surprisingly badly considering its domination of British wartime industry and the British imagination. RAF Fighter Command did much better, three of the above being fighter stories and pilots always played a large role in any POW drama. But there were only two bomber films made during this period, and most people could probably name only one of them, *The Dam Busters* (1954), the other, *Appointment in London* (1952), is hardly known at all.

With the fresh explosion of British war films in the fifties, as the nation began to relive its glories, *The Dam Busters* was simply sitting-up and begging to be done. *The Dam Busters* was a great box office success and has become a British cultural icon. The reason for this is simple. The film reflected the way the British people wanted to remember the war and the way they preferred to think of Bomber Command. Though the raid caused great loss of life it seemed cleaner than the razing of Hamburg or Cologne. It was a precision raid carried out by a dedicated few. The odds were stacked against them and yet skill, daring and teamwork paid off. Busting the dams was about young men testing their skills against a legitimate industrial target. The bombing war the British wanted to remember. For the British the raid, immortalised in the film, was – and is – a vital touchstone of national identity and a reminder of how we fought. Doubts about the morality of the British bombing war were hidden by the film. It was also a story already well known. The raid on the dams was a cultural phenomenon long before the film.

The plot of the film was straightforward, based on Paul Brickhill's best-selling account of the raid, *The Dam Busters* (1951). Brickhill's *Reach for the Sky* was to receive a similar cinematic treatment a few years later. Like the wartime films the plot stressed the Commonwealth make-up of 617 Squadron. As with the wartime films this was nothing more than a reflection of the truth.

The reassuring stress on the skilful and precision nature of the raid played a big part in the movie. As a consequence the training and accuracy demanded of 617 Squadron is heavily emphasised. Wallis (Michael Redgrave) can perhaps be heard to make a veiled criticism of the area bombing campaign at the very start of the film. He is seen standing in the garden talking to the village doctor. They hear bombers pass overhead, Wallis turns and replies to the doctor's statement that the Germans won't be able to take many more heavy raids:

> They wouldn't if we could really get at them. But we don't. It's like trying to kill a giant by firing at his arms with thousands of pea shooters instead of one clean bullet through the heart. Well, you know what happened when they tried to wipe out London.

Harris is portrayed as a gruff, no-nonsense man. In fact it was very close to reality. His first appearance is during the planning session of a maximum effort raid to 'see if we can't knock out Essen'. It was therefore exactly the sort of raid the screen Wallis believed was pointless. Later sequences show Gibson drum-in the need for pinpoint accuracy and exact timing to his men. Very different to the Harris preferred approach.

Richard Todd played Guy Gibson. Such was the impact of the film that Todd has somehow become Gibson and Gibson has become Todd. He is irrevocably linked with his portrayal of Wing Commander Guy Gibson and Gibson's real character has been swallowed into it. Public knowledge of Gibson is synonymous with Todd's interpretation. Gibson is the symbol of the film and its mood. He is presented as stoical and absolutely dedicated. The British people liked to think of themselves in this way.

In Todd's portrayal of Gibson many of the realities of the British bombing war were downplayed. Gibson himself was a man under strain. His job was to lead men in terrifying situations. To stay calm when the natural instinct was to run away. Prematurely aged, jumpy and irritable he was often not a pleasant man to be with. The real Gibson was like many other Bomber Command aircrew. Tense, often tired, desperately in need of genuine relaxation and a touch coldhearted because that was the only way to survive. But this was not the way the public wanted its heroes between 1939 and 1945, and it was not the way they were going to be shaped in the wake of victory.

The Bomber Boys had been mythologised as jolly young men. As relatively few attempts had ever been made to ascertain their real opinions or characters the image remained. It ignored much. It certainly ignored shocking facts like the VD levels. A similar avoidance of reality was seen in *The Dam Busters*. The screen Gibson displayed absolutely no interest in the opposite sex, or his own. The focus of his emotions is his dog. 'Nigger', the labrador, meant everything and is shown as the mascot of the squadron. On the day of the raid Nigger is run-over and Gibson is seen staring at the dog's scratch marks on the door. Todd played Gibson as a man so obsessed by his job that he has no time for romantic involvement. But reality was far more interesting. Gibson was married. He had fallen in love with a young dancer he had seen in a review and married her after a short courtship. His relationship with his wife Eve was volatile, but old comrades remembered that he had a glamorous portrait photograph of her by his bed. Though he often worried about Eve's fidelity, especially as she was in London while he was out in Lincolnshire, it did not stop him from sleeping with a fair number of WAAFs and wives. Gibson the real man, the man who was like so many of his colleagues, did not fulfil the stereotype. Todd and *The Dam Busters* turned him into a stock British hero. It saved too much introspection about the bombing war and the effect it had on the men who fought it.

A far more realistic interpretation of the bombing war was contained in the film *Appointment in London* (1952). But it did not do well at the box office. It implied that the British people far preferred the cosy myth they were buying into. If they had to think about bombing they preferred to think of glorious precision raids carried out against the odds. The harsh realities of life in Bomber Command as portrayed in *Appointment in London* threw up too many difficulties. *Appointment in London* was written by John Wooldridge, a former bomber pilot and colleague of Guy Gibson in 106 Squadron. Gibson had distrusted Wooldridge as an intellectual and aesthetic and the two kept a respectful distance from each other. Wooldridge's portrait of Squadron Leader Tim

Mason (Dirk Bogarde) bore more than a passing resemblance to Gibson. The story follows the lives of members of the fictitious 188 Squadron of Lancasters in 1943.

That no one picked up on the similarities between Gibson and Mason at the time is a tribute to the power of the Gibson legend. At the start of the film Mason has completed 87 missions and only needs to get to 90 to be absolved from flying ever again. However, he is on the verge of some sort of nervous disorder. Mason suffers the usual catalogue of semi-neurasthenic complaints: poor sleeping patterns, general snappiness and irritability. This is very close to the real Gibson. It was also very close to the real lives of thousands of bomber crew. As the pressure mounts on Mason, it is noted that one of the greatest stresses a man has to carry is the fear of being afraid and showing fear. Gibson, like his fellow crew, overcame this by resigning himself to the fact that he would never see out the war (indeed he was killed just after his twenty-sixth birthday).

Though Gibson had an interesting sex life he had a keen belief that men, pilots especially, should not have their wives living near the base as it distracted them from concentrating on their jobs. In *Appointment in London* Mason has exactly this trait, telling off one of his pilots for constantly trying to communicate with his wife.

Mason is forbidden to fly by Bomber Command Headquarters and the Air Ministry for both reasons of his state of mind and that he has now reached such a state of experience that he is more important on the ground. Like Gibson, however, he manages to wangle his way round it, unlike Gibson he comes back.

In other respects the film shared the same aspects as earlier bomber films. The crews were very definitely Commonwealth in composition. Bill Kerr, the Australian actor, played the Australian pilot. Unlike earlier films, *Appointment* actually shows a West Indian aircrew member. The white dominions usually provided the Commonwealth composition in film interpretations.

Appointment in London must have touched a chord with airmen thanks to its authenticity. The rituals and routines of life on a bomber station are caught perfectly. Most significantly, the sense of fate and the need to either accept it or propitiate it with lucky charms. The night Pilot Greeno is lost is put down to two fateful interventions. Firstly, the fact that Mason is not leading the squadron as usual and secondly, to the fact that Greeno had lost his lucky charm, a harmonica, not long before they had set out. This sense of fate waiting for its moment grows as the film progresses and plays still further on Mason's nerves. He longs to face it down and chalk-up his last mission. His chance to get back into the air has a mad twist to it, one of the strange facts of war. One of the Lancasters has trouble with its bomb-bay doors, just before take-off they buckle crushing an armourer to death, forcing Mason to rally the crew into another Lancaster taking him with them.

The film showed the corollary of the high-tension lives of the aircrew by giving full vent to the intensity of the off-duty moments. When the popular Greeno is lost Mason orders a mess party and clearly wants everyone to have a good time, get drunk and so find the strength to carry on. One of the rituals of the party is the dipping of feet in a sooty bowl of water, climbing a ladder and putting footprints on the ceiling. Wooldridge knew his stuff and it shone through in *Appointment in London*.

But a gap with other bomber films opened up in the portrayal of the main raid. The authenticity is matched by the drama. The raid is on secret installations for the making of a new weapon. It therefore seems to be loosely based on the raid on Peenemünde. At the briefing heckling and ironic whistling accompanies the predictions of the Meteorological Officer. In all earlier films the stress on absolute and complete intelligence is very heavy. Mason tells the men that it will be 'a straightforward saturation attack by Bomber Command' – quite a way from the insistence on pinpoint accuracy. The sequences over the target, liberally spliced with real footage, are quite excellent. The commentary of a Master Bomber heard on the soundtrack appears to be from genuine recordings. All the problems of trying to get something as big and vague as 'saturation bombing' right are heard. The Master Bomber's commentary with its constant repetition beats out its rhythm: 'bomb on the green, bomb on the green... you're bombing on their red they're miles out, bomb on the green.' Veterans must have seen the vivid colours of the Target Indicators flashing before their eyes as they watched the film. Despite the urgings of the Master Bomber the accuracy does not improve. Finally, the Master Bomber states in exasperation 'we've not even hit a ruddy cow.' He tries to put more markers in the right place, but is hit and goes down. At this point Mason decides to step in and act as co-ordinator of the attack, carefully taking his crew in, hitting the target and starting a grand fire for the rest of the bomber stream to aim at. Mason then comes back in triumph, leaving him free for his Appointment in London, the awarding of the DFC at Buckingham Palace with other members of his crew and Greeno's widow who collects her husband's award.

Why *Appointment in London* has been ignored and *The Dam Busters* has received such interest is a curiosity on the surface. But scratch the surface and it is easily explicable. *The Dam Busters* is the way the British public wanted to remember their bomber war. A war of simple, uncomplicated, dedicated heroes, doing a job with skill and tenacity, underlined by the morality and decency of the cause. *Appointment in London* shows a man on the verge of cracking-up, shows a bombing mission on the verge of becoming a fiasco. It makes reference to bombs falling everywhere but on the target. Much closer to the truth of many Bomber Command operations, but not a reality that was easily palatable in the wake of Dresden. There is indeed a long way between the dams and Dresden, at least in terms of immediate reactions, memories and images.

The fifties saw a determined campaign of forgetting and redrafting. If the bomber war was going to be remembered, it was to be in a particular way. The controversial edges were to be shaved off. Publication figures for books on Bomber Command provide evidence of the neglect of the decade. Around 570 books on Bomber Command were published between the end of the war and 1996. Of these only 38 were published in the fifties. Interestingly, 12 of these were works of popular fiction, including such titles as *Night be My Witness* (1952); *Faith is a Windsock* (1952); *Johnny Kinsman* (1955); *Maximum Effort* (1957) and *That Great Hunter* (1959). Interestingly, however, the fiction always carried elements of truth in it. The endurance and bravery of the aircrew are stressed in these works, and occasionally the horror too. But they are largely devoid of descriptions of the targets, or the effects of the bombing. Large fires in target cities are mentioned, but moral justifications are avoided as are precise comments about what was happening on the ground. The British people did not want to be bothered with this aspect and the government was keen to avoid it too.

Bomber Command was remembered in other ways. In October 1953, the Queen opened the Imperial War Graves Commission's memorial to the missing of the RAF at Runnymede. But this was a memorial to the missing of all branches of the RAF. A specific Bomber Command memorial, in the form of stained glass windows, was unveiled at Lincoln Cathedral in May 1954. In February 1956 Lord Trenchard died and his ashes were buried in Westminster Abbey. The passing of Trenchard marked the end of an era and perhaps opened the way to reassessments and new interpretations.

The 1960s was a decade of questioning, it was a decade of action and reaction. History was a subject which entered a dynamic period in which standard interpretations were re-examined, and new, shocking theses offered. The two world wars became foci of interest. The First World War began a cycle of fiftieth anniversaries from 1964 that encouraged a renewed interest in the conflict. It was an interest which had already been stoked by the publication, in 1961, of Alan Clark's provocative work *The Donkeys*. *The Donkeys* claimed that British generals wasted their men on the Western Front in a series of disastrously planned and executed battles. Thus it became the fashion to see fault in leaders and encouraged a spirit of 'debunking'. The Second World War was to attract a similar treatment. In 1959 the twentieth anniversary cycle began and this, too, had the effect of stimulating interest in the conflict and provoking reassessment.

Ironically, the greatest stimulus of dissent and ally of radicalism in understanding Bomber Command was an official publication. In 1961 the four volumes of the Official History, *The Strategic Air Offensive Against Germany, 1939-1945*, were published. The volumes were written by the combination of an established academic, Professor Sir Charles Webster of the London School of Economics, and Noble Frankland, a former navigator in Bomber Command, who had become a historian.

Frankland had worked in the Air Historical Branch of the Air Ministry and so had firsthand knowledge of the campaign and had already seen some of the documents. His doctoral thesis was also on the British bombing campaign and was to become the central theme of the Official History. However, it was a thesis which questioned many of the assumptions made about the nature of bombing and the bombing war itself.

The gestation of the Official History was a long and complex affair. The Air Ministry began the search for suitable historians in 1947. A large list was duly examined and various candidates were considered. In May 1950 Sir Charles Webster was approached. Being a historian of foreign policy and international relations it was felt that Sir Charles might need help from someone with expertise in the actual subject. A year later Frankland was formally appointed as Webster's co-author.

The Official History then took ten years to write, such was the huge task involved. The authors had to examine the myriad papers generated by Bomber Command and the Air Ministry during the war. Frankland also had to use a considerable amount of ingenuity and stamina to get the funding for a trip to the States. This was a vital part of the project, for it allowed a comparative approach with the strategy of the USAAF. In addition to this, Webster was determined to know exactly what the experience of flight in a bomber was like and so a special set of flights had to be arranged for him. Webster then settled down to write the narrative sections with Frankland writing the analyses. Each then read the other's work.

One of the trickiest tasks was ensuring balanced portrayals of the commanders involved. They were, of course, nearly all living at this time. Webster visited Harris in 1952 and was much charmed by him. However, Frankland has since written that Harris soon became highly suspicious of the motives of the Official Historians and his early spirit of co-operation dried up. Harris had probably heard of Frankland's controversial doctoral thesis. Frankland claims that Harris was sent drafts but refused to read them. Harris's official biographer has countered this claim. According to Saward, Harris received a final draft giving him little chance to add comment or annotations. Realising this Harris refused to have anything to do with it.

Portal was a different case altogether. He retained an open mind, reading and commenting on draft sections, only becoming worried when the question of publishing letters, documents and papers came up. Tedder proved to be co-operative and frank. Ludlow-Hewitt read sections and added some comments as did Slessor and Saundby. With Harris seemingly sidelined by his own actions, the big problem came in the form of Peirse. According to Frankland Peirse hinted at a libel action in a personal meeting with the authors. Then came the controversy over the inclusion of official papers. The government was extremely reluctant to allow the inclusion of the Churchill papers on Dresden. Webster and Frankland stood firm. They said the Official History would only make sense if it included the official papers. It then became a complex legal matter as questions of Crown privilege and individual copyright over the papers and documents were debated. Eventually the problems were cleared up and the Prime Minister gave his consent to publish. Sadly, Webster did not live to see the publication day, October 2 1961, for he died seven weeks earlier. But it did save him from the furore the volumes caused.

The controversy lay in Frankland's thesis. He argued that the pre-war Air Staff had worked on the understanding that the air was a frontier that could not be completely defended. Therefore the bomber could, and would, get through to cause massive damage to the enemy. A revolutionary concept came out of this. Until the conquest of the air all wars had relied upon defeating an enemy force first. Thus navies had to win their battles before they could blockade an enemy, armies had to win their land campaigns before they could enter enemy capitals in triumph. By contrast, a bombing force could avoid battle *and* impose a blockade *and* attack an enemy capital. Frankland argued that this concept had been put into practice in the war, but had failed.

His main point of reference was Mahan's understanding of sea power. Admiral Mahan's influential works, *The Influence of Sea Power upon History, 1660-1783* (1890) and *The Influence of Sea Power upon the French Revolution* (1892), had stated that sea power was effective only when complete mastery of the seas had been gained. This may seem self-explanatory, but he was actually making a more complex point. He demonstrated that Louis XIV had realised he could not defeat the British fleet and so had turned to a war of commerce raiding instead, a *guerre de course*, to strangle British trade. It was a fine plan, but it did not work because at no point did it directly challenge Britain's control of the sea. Similarly, the German u-boat threats in both world wars caused huge scares, but they were not enough to wrest naval power from Britain. Frankland suggested these lessons could be applied to the air war. He believed the British bombers were the equivalent of Louis's ships. Unable to beat the daylight defence of the Luftwaffe, the British turned to a nightly *guerre de course*, hoping to destroy Germany in this way. But this consigned the British efforts to a list of similar failures. Bombing became effective only once the German defences had been directly attacked and destroyed. In other words, only once the long-range fighter had taken out the Luftwaffe thus achieving allied mastery of the skies, were the bombers given their chance to get on and do their job. Such an interpretation was a direct refutation of much of the Trenchard doctrine and condemned much of the British bombing war as a sheer waste of time and effort. When these themes were developed in the Official History it resulted in a comprehensive reappraisal.

Webster and Frankland also revealed how much time was wasted in Ministry of Economic Warfare suggestions and predictions. The complete failure to understand the German wartime economy was exposed. Both the Ministry of Economic Warfare and Harris were portrayed as setting unrealistic targets. But they did not write-off the role of the bomber completely, for they stressed its part in achieving victory for the allies. However, this was a message lost in the more shocking revelations.

The newspapers and journals all waded in with comments on the volumes. The Military Historian, Michael Howard, reviewed it for *The Times Literary Supplement*. He found it to be a model of balanced argument and comment and praised it 'as an achievement without parallel in military history'.[24] Reflecting the changing attitudes of the times, he concluded on the fact that he found the ordinary Germans, who carried on with their daily lives, the true heroes of the work. A.J.P. Taylor also felt the work was of an extremely high standard, calling it 'a model of scholarly accuracy and impartiality' in the *New Statesman*. Gavin Lyall wrote a generally favourable review for the *Spectator*, but wanted to know why Churchill was not identified more strongly as the man in ultimate charge. Lyall argued that if Harris was wrong it was because Churchill was wrong, and added it 'is here, but it is written between the lines'.[25] Richard Crossman's review filled five columns in the *Sunday Telegraph*, which carried such headlines as 'Row Breaks over Last-War Bombing', 'Sir Arthur Harris's Retort to Charge of Costly Failure' and 'Bombing Victory That Never Was'. His balanced review noted the high casualties of the campaign. He reminded people of how a new Passchendaele had arisen from a strategy designed to avoid such an outcome.[26] Was anyone entitled to call the campaign a 'costly failure'[27], asked the *Daily Express* in which the leader noted that 'truth must be served'. Bennett, formerly of the Pathfinders, condemned the history in the *Evening Standard*.[28] Frankland has pointed out that this piece was ghost written and that Bennett actually agreed with him on the bulk of his interpretation. *The People* ran the headline

'Now it is officially admitted we killed 180,000 German Civilians in vain'.[29] What such responses revealed was that many British people believed the bomber offensive was a great success *and* that the deaths of German civilians were acceptable because it brought about victory. The majority of British people were shocked to find the great bombing campaign had not worked as well as they thought. They were also shocked because the long concealed, half-known truth was exposed. The British bombing campaign had set out to hit German civilians. Reliance on the idea of accidental deaths was no longer an option. Accidental deaths were the greatest myth and it had been torn open. It was a shock to be brought face-to-face with it after so many years juggling with that fact. The realities of British bombing, carefully suppressed for such a long time, were brought back to the surface by Webster and Frankland. The twisting of the truth into a comfortable set of memories was exposed. What the people had known during the war, and carefully forgotten since, was resurrected. Having forgotten that the British bomber was a brutal bludgeon, it was a shock to have such a pointed reminder. The violence unleashed with their help was revealed. The desire to slough it off on someone else was becoming stronger.

An atmosphere of bunking and debunking was becoming the new orthodoxy. A year before the Official History appeared Martin Caidin's book *The Night Hamburg Died* was published. The work was highly emotional and sought to draw out the full horror of the raids of July 1943. He claimed that 'not even the atomic bombings of Hiroshima and Nagasaki equalled the flaming devastation sown in the Hanseatic port.' Bomber Command was portrayed as a force obsessed with its ability to cause wanton destruction:

> the Royal Air Force continued its mission of piling ruin upon ruin in German cities, slaughtering tens of thousands of workers, injuring hundreds of thousands, burning vast sections into rubble, immobilising millions of workers, and extinguishing the economic substance of the Reich.[30]

At least Caidin seemed to give grudging respect to the role the bombers played in destruction of the Nazi war economy. No such admission was made in David Irving's 1963 work *The Destruction of Dresden*. Irving's approach was sober and measured. It was also backed up by a great deal of research. He argued that the bombing was out of all proportion to the military significance of the city. Refusing to blame Harris, he laid the blame at the feet of the government, saying Bomber Command merely carried out its orders.

The Times Literary Supplement praised the work, but believed it was motivated by communist stories put about in the east that the raid was a piece of western, capitalist terrorism.[31] Irving wrote back to remind the reviewer he had interviewed only former residents of Dresden now living in West Germany, as he feared current residents were over duly influenced by communist propaganda.[32] For Richard Crossman, reviewing it in the *New Statesman*, the lack of east German witnesses was a flaw.[33] He also added that the raid was a crime against humanity, 'whose authors would have been arraigned at Nuremberg if that Court had not been perverted into a mere instrument of Allied vengeance.' He concluded: 'Bomber Command… was never forgiven for carrying out the War Cabinet's orders with such wanton efficiency. It has never been given either a national memorial or a campaign medal, and its Commander-in-Chief was excluded by Earl Attlee from the victory honours list of January 1946.' Crossman clearly wanted to help set the record straight, but it was becoming a very hard job for the public was witnessing the exhumation of old skeletons.

The modern memory was taking shape. In 1945 Dresden was just another raid for most British people. By the early sixties the consequences of that raid were coming before the public. Dresden was coming to prominence, but it was a prominence shaped by the nature of the post-war world. With the Soviet authorities intent on forming East Germany in its own image it was convenient to present the bombing of Dresden as the continuation of the oppression of the German people by the Nazis. In the light of this it suited both British and American governments to allow the Dresden raid to be seen as the result of Harris's policies, rather than of part of their own allied strategy. The regeneration of Coventry, and the opening of the new cathedral, changed the atmosphere still further. Coventry, and its cathedral, became a symbol of reconciliation between Britain and Germany. It was an admission that both sides suffered and both sides could forgive while never forgetting. Added force was given to this feeling by Benjamin Britten's *War Requiem*. Though ostensibly a piece about the Great War – Britten used Wilfred Owen's poetry and sections of the Latin requiem mass – it had a wider significance. Britten wanted it to be an act of reconciliation between the Second World War combatants. He had originally envisaged the main roles to be performed by singers from Russia, Germany and Britain. It was premiered in the new Coventry cathedral in 1961 and then received its German premiere in Dresden in 1965. The modern image of Dresden as nothing other than a byword for wanton destruction was taking shape – nearly 20 years after the event.

The Official History had set the standard for other historians to follow. The strategic air war had been returned to its controversial origins. The 1970s saw the trend continued and that of a continuing empathy with the German people who had suffered the storm of bombs. It was also a period in which more and more studies began to make use of interviews with ordinary airmen and ground crew, providing the human story behind matters previously discussed only in terms of high strategy. The People's War was taking on more significance.

Len Deighton kicked off the decade with his powerful novel *Bomber*. Deighton had served in the RAF and had taken a keen interest in Bomber Command in his teens during the war. The novel told the story of one maximum effort raid on the fictional Ruhr town of Altgarten, located near Krefeld, in June 1943. As well as telling the story of the Bomber Command personnel involved, Deighton's sweep covers the German civilians of Altgarten and a Luftwaffe night-fighter and control station in the Netherlands. It is made clear that not all Germans were Nazis. Further still, ordinary Germans suffered at the hands of the Nazis. This was an interpretation of the Second World War that was gaining acceptance at the time.

Bomber was a product of its time. The satirical and ironic elements of *The Donkeys* and *Oh What a Lovely War* influenced it, as had the war in Vietnam. The 'blurb' on the jacket of the book made comparisons with the charge of the Light Brigade and the bombing in Vietnam. Deighton himself admitted that the genesis of the novel lay in an irony. A friend who was in the RAF during the war told him that Lancasters liked flying with Stirlings as their lower ceilings made them more attractive to night-fighters. 'This wasn't the sort of war I was reading about in the newspapers, and it wasn't the sort of war that the cinema has been serving up ever since.'[34]

The press reactions were favourable, with relatively few exceptions. The *New Statesman* was one of the few finding it just too obsessed with technical matters;[35] the *TLS* made a similar point, but felt that its 'dispassionate recording of horror... [makes] us feel such horror is unrepeatably outrageous'.[36] But the *Daily Mail* praised it as 'masterly', which was also the term used in the *Spectator*, while *The Times* stated: '*Bomber* develops into a tearing, terrifying denunciation not just of war, but of the irreversible mechanical processes that govern war and, increasingly, the world.[37] He uses a detached, emotionless style which wields tremendous power. At times an actively painful experience.' It was obvious that the novel, though about the Second World War, and highly authentic, was also felt to have a relevance to the modern world. For from the end of the Second World War the debate about bombing was intimately connected to fears of atomic, and then nuclear, war. Recent history and current events had coloured understandings of the strategic air campaign.

The generally critical and questioning approach to Bomber Command was further reinforced in the seventies by its interpretation in the highly praised and highly successful Thames Television series, *The World at War*. Episode twelve examined the bomber war, *Whirlwind, Bombing Germany September 1939–April 1944*. The episode was written by Charles Douglas Home, and implied that much of the campaign was a waste. An edge of satire was also introduced, for clips from *Target for Tonight* were used alongside a highly ironic commentary, read by Laurence Olivier:

> Patriotic films had no difficulty in giving the impression that pluck and determination and a diet of raw carrots could overcome the law that says you cannot see in the dark... Of course once the target was reached it was a piece of cake – provided you were just blowing up a studio model – the truth was different.

Reviewed in the *Daily Mail*, it was praised as an even-handed programme with a good sense of perspective which gave due respect to the bravery of the pilots and crews. However, it also remarked that the episode 'showed the long campaign to have been murderously indiscriminate and often ineffective'.[38] The sense of a schism having opened up between wartime values and those of the new orthodoxy was perceptible in the reviewer's comments on the use of wartime newsreels: 'Heard today, those newsreel voices make one cringe, or sigh. They are as alien to present outlooks as the Bayeux Tapestries – and were acceptable and effective only 30 years ago.' 'Acceptable and effective only 30 years ago' reveals the rejection of the justification of the bomber campaign. The generations that had grown up since the war in the confused silence about the bombing campaign were bound to come to the conclusion that there was something shameful about it. Instead of trying to understand it they were mystified and repulsed. Finding it hard to believe that the British people could have had any inclination of the real nature of the campaign they found it easier to blame Harris and his men.

In 1973 Martin Middlebrook began his cycle of Bomber Command books with *The Nuremberg Raid*. Like Deighton, Middlebrook's works stress the stories of the individuals involved, both British and German. Middlebrook's works are distinguished by their accessibility coupled with their meticulous research and clear structure. He followed up the success of this formula with *The Battle of Hamburg* (1980); *The Peenemünde Raid* (1982); *The Bomber Command War Diaries* with Chris Everitt (1985) and *The Berlin Raids* (1988). Ironically, given the condemnation of Harris and what his men had done, Middlebrook was successfully putting the other side of the case. After years of neglect the real airman's war was brought to public attention. The Official History had been largely critical of the strategy, but it had not told the story of the men at the sharp end. Here the public was given the chance to see that the men involved were ordinary, young people. They came from ordinary backgrounds. They were not ruthless killers or amoral criminals. They were sons, husbands, dads and boyfriends too. They were hoping to end the war quickly and wanted to get back to their everyday lives. They were killed in thousands. In describing the lives of aircrew, and providing a new perspective, such histories could only make it worse for Harris. Harris looked even more like a man driven by an insane dogma, a man who did not care, a man beyond the control of his political masters. For only such a character could put men through the ordeals and rigours of bombing Germany night after night.

In 1982 Alexander McKee's work *Dresden 1945: The Devil's Tinderbox* was published. McKee set out to prove that the raid might have been down to allied policy, but was carried out with fiendish enthusiasm by Harris. His interpretation of events is heavily coloured by his own wartime service in the army, in which he saw the ruins of French and German towns, caused by allied bombs. His very first line sets the agenda and tone for the rest of the book: 'Dresden was a famous massacre from the start.'[39] It was also factually wrong, for it implied a far greater initial knowledge of the raid, thus helping to buttress the idea that Dresden had always been a popular *cause celebre*. McKee's narrative made many confusing and contradictory statements: 'After the war, in his book, the bomber commander [Harris] was to try to evade responsibility for the Dresden massacre by saying that the orders for it had come from above his level. This was true, so far as it went.'[40] Later he completely contradicted himself: 'It was the Prime Minister himself who in effect had signed the death warrant for Dresden, which had been executed by Harris... They were all in it together... and the Prime Minister most of all.'[41]

He took a great delight in condemning Harris and his character:

a great deal depended on how much the crews believed in their leaders. Some did, but there were many who nicknamed Harris 'the Butcher' not so much because he cared nothing for the lives of German civilians but because they believed that he cared nothing for their own either.[42]

He also quoted a Scots-Canadian navigator who claimed that Harris was 'an air force twin for Haig of the Somme, Ypres, Passchendaele. One thing about Harris, though, he played no favourites. He was just as willing to sacrifice Brits as Canadians.'[43] Finally, when referring to Harris's dealings with the Official Historians, he noted: 'In Harris's background world, people died in theory; but Frankland had been over Germany where they died in fact.'[44]

But far from finding the Official Historians credible, McKee argued they failed to condemn the area campaign and the Dresden raid with sufficient vigour:

> The condemnation of the British official historians was restrained. Having quietly equated area bombing with a policy of terror, they referred to 'vast havoc of the continuing area offensive culminating in the destruction of Dresden'. That was the verdict of Webster and Frankland in 1961.[45]

McKee provided a powerful example of the confused rhetoric and moralising the bombing war had thrown up. It was not new, for during the war itself there was equal confusion. Harris was actually, and rather ironically, being vindicated. Sinclair should have made a clear and unequivocal statement about British bombing in the House. It would not have stopped debate. Far from it. But it would have given a firm factual base from which debate and discourse could be launched. The silence and contradictions have led to a continuing malaise.

In 1983 the RAF Museum at Hendon, North London, finally opened a permanent display dedicated to Bomber Command. It is a mark of the trepidation with which even the RAF treated the campaign that it took nearly 40 years for such a display to be opened.

Interest in Bomber Command was increasing the whole time and it was given a massive boost in the mid-eighties by the high profile fortieth anniversary cycles and the death, in April 1984, of Sir Arthur Harris. The death of Harris was bound to cause controversy. Arguments, old and new, were aired, but it was impossible to strike a new, more rational balance for there was too much baggage to slough off. The obituary in *The Times* avoided making too many controversial statements, commenting instead that 'Harris may fairly be considered to have been treated somewhat churlishly in the aftermath of hostilities', and that he and his campaign 'undoubtedly made a considerable contribution to the winning of the war in the west'.[46] The *Daily Mirror* reported that Harris had been labelled 'the "Butcher" for his saturation bombing of German cities.[47] Air Marshal Sir Michael Beetham defended Harris's reputation at the memorial service, saying 'his area bombing of cities has been strongly criticised in some quarters but in practice there was no alternative if there was to be an offensive at all.'[48] But not all responses were so restrained or measured. For George Gale Harris was nothing but an indiscriminate murderer, he was little better than the Nazis. He wrote in the *Daily Express*: 'it is a terrible thing to say, but it is, nonetheless, my opinion that Harris's blanket bombing of German towns when victory was assured was a crime against humanity.'[49] This was presumably a reference to Dresden. A taboo had been aired in a popular newspaper. The British war effort had been equated with Nazi crimes. Many people might have been thinking it, might have felt it for years, but had been too appalled to voice it. Gale did it. A response was inevitable. An ex-Bomber Command navigator wrote to the editor, but his tone revealed that even he had doubts about Dresden:

> I can state positively that the MAIN targets of our bombers in the last fifteen months of the war, with the possible exception of Dresden, were largely military and transport centres – including the flying bomb launching sites, from where war was launched against British civilians... The Germans started the whole shooting match, and having sown the wind they reaped the whirlwind.[50]

But Gale had also opened up the whole foggy memory of the bombing war. Those who wrote in to oppose him provided a host of different arguments. They revealed that solid justification for the strategic air campaign was (and is) missing because the basic knowledge of it was (and is) missing. One correspondent (who did not reveal whether he or she had served in Bomber Command) claimed the raids were never aimed at civilians and always had specific targets in mind.[51] Yet another wrote: 'I had been fighting the war for over five years, and I was in favour of anything that would bring it to an end in Europe.'[52] A former bomber pilot, A.G. Goulding, wrote many letters to both Gale and his editor Sir Larry Lamb pointing out inaccuracies and different interpretations.[53] His correspondence wasn't actually published, but he included it in his 1985 memoirs *Uncommon Valour*. It resulted in Lamb refusing to enter into any further debate with Mr Goulding. He certainly never answered Goulding's charges of poor research and repetition of established myths without checking the actual record.

With Harris's death, his family authorised Dudley Saward, a former member of staff at Bomber Command, to publish his biography. It is a competent piece, but in trying to defend Harris on all counts it ends up massively overstating the effectiveness of Bomber Command. Solly Zuckerman picked up on exactly this trait in his review for the *Sunday Times*.[54] But its worse feature is its lack of backbone. Harris knew what he was up to and was not afraid of it. The one element he did not lack was resolution. In trying to explain away, rather than simply explain, Saward painted an anodyne Harris. Whatever one might think of Harris, he deserved better than that.

A far more interesting and significant investigation of Harris's character came from outside the realms of traditional history and biography. In 1989 the BBC produced Don Shaw's play, *'Bomber' Harris*, as part of its series of programmes marking the fiftieth anniversary of the outbreak of the war. The *Guardian* carried a feature on the production a month before its broadcast. That legends and myths about Harris still abound was proved by the introduction to the piece: '*The RAF's strategic bombing policy was largely Harris's brainchild*, and he defended it until the bitter end, in the face of mounting evidence that it simply wasn't working.'[55] [emphasis added] John Thaw, who played Harris, said he had studied the character and ideas of Harris and stated: 'Harris's argument was that if you're going to have a war, everybody's in it – men, women and children.'[56] Shaw added his thoughts, for him Harris's strength was his refusal to see war as anything other than a very messy business:

He was one of the great realists of the war on our side, in that he accepted that war is a bloody terrible business, it's pure savagery, and it's pointless pussyfooting about saying 'let's ban chemical weapons or nuclear weapons'. The only way to deal with it is to get it over as quickly as possible.[57]

For Shaw Harris was not a war criminal for he 'did not want to kill six million people. The other guy did. That's the essential difference. Harris wasn't acting with base motives'.[58]

As with Deighton's *Bomber*, the mixture of fact and fiction made for an extremely moving whole. The *Financial Times* reviewer felt it was important for showing that 'the last notions of romance and chivalry were disappearing from earthly warfare. The old rulebooks were about to be atomised. Asked about the ethics of bombing, Bomber Harris replied: "There aren't any."'[59]

Harris and Bomber Command are still the black sheep of the British popular memory of the Second World War. This memory relies upon an incomplete and inaccurate knowledge. But even those who are trying to rehabilitate the memory use inaccuracies, or have gaps in their knowledge. The most often heard defence is that the Command never set out to kill German civilians. Clearly, that was not the case. Historians have tried to take a more measured line, pointing out that if it was an atrocity, it was an atrocity for which the wartime government must take responsibility. But there seems precious little evidence of this interpretation actually seeping into the popular consciousness.

At the end of the war, during the last days of the coalition, the government moved to distance itself from Harris and the Command. Attlee's Labour Government was to continue that trend. It was not wholly understood at the time, though some guessed why, measuring the silence by their own private qualms. But in the changed atmosphere of the sixties it became the new orthodoxy. It was also an orthodoxy which seemed to gain credibility by yet another government statement, the Official History. The Cold War made it politic to encourage the idea of a rogue unit, operating outside government control. Now, with the movements towards European integration the desire is similar.

Over 50 years after the events the rumble of Bomber Command engines still echo, while the vapour trail of truths, half-truths, confusions and lies about its role can be traced back to the day the war broke out.

Conclusion

On the outskirts of the German town of Kleve stands a Commonwealth War Cemetery. It is in a beautiful spot. Surrounded by the trees of the Reichswald, the Commonwealth War Graves Commission fulfilled the dreams of Rupert Brooke. This is a corner of a foreign field forever England. The trees shade the graves and in summer flowers add splashes of colour across the simple white Portland stone headstones of the dead. They are arranged in neat rows, providing a straight promenade down to the Cross of Sacrifice. But this English garden also commemorates men from the Dominions and occupied countries. For this English garden contains 3,971 RAF men, more than any other cemetery in Germany. The dead lie in perfect peace. Given the awful ways in which they died it is consoling to see such a beautiful and tranquil place. They lie in peace in the land they did their best to destroy.

Was it all worth it? Was it worth the loss of 55,573 officers and men of Britain, the Commonwealth and the occupied countries? Men who were often trained specialists and technicians. The sorts of men desperately required for rebuilding the post-war world. The casualties were shocking – as they still are. But compared with the millions who died on the Eastern Front or in China they are tiny. The shock came in the constant attrition of men from a small island. Every man was a volunteer. Every man was someone special. There were no conscripts among the aircrew. However, this might seem a more effective way for a small country with a limited population to fight a sprawling war. The corollary was the greater sharpness of losing them. 125,000 men and women served in Bomber Command. This relatively compact force must have felt those losses keenly. Did their efforts and their deaths shorten the war and play a worthwhile role?

Opinions on the efficacy of the British – and indeed whole allied – air strategy are as divided today as they were during the war. At the conclusion of the war the British and American governments formed Bombing Survey Units. The British government revealed its desire to brush Bomber Command under the carpet by constituting a pitifully small team. A quick fix was required. No one wanted to be reminded of it. Professor Zuckerman took charge of writing the overall appraisal and concluded that more attention should have been paid to communications. In effect he damned the area campaign as a waste of resources. The Air Ministry filed away the report and did little with it. Thankful to have done with the whole affair the government was equally happy to see it disappear into the mist. The hearts and minds of the new Germans were very important to them. It was regarded as best not to rub home the bombing war in any way whatsoever. With the Nuremberg war crimes tribunal up and running there was also the desire to avoid any charges of similar complicity in crimes against humanity. Rather than stand up and make a clear statement about bombing, the British government once again ran from the opportunity. As part of this enforced silence Harris suffered the ignominy of having his despatch withheld from the public. It was a miserable insult to deliver for a final despatch was traditionally an instrument in which a commander expressed his full thanks and gratitude to the men under his command by summarising their work. The men of Bomber Command were deliberately denied their share of honour by this action.

The American Bombing Survey was a much more thorough instrument than its British equivalent. The air force was keen to examine the effects of its cherished precision daylight campaign. A host of experts was drafted in and the American team swept up documents and witnesses with a huge appetite. Rather shockingly for the American advocates of air power this report too concluded with a cool assessment. One member of the team, the young economist J.K. Galbraith, damned the entire struggle as a waste of time.

Critics of the campaign have used the surveys to support their theses. But the surveys were not as all-encompassing, nor as methodical as they credited themselves to be. The British survey in particular lacked real depth thanks largely to the strain imposed on its small team.

For the doubters the bombing war failed to destroy the German war machine. There is plenty of evidence to support this case. Though German cities resembled moonscapes by 1945, German industry survived until the last. The German war economy had, indeed, got stronger during 1943-44. It can also be shown that the German air force was never destroyed in the factory as the Pointblank Directive ordered, but by the long-range allied fighters. Air supremacy was only achieved by attrition of the air force in the air, not by choking it on the production line.

A persuasive critique of the policy can therefore be made without requiring too much hard work. The task of defending the strategy has also been made much harder by the fantastic claims made by the airmen during the war. If Harris and Eaker had moderated some of their most dogmatic statements about the ability of the bomber to end the war they might have gained a more reasoned appraisal from subsequent commentators. The airmen gave their critics a large target to snipe at by refusing to admit that the bomber was a superb weapon in a 'mixed economy of warfare'.

Harris claimed he never had the chance to prove his thesis and had been judged on an incomplete experiment. He certainly had a degree of legitimacy. The bomber force was never built up to the size Portal thought necessary. Further, the bomber force that was available often found itself a maid-of-all-work. Bomber Command carried out a host of ancillary roles. Thousands of mines were laid, spies and agents were dropped in France, supplies were dropped to resistance forces, propaganda leaflets were delivered. The work of Bomber Command often had more in common with the work of its sister force Transport Command than carrying bombs to the enemy. Harris was also denied the chance to see through his strategic campaign. The Battle of Berlin may have been a defeat, but it can be argued that he had not lost the bombing war. Instead of moving into the next battle he was deflected into a tactical force. Ironically, it is in the tactical application of the Command that both critics and supporters have come together. Between the spring of 1944 and the spring of 1945 Bomber Command was nothing less than brilliant. Targets, great and small, were taken out by the bombers providing invaluable service to the invading armies. British and American army casualties would have been much higher had it not been for the work of the bomber forces.

On a wider scale, there are many potent arguments in favour of the effectiveness of the area campaign strategy. German offensive air power was negated by bombing. The Luftwaffe took less and less part in offensive activities and became a force devoted to defending the Reich. When combined with the ability of allied long range fighters to engage and knock-out the enemy the attrition rate became an intense strain for the Germans.

The area offensive and the American strategy led to the dispersal of German industry. This tactic allowed German production to continue and made it harder for the area offensive to cause further damage. But it was forced upon the Germans by the non-stop aerial offensive. Every production process dispersed meant longer to complete each process. Raw materials, components and labour had to be spread over large areas. It created a great strain on the German transport system.

In order to negate the effects of the air campaign, Hitler resorted to more and more wasteful and fantastic schemes. To hit back at the British people Hitler demanded the v-weapons scheme. But the project swallowed German skilled labour and engineering prowess needed elsewhere. It deflected from many other aircraft developments and fatally interrupted the production of jet fighters. Alongside the v-weapons project Hitler indulged in the fantasy of transferring German industry underground. In a vastly expensive and time-consuming effort German workers, supplemented by levies of slave labour, sought to construct over 93 million square feet of floorspace. By the end of 1944 only 13 million feet were completed. Over half a million men were employed and the materials used drained the German wartime economy still further.

By 1944 Bomber Command was making considerable in-roads into the German fuel supply and production system. Domestic oil production fell from 673,000 tons in January to 265,000 tons by September. Gas supplies too were severely disrupted. The Battle of Berlin helped reduce the city's gas stock from 2.25 million cubic metres in 1943 to 480,000 by March 1944. Berlin's electricity supply was eroded in an equally dramatic way. In 1943 Berlin received 2,297 million kilowatts, but in 1944 it only received 1,946 million.

In every way the allied air campaign affected and influenced the German war economy. Most importantly, it diverted the German war effort from offensive produc-tion to defensive. Anti-aircraft guns, searchlights, radar sets and fighters were built almost exclusively for the defence of the Reich. For the Wehrmacht troops suffering on the Eastern Front, the air offensive occurring thousands of miles behind them was as much of an enemy as the Red Army. The armies at the front were not just drained of equipment manpower was held at home too. In 1942 there were 439,000 men and women engaged in air defence services, by 1944 it had risen to 889,000. The spring of 1944 saw 68 per cent of Germany's fighters consigned to home defence. There were 14,489 heavy guns and 41,937 searchlights dedicated to the protection of the Reich heartland. 2.7 million working days were lost repairing bomb damage, demanding 800,000 workers. However, this deflection and redeployment of war industries was not the original intention of the air campaign. The campaign had been designed to obliterate production completely rather than deflect it. But that should not detract from the very real drain the campaign had on Germany's ability to wage war.

Germans found themselves under siege. The allied campaign pounded away without let. Every night the British smashed away at German nerves. The strategy against morale became progressively more effective. Just as the British people had done, Germans emerged from their shelters each morning and attempted to continue their everyday lives. Unlike the British people, they were never given a chance to recover completely. Night after night, week after week, month after month it ground on. People became withdrawn, apathetic, listless, melancholic. The ruthless Nazi system of government made it impossible for revolution or mass civil unrest to break out, but the Nazis could not make exhausted men work harder or more efficiently. From January to November 1944 Mainz existed in an almost permanent state of air raid alarm. It amounted to 540 hours, or almost ten weeks of work. Absenteeism soared. Evacuation forced massive disruption. The numbers of evacuated people placed great strains on the reception areas. Over five million people were made homeless. Somehow the German economy had to find room to make extra beds, sheets, cooking utensils, boots and shoes for the millions left homeless and billeted in rural areas.

Men fighting at the front were affected. The most potent justification of their efforts was the thought of protecting their loved ones at home. Their only dream was to return to their wives, children and homes. But letters home remained unanswered, for their homes had disappeared. Between 300,000 and 600,000 German civilians lost their lives by bombing. In effect the soldiers at the front were fighting for nothing, for their efforts did little to protect the sanctity of the Fatherland.

As German endurance dipped British morale turned upwards. For the British the bombing campaign was justifiable retribution. Every crime the Nazi system imposed on the world was paid back with a vengeance. The bomber was a symbol of Britain's dedication and independence. From the moment America joined the war Britain was bound to become the most junior partner in the Soviet-US-British alliance. The bomber and the area offensive were a completely independent contribution to the war. Every Lancaster summed up Britain's ruthless desire to win. It was a ruthlessness there from the earliest days of the war. A ruthlessness that had shown itself well before the first German bombs fell on Britain. In July 1940 the British Mediterranean fleet had shelled the French fleet to pieces. Rather than allow the warships of a former ally to fall into German hands the British killed hundreds of French sailors. It was devastating. It was shocking. It was ruthless. It was a modern war of national survival. If Britain had the resolution to slaughter allies no one should be surprised at the force unleashed against the Germans. The campaign was also vital for Britain's self-esteem. Every Lancaster proved Britain was fighting the Germans. Every Lancaster was also proof of sovereign power. Britain was not merely a nephew of Uncle Sam. Prior to June 1944, every Lancaster sent over German territory was also a reminder to Stalin that Britain had launched a second front. Moreover, the front was over the heartland of the Reich itself.

The crews that carried out the policy thought little of what they were doing. Rod Rodley admitted to never considering what a bomb could do to the human body.[1] But nor did the majority of British people. John Gee recalled never coming across anyone who challenged his role during the war. It certainly never occurred to him to think too much about what he was doing.[2] Lord Mackie, who served as an observer, accepted his role without much pity, the situation did not allow it. 'We had to accept that in modern war civilians were killed. In our eyes we were in a desperate situation, and we knew it. The trials of the German nation did not worry us an awful lot.'[3] 'I just cannot and will never accept that bombing Germany was immoral,' stated Sir John Curtis, a former navigator.[4] They had a job to do. They were there to bomb Germany. The Germans wanted to shoot them down and kill them in large numbers. This made the bombing campaign a relatively easy problem to deal with. In the struggle for self-preservation wider moral debates were side-lined.

Whether the area campaign, and its targeting of civilians, is morally justifiable is an extremely difficult question. The element missing most clearly in modern discussions is a genuine understanding of the time. Modern critics constantly under-estimate the desperate atmosphere of 1941-2. The value of hindsight is employed too readily. It is assumed that the British government and people knew the war would end in their favour. But in 1941-42 no one knew the German offensive in Russia was a huge blunder. No one knew the Japanese empire could be curtailed. No one knew how long Britain would be hemmed in, unable to strike at the heart of its enemies. This was the atmosphere in which the area campaign matured.

During the conflict itself the British people were informed by a constant stream of stories, leading articles, pamphlets, books, newsreels, radio broadcasts, recordings and films about Bomber Command and the strategic bombing campaign. Much of the material was contradictory. It was said that the British were flattening large sections of Germany and this was felt to be right. But, it was also said that the British were by no means aiming at defenceless citizens. There was a fracture line of contradiction and confusion running through public knowledge of the campaign. Despite this the British people had a shrewd idea of what British bombing of Germany meant. It may have been an incomplete knowledge, and it may have made them feel uncomfortable at times, but they lived with the idea of bombing because they were in the frontline of a vast war. There was a much cruder, simpler justification too, and it could be used to justify almost anything – *they started it*. The Germans had started the war *and* indiscriminate bombing. The British developed it and used it as a scorching, searing instrument of retribution. The words of Hosea's Old Testament prophecy have been used with regard to the British bombing campaign almost to the point of cliché. But that does not stop them from having the ring of historical authenticity. The feeling of most

British people between 1941, when the British bombing campaign began to gather pace, and 1945, was that the Germans had sown the wind and were now reaping the whirlwind. A whirlwind which, it was felt, they fully deserved. Only after the war when other factors came into play would the image of Bomber Command and Harris be altered. The image in the shadows of British minds. The British liberal conscience, audible, but only just, during the war itself, reasserted itself and reshaped the memory of the bombing war. Ironically, it was aided by many of the men who had held authority over the work of the Air Ministry and Bomber Command.

Bomber Command was the only weapon we possessed. People forget that the British Army for four years did nothing. They stayed in England training, equipping and preparing for the eventual invasion. Bomber Command was available and had to be used every day and every night, weather permitting. Had that force been available and Churchill had got up and said, in the House of Commons, 'Well, we have this large bomber force available, but I'm afraid we mustn't use it because as it operates at night we can't be sure of hitting specific targets, and a lot of women and children will get killed', the British people would have been outraged. They would have said, 'Not attack them because civilians might get killed? Have you gone mad? Hitler's been killing civilians all over Europe, including England.' If Churchill had said that he wouldn't have survived as Prime Minister.

Morality is a thing you can indulge in an environment of peace and security, but you can't make moral judgements in war, when it's a question of national survival.
Charles Patterson, pilot.[5]

Living in a world free from the shadow of Nazism is something to be sincerely grateful for. Living in a Britain unravaged by invasion is something to be sincerely grateful for. And, for my own part, I am also intensely grateful at not having been called upon to play any role in that struggle. I have lived in mental and physical comfort because so many did not. Easy judgements were my birthright because so many made difficult ones.

Per Ardua Ad Astra

Bomber Command and the War Artists Scheme

In 1939, as in the Great War, a body was assembled with the purpose of creating an artistic record of the conflict under the title War Artists Advisory Committee. Sir Kenneth Clarke, director of the National Gallery, chaired the committee. The body commissioned works and liaised with the artist and service they were assigned to cover.

Eric Kennington, an established artist who had worked for the War Artists Scheme and British War Memorials Committee in the Great War, was commissioned for RAF portrait work. In this capacity he executed fine portraits of Portal and Harris, as well as ordinary crew members of Bomber Command. The Committee, at a cost of twenty five guineas each, then bought these portraits. Kennington then had his contract switched directly to the Air Ministry. It is clear from his correspondence (which can be found in the Imperial War Museum's art department archive) that he was far from happy with the Public Relations Department of the Air Ministry. He felt it was incompetent and interested only in the minutiae of the paintings, such as whether medal ribbons and buttons were correct.

Air Commodore Peake, who was in charge of liaising with the artists, seems to have been highly distrustful of them. Not only did he exasperate Kennington, he also angered and insulted another artist of high repute who had also had works commissioned during the Great War, Paul Nash. The bombing aeroplanes fascinated Nash, he likened them to whales and prehistoric creatures. He set about his commissions of scenes on bomber stations with great enthusiasm. As well as producing paintings, he also wrote a short pamphlet, *Aerial Creatures* (1944). A string of excellent canvases followed, showing a variety of scenes. However, Peake did not like his work at all and was a steady irritant to Nash. But Nash did manage to get his works displayed. They went on tour and formed an exhibition at Manchester City Art Gallery in the spring of 1941. Finding Peake just too difficult to get along with he eventually parted company with the Air Ministry. Clarke wrote to Nash, and commiserated with him: 'We have told them how foolish they are in very strong – I might almost say insulting – terms, but I am afraid there are a certain number of them led by Peake who yearn for the Royal Academic style, and are determined to have it.'

They got it in the form of Dame Laura Knight. In July 1943 she was asked to produce 'a large painting of a bomber crew either setting out or returning'. There then followed some debate as to the pay, for the initial suggestion had been 300 guineas but the Treasury wanted it to be £300 instead. Once this matter was clarified – it appears that the payment was in guineas rather than pounds – she set off for RAF Mildenhall to start work. 'Take Off' was complete by February 1944 and shown at the Royal Academy in March. Her work clearly impressed the staff and crew at Mildenhall for photographic copies were requested from the station.

Other artists commissioned to produce works depicting Bomber Command include Sir William Rothenstein (who also ran into difficulties with the Air Ministry); S.B. Jones; Mervyn Peake (no relation to the above); Frank Woolton; H.W. Hailstone and Keith Henderson. The works of the artists mentioned were usually displayed at the National Gallery and as part of touring exhibitions. The paintings gave an added dimension to the public's knowledge and visualisation of the bombing war. For the details of artists' contracts and correspondence with the War Artists Advisory Committee see bibliography.

For more detail on Second World War art see Alan Ross, *Colours of War*, London 1983.

. . . .

Journey Together (1945) and *The Way to the Stars* (1945)

Journey Together was made by the RAF Film Production Unit in 1944. The RAF Film Production Unit had come into being in the late summer of 1941 and had made a series of minor instructional and training films; *Journey Together* was the culmination of its work. The film concentrated on the training of bomber crews and Terence Rattigan's script made some important points. As had become standard practice the film showed a cross-section of recruits representing all classes. But Rattigan's world did not make any genuine concession to the idea of a truly new Britain: class differences are eroded slightly, rather than replaced. This came out in the fact that Aynesworth (Jack Watling) is an upper class Cambridge graduate. He is actually not as technically proficient as his lower class chum David Wilton (Richard Attenborough), but his gentlemanly panache and style make him a natural pilot, whereas Wilton is always a bit too much like an eager tradesman. Wilton is therefore turned down for further pilot's training and has to accept the role of navigator. The bulk of the training takes place in the USA and Canada, where Edward G. Robinson makes a cameo appearance as McWilliams, a USAAF flying instructor. This emphasised the nature of the *Journey Together*. Both bomber crews and the allied nations were making a journey together.

Wilton thinks the job of the navigator is neither as glamorous, nor significant as that of a pilot. This attitude is knocked out of him by one of his instructors who deliberately gets lost forcing Wilton to think hard and do his job properly. When Wilton joins Aynesworth on operations they get shot down and it is only due to his excellent navigational skills that their last signal allows RAF Coastal Command to direct their rescue operation.

The film is significant for showing the everyday routines within the service.

Just beating *Journey Together* to the screen was another Terence Rattigan screenplay, *The Way to the Stars*, based on his play *Flare Path*. *The Way to the Stars* does not contain many flying scenes, but managed to convey the stresses of being a member of a bomber crew. Its atmosphere of quiet reflection was acceptable largely because it was clear that victory was in sight. Indeed, the film opens with the camera tracking over an abandoned airfield and its buildings implying that the airmen have packed-up and gone back to their peacetime lives.

The film concentrated on the Anglo-American relationship by showing how the USAAF take over a British airfield and yet continue close co-operation with the RAF and extend their friendship to the local people. The early scenes are dominated by Toddy (Rosmund John), owner of the local hotel and her husband David Archdale (Michael Redgrave). Archdale is the leader of a squadron of Blenheim daylight light bombers. The time is 1940, which would have reminded informed viewers, particularly the few fortunate survivors of those squadrons, of the murderous attrition rate from which they suffered at that point. Indeed, it is not long before Archdale himself is killed after losing his lucky charm. (The reliance on a charm has a ring of authenticity about it.) The rate of attrition and the erosion of the pre-war RAF leads Archdale to conclude that 'there aren't any amateurs and professionals any more, just good pilots and bad pilots. The good pilots stay alive and the bad ones don't... and even that's not true any more.' Such fateful and resigned comments have an air of truth about them, but they are ones that could only have been made when victory was well within sight. Penrose (John Mills), one of Archdale's young pilots takes over the squadron, and he too becomes more and more withdrawn, scared to get involved with Iris, the woman he secretly loves. He does not feel it is worth making any permanent plans in wartime and so decides to avoid her. Only when listening to Toddy's advice does he declare his real feelings to her.

Doubtless, it was this romantic interest which helped the film become one of the big money-makers of 1945. The press certainly loved it seeing it as a perfect statement of both Anglo-American co-operation and British values. For a film only marginally concerned with bombing itself, it nevertheless highlights many truths about life within Bomber Command. The spirit of everyday life and attitudes in the Command is caught perfectly.

Bomber Command Chronology

1936

July 14   Bomber Command formed

1937

September 12   Air Chief Marshal Sir Edgar Ludlow-Hewitt appointed Air Officer Commanding Bomber Command

1939

September 1   German invasion of Poland
2   Advanced Air Striking Force (10 Battle squadrons) to France
3   Britain and France declared war on Germany
3/4   First night of leaflet-dropping on Germany
4   First attack on the German fleet

December 14   Heavy losses in North Sea shipping searches
17   Empire Air Training agreement signed
18   Heavy losses in North Sea shipping search off Wilhelmshaven. Bomber Command forced to reconsider daylight policy

1940

March 17   Attack on seaplane bases on Sylt
28   Air Marshal Charles F.A. Portal created Air Officer Commanding Bomber Command

April 9   German invasion of Denmark and Norway
11   Attack on Stavanger airfield – first raid against a mainland target
13/14   First minelaying operation by the Command

May 10   German invasion of Holland, Belgium and Luxembourg
10/11   First Bomber Command raid on German mainland
12-14   German breakthrough across the Meuse. Heavy Battle and Blenheim losses
14   German bombing of Rotterdam

15	Bombing east of the Rhine authorised by War Cabinet
26-June 4	Evacuation of Dunkirk
June 10	Italy entered the war
11/12	First bomber raid on Italy
15-17	Remains of AASF rejoin Bomber Command
17	Armistice requested by France
August 10	Beginning of the Battle of Britain
12/13	Dortmund-Ems Canal attacked
24/25	First German bombs on central London
25/26	First bombing raid on Berlin
September 7/8	Beginning of 'blitz' on London
8	Intensive Bomber Command attacks on airfields and ports
13/14	Intensive Bomber Command attacks on invasion barges
23/24	Raid against Berlin by 119 bombers
October 4	Air Marshal Sir Richard Peirse created Air Office Commanding Bomber Command
25	AVM Sir Charles Portal Chief of the Air Staff
30	First Directive sanctioning area bombing
31	Official date for the end of the Battle of Britain
November 14/15	Heavy German air raid on Coventry
16/17	131 aircraft to Hamburg, single most intensive raid to date
December 16/17	First major area attack against Mannheim, 134 bombers

1941

January 1/2	Attacks on Bremen
2/3; 3/4	
February 24/25	First Manchester operation
March 10/11	First Halifax operation
15	'Battle of the Atlantic' (Maritime) Directive
30/31	Start of intensive series of raids on warships *Scharnhorst* and *Gneisenau* in Brest
April 6	German invasion of Greece and Yugoslavia

May 8/9	Largest Bomber Command operation to date. 359 aircraft gathered for attacks on Hamburg and Bremen
June 22	German invasion of the USSR
23	First chain of three GEE stations completed
July 4	Low-level daylight raid by Blenheims on Cologne
August 12	Daylight raid by 53 Blenheims on Cologne power stations
18	Butt Report completed and presented to government
November 7/8	Raid on Berlin results in 21 of 169 aircraft lost. Command ordered to scale down operations to conserve force
December 7	Japan attacked Pearl Harbor
8	British and US declaration of war on Japan

1942

January 4	Churchill, in Washington for the first conference with the newly allied USA, dismisses Peirse after considering Berlin debacle
8	Peirse created C-in-C SE Asia Air Forces
February 12	Escape of *Scharnhorst* and *Gneisenau* through the English Channel
15	Fall of Singapore
20	Air Marshal Sir Arthur Harris takes up his place as AOC Bomber Command
March 3/4	Raid against Renault factory at Billancourt. First Lancaster operation
8/9	First major use of GEE – against Essen
10/11	First large-scale bombing operation by Lancasters
28/29	Major attack on Lübeck
April 17	Daylight raid against MAN works at Augsburg
23/24	First of four heavy raids on Rostock
29/30	Last bombing operation by Whitleys
May 30/31	First 'Thousand Bomber Raid' – against Cologne. First operation by Mosquitoes
June 1/2	Second 'Thousand Bomber Raid' – against Essen
25/26	Third 'Thousand Bomber Raid' – against Bremen. Last operation by Manchesters

| July 5 | Cabinet gave permission for use of magnetron valve in H2S |

August 15	Pathfinder Force formed
17	First USAAF raid
17/18	Last Bomber Command operation by Blenheims
18/19	First Pathfinder Force operation

| September 14/15 | Last operation by Bomber Command Hampdens |
| 19 | First daylight raid on Berlin (by Mosquitoes) |

| October 17 | Lancaster daylight raid on Le Creusot |
| 22/23 | First raid on Italy by over 100 bombers |

| November 8 | Allied landings in North West Africa |
| 11 | German occupation of Vichy France |

| December 6 | Daylight raid on Philips' works at Eindhoven |
| 20/21 | First OBOE operation – against Lutterade power station |

1943

January 21	Casablanca bombing directive
25	Pathfinder Group (8) formed
27	First USAAF raid on Germany
30	Mosquito raid on Berlin to interrupt 10th anniversary of Nazi government
30/31	First operational use of H2S – Hamburg

| February 2 | German capitulation at Stalingrad |
| 4 | 'Anti-U-Boat' Directive to Bomber Command (Much of the rest of the month was taken up by attacks on u-boat plants and against the French base ports) |

| March 5/6 | Battle of the Ruhr opens with attack on Essen |

| April 16/17 | Attempted attack on Skoda works at Pilsen |

May 13	Axis surrender in North Africa
16/17	Dams raid
23/24	826 aircraft against Dortmund. Biggest raid since previous summer
31	Last raids by 2 Group before leaving Bomber Command

| June 10 | Final refinement of Casablanca directive – Pointblank |
| 30 | First Serrate operation |

July 10	Allied invasion of Sicily
24/25	Opening of Battle of Hamburg, debut of Window
August 2/3	Last day of Battle of Hamburg
7/8	First use of 'Master Bomber'
16/17	Last attack on Italy
17/18	Attack on Peenemünde
23/24	Attacks on Berlin, opening 'scuffles' of Battle of Berlin
September 3	Allied invasion of Italy
8	Italy signs Armistice
22/23	First 'spoof' raid – on Oldenburg, main force to Hanover
23/24	First OBOE marking for main force
October 4/5	First operational use of GH
7/8	First Airborne Cigar operation
8/9	Last Bomber Command operation by Wellingtons
22/23	First Corona operation and heavy raid on Kassel
November 3/4	First blind-bombing by GH Lancasters
18/19	Beginning of the main Battle of Berlin (fifteen major attacks in next three months)
December 3	Formation of 100 Group
16/17	Intruder operations begin
20	Crossbow attacks against v-weapon sites begin
23	General Eaker appointed Marshal of the American Air Force, General Doolittle to Eighth Air Force. General Eisenhower appointed Allied Supreme Commander.

1944

February 15/16	Heaviest attack on Berlin to date, 891 aircraft
18	Amiens prison attack by Mosquitoes
23/24	Start of 'Big Week' against German aircraft industry
24/25	734 aircraft to Schweinfurt
March 4	First USAAF attack on Berlin
6/7	Opening of Bomber Command attacks on French railways in preparation for Overlord
24/25	Last major Bomber Command raid on Berlin
30/31	Bomber Command's heaviest loss of war, 94 from 795 aircraft sent against Nuremberg

April 14	Allied strategic bombers placed under Eisenhower's command
26/27	Unsuccessful attack on Schweinfurt
May 3/4	Attacks on German airfields in France begins
9/10	First major attacks on coastal batteries in Pas de Calais
June 4/5	Heavy attacks in direct support of invasion forces
5/6	D Day
6/7	Communications interdiction raids in Normandy
8/9	First 'Tallboy' dropped on Saumur tunnel
13/14	First V1 attack on Britain
14	First daylight raid by Bomber Command since June 1943
16/17	Opening of intensive series of raids on v-weapons sites (until September)
July 7	Large raid on Caen in support of British forces
18	Bombing in support of Operation Goodwood
24/25	Area campaign resumed with attack on Stuttgart
August 14	Bombing in support of advance to Falaise
23	Paris liberated
27	First major daylight raid against Germany (Hamburg) since August 12 1941
September 3	Brussels liberated
8	First V2 falls on London. Last bombing operation by Stirlings
16/17	Operations in support of Operation Market Garden
23/4	Dortmund-Ems Canal breached
October 6/7	New Battle of the Ruhr opens against Dortmund
14/15	Intense set of raids against Duisberg and Brunswick
23/24	1055 aircraft against Essen
25	771 aircraft against Essen, Krupps destroyed
28, 30/31	Intense raids against Cologne
November 2/3	Heavy raid on Düsseldorf
4/5	Heavy raid on Bochum. Major breach of Dortmund-Ems Canal
12	*Tirpitz* sunk
December 6/7	Major raid on Leuna
16	German offensive in Ardennes
19-26	Attacks on German communications and airfields
26	Ardennes offensive halted

1945

January 1/2	Mittelland Canal breached
5/6	Heavy attack on Hanover
7/8	Last major raid on Munich
February 13/14	803 aircraft against Dresden
14/15	717 aircraft against Chemnitz
20/21	Mosquitoes attack Berlin in the first of 36 consecutive nightly raids
21/22	Opening of campaign to seal-off Ruhr. Mittelland Canal breached again
March 11	1079 aircraft against Essen
12	1108 aircraft against Dortmund
14	First Grand Slam raid on Bielefeld Viaduct
27	Farge u-boat shelter ruined by Grand Slams
27/28	Last v-weapon attack on Britain
April 6	Area offensive discontinued
9/10	*Admiral Scheer* sunk in attack on Kiel
14/15	Potsdam attacked
16	*Lützow* sunk in attack on Swinemünde
18	Surrender of German troops in the Ruhr
20/21	Last Mosquito attack on Berlin
22	Wangerooge and Berchtesgaden attacked
25/26	Last heavy bomber operation (on refinery at Tönsberg, Norway)
30	Suicide of Hitler
May 2	Russians capture Berlin
7	Germany capitulates
8	VE Day

Notes

Introduction

1.   Information taken from Martin Middlebrook, *The Nuremberg Raid 30-31 March 1944*, Harmondsworth 1980, pp 234-5.

2.   *Spectator*, July 28 1984.

Chapter One

1.   Details taken from Larry Melling 'Diary of a Pathfinder' in Martin W. Bowman, *RAF Bomber Stories, Dramatic first-hand accounts of British and Commonwealth airmen in World War Two*, Sparkford 1998, pp 131-138.

2.   The Treaty of Locarno was signed by France, Germany and Belgium and guaranteed by Britain and Italy. It sought to create a new climate in European relations by clarifying and modifying elements of the Treaty of Versailles (1919).

3.   T.E. Lawrence, *The Mint*, Harmondsworth 1978 edition, p 58.

4.   Arthur Harris, *Bomber Offensive*, London 1947, p 13.

5.   Guilio Douhet (1869-1930) commanded Italy's first aviation unit in the Great War. In 1921 he published *The Command of the Air*, which advocated a policy of strategic bombing against enemy cities by independent air forces. His book was translated into many languages and became an influential text. William Mitchell (1879-1936) was an American, who had also gained experience of air warfare during the Great War. He quickly came to the conclusion that strategic bombing and parachute operations were the key to success in a future conflict. His enthusiasm for his ideas led to him making many enemies in the army and navy, forcing his dismissal in 1925.

6.   Quoted in Max Hastings, *Bomber Command*, London 1979, p 46.

7.   Quoted in John Terraine, *The Right of the Line: The RAF in the Second World War*, London 1985, p 82.

8.   Ibid, p 83.

9.   Details taken from Larry Donnelly, *The Whitley Boys, 4 Group Bomber Operations 1939-1940*, Walton on Thames 1991, p 15.

10.   Details taken from Richard Overy, *Bomber Command 1939-1945, Reaping the Whirlwind*, London 1996, p 19.

11.   Details taken from Overy, p 16.

12.   Details taken from Donnelly, p 21.

13.   Details taken from Overy, p 17.

Chapter Two

1. *Daily Express*, September 5 1939.
2. John Ware, *The Lion Has Wings*, London 1940, p 74.
3. Ibid.
4. Ibid, p 87.
5. *News Chronicle*, June 2 1942.
6. *Motion Picture Herald*, November 18 1939.
7. Quoted in Overy, p 44.
8. Ibid, p 70.
9. Details taken from Donnelly, p 39.
10. Quoted in Hastings, p 35.
11. Quoted in Charles Webster and Noble Frankland, *The Strategic Air Offensive Against Germany, 1939-1945*, London 1961, Vol I p 198.
12. PRO AIR 14/85.
13. The Bomber Command Daily Bulletin of December 19. PRO 14/85.
14. *Daily Express*, December 19 1939.
15. Details taken from Hastings, p 35.
16. Harris, p 36.
17. Details taken from Overy, p 31.
18. Ibid, p 68.
19. Details taken from Donnelly, p 53.
20. Quoted in Overy, p 32.
21. Quoted in *The Times*, January 29 1940.
22. Harris, pp 36-7.
23. *Daily Express*, March 20 1940.
24. Details taken from Donnelly, p 79.
25. *Daily Express*, March 21 1940.
26. Details taken from Overy, p 44.
27. Details taken from Donnelly, pp 94-6.
28. Quoted in Overy, p 44.
29. *Daily Express*, May 13 1940.
30. *Daily Express*, May 15 1940.
31. *Daily Telegraph*, August 27 1940.
32. *Daily Telegraph*, September 26 1940.
33. Quoted in *Daily Express*, May 17 1940.
34. *Daily Mirror*, May 18 1940.
35. *Daily Express*, May 17 1940.
36. *Daily Mail*, May 28 1940.
37. Details taken from Hastings, pp 65-6.
38. Details taken from Donnelly, p 184.
39. *Daily Mail*, June 13 1940.
40. Quoted in Overy, p 54.
41. Martin Middlebrook and Chris Everitt, *Bomber Command War Diaries: An Operational Reference Book*, London 1985, p 56.
42. Details taken from Overy, pp 52-3.

43. Quoted in Webster and Frankland, Vol IV, p 113.
44. Ibid, Vol I, p 150.
45. *Daily Mail*, September 25 1940.
46. *Daily Sketch*, September 25 1940.
47. *Daily Telegraph*, August 27 1940.
48. *Daily Telegraph*, September 26 1940.
49. *Daily Mail*, September 10 1940.
50. *Daily Mirror*, September 12 1940.
51. Ibid.
52. *Daily Express*, November 12 1940.
53. *Daily Express*, January 3 1941.
54. British Movietone News, December 5 1940.
55. BBC November 24 1940. R34/857.
56. Memo to Governor General BBC, January 25 1941. R34/856/1.
57. Ibid.

Chapter Three

1. Details taken from Overy, p 75.
2. *Daily Mirror*, March 12 1941.
3. *Daily Telegraph*, February 12 1941.
4. *Daily Telegraph*, March 14 1941.
5. Quoted in Hastings, p 116.
6. Quoted in Webster and Frankland, Vol IV, p 128.
7. Middlebrook and Everitt, p 123.
8. *Daily Mirror*, March 14 1941.
9. Details taken from Overy, p 65.
10. Details taken from Charles Patterson, 'Blenheim Boy' in Bowman, pp 59-68.
11. Details taken from Basil Craske, 'Whitley wanderings' in Bowman, pp 28-39.
12. Harris, p 47.
13. Webster and Frankland, Vol I, p 165.
14. Quoted in ibid, Vol IV, p 136.
15. Ibid, p 135.
16. Ibid.
17. Details taken from Overy, p 70.
18. Quoted in Hastings, p 121.
19. Quoted in ibid.
20. *Sunday Dispatch*, October 5 1941.
21. *Daily Telegraph*, March 12 1941.
22. *Daily Express*, July 8 1941.
23. *Daily Mirror*, September 9 1941.
24. *Daily Mail*, September 9 1941.
25. *Daily Telegraph*, October 14 1941.
26. Michael Balfour, *Propaganda in War 1939-1945*, London 1975, p 201.
27. *Daily Telegraph*, April 10 1941.
28. Ibid, April 14 1941.

29. Ibid, April 16 1941.
30. Ibid, April 19 1941.
31. Ibid, April 22 1941.
32. *News Chronicle*, May 2 1941.
33. Quoted in Balfour, p 201.
34. *The Times*, April 28 1941.
35. *Daily Sketch*, May 19 1941.
36. *Sunday Dispatch*, May 18 1941.
37. *Fortnightly Review*, June 1941, pp 67-70.
38. Ibid, July 1941, pp 556-8.
39. *Spectator*, September 12 1941.
40. *Daily Telegraph*, April 16 1941.
41. *Daily Telegraph*, April 19 1941.
42. *Spectator*, October 3 1941.
43. *Sunday Dispatch*, August 3 1941.
44. *News Chronicle*, May 2 1941.
45. *The Times*, November 13 1941.
46. *Daily Telegraph*, November 4 1941.
47. *Daily Telegraph*, November 5 1941.
48. Harry Watt, *Don't Look at the Camera*, London 1974, p 150.
49. Quoted in K.R.M. Short 'RAF Bomber Command's *Target for Tonight* (1941)' in *Historical Journal of Film, Radio and Television*, Vol 17, No 2, 1997, p 184.
50. Details of press reaction taken from Short, pp 195-200.
51. Watt, p 152.
52. Air Ministry, *Bomber Command: The Air Ministry Account of Bomber Command's Offensive Against the Axis, September 1939-July 1941*, London 1941, p 32.
53. Ibid.
54. Ibid, p 28.
55. Ibid, p 104.
56. Ibid, p 114.
57. Ibid, p 122.
58. Ibid.
59. Ibid.
60. Ibid, p 127.
61. Ibid, pp 126-7.
62. *Times Literary Supplement*, October 11 1941.
63. Details taken from Overy, p 69.
64. *Daily Express*, November 10 1941.
65. *Daily Sketch*, November 10 1941.
66. *Daily Sketch*, January 9 1942.

Chapter Four

1. *Daily Mirror*, February 13 1942.
2. Quoted in Antony Aldgate and Jeffrey Richards, *Britain Can Take It: British Cinema in the Second World War*, Oxford 1986, p 126.

3.   Quoted in Webster and Frankland, Vol IV, p 148.

4.   Quoted in Hastings, p 112.

5.   *Daily Mirror*, March 5 1942.

6.   *Daily Express*, February 20 1942.

7.   *Daily Telegraph*, June 1 1942.

8.   Quoted in Overy, p 83.

9.   *Daily Mirror*, April 20 1942.

10.   *The Times*, April 20 1942.

11.   Hastings, p 109.

12.   Quoted in Overy, p 60.

13.   *Daily Mirror*, April 25 1940.

14.   *Daily Express*, April 25 1940.

15.   *Daily Express*, April 25 1940.

16.   *Daily Sketch*, April 25 1940.

17.   *The Times*, April 30 1942.

18.   *Spectator*, May 1 1942.

19.   Ibid.

20.   *Daily Mirror*, December 7 1942.

21.   *New York Times*, November 2 1942.

22.   Terraine, p 487.

23.   *Daily Mirror*, June 1 1942.

24.   *Daily Express*, June 1 1942.

25.   Ibid.

26.   *Daily Telegraph*, June 1 1942.

27.   *News Chronicle*, June 2 1942.

28.   *Daily Mail*, June 1 1942.

29.   BBC R/34/261.

30.   British Paramount newsreel June 9 1942.

31.   British Universal newsreel June 8 1942.

32.   British Movietone newsreel June 8 1942.

33.   British Gaumont newsreel August 6 1942.

34.   PRO AIR 20/4229. Memo June 28 1942.

35.   CP1290 Un-numbered National Savings Movement disc recording shortly after June 1 1942.

36.   Quoted in Overy, p 109.

37.   Details taken from Denis Richards, *The Hardest Victory: RAF Bomber Command in the Second World War*, London 1994, p 334.

38.   Details taken from Richards, p 335.

39.   Ibid.

40.   Details taken from Overy, p 168.

41.   Details taken from Overy, p 169.

42.   *Spectator*, July 17 1942.

43.   *Listener*, November 5 1942.

44.   Quoted in Webster and Frankland, Vol IV, p 258.

45.   Quoted in Hastings, p 185.

46.   Quoted in Overy, p 76.

47. Quoted in Hastings, p 179.
48. *The Times*, April 20 1942.
49. *Spectator*, March 19 1943.
50. Details taken from Tom Wingham, 'It just couldn't have happened' in Bowman, pp 79-85.
51. *Daily Mirror*, May 25 1942.
52. *Daily Express*, June 1 1942.
53. OEA 10027-1. HMV RAF II.
54. *The Times*, May 18 1943.
55. *Daily Mirror*, May 18 1943.
56. *Daily Express*, May 18 1943.
57. Quoted in Richard Thomas, *Guy Gibson*, London 1994, p 175.
58. *Daily Sketch*, May 19 1943.
59. Quoted in Thomas, p 80.
60. Quoted in Middlebrook, *Hamburg*, p 244.
61. *The Times*, August 9 1943.
62. *Daily Sketch*, July 29 1943.
63. *Daily Mirror*, August 19 1943.
64. British Paramount newsreel August 12 1943, British Universal newsreel August 12 1943.
65. Gaumont British newsreel August 12 1943.
66. *Daily Express*, July 29 1943.
67. *New Statesman*, January 23 1944.
68. *The Times*, September 14 1942.
69. British Movietone newsreel August 13 1942.
70. *Daily Express*, March 8 1943.
71. *Daily Mirror*, August 18 1943.
72. *Daily Sketch*, August 25 1943.

Chapter Five

1. Details taken from Martin Middlebrook, *The Berlin Raids*, London 1988, p 43.
2. *Daily Express*, August 4 1943.
3. *Daily Mirror*, August 25 1943.
4. *Daily Express*, August 25 1943.
5. *Daily Telegraph*, August 25 1943.
6. 12RM15264/5. BBC acetate recorded August 4 1943.
7. BBC Written Archives Centre, R46/8/1 File 1 1942–1947.
8. CP1313. Un-numbered disc for the National Savings Movement. Recorded shortly after January 17 1943.
9. Details taken from Richards, p 311.
10. Details taken from Middlebrook, *Berlin*, p 135.
11. Quoted in Overy, p 150.
12. Quoted in Overy, pp 150-1.
13. Details taken from Hastings, p 215.
14. Quoted in Middlebrook, *Berlin*, p 332.
15. Quoted in Ibid, p 333.
16. Quoted in Ibid.

17. *Daily Mirror*, November 20 1943.
18. *Daily Mirror*, December 4 1943.
19. *Daily Express*, November 24 1943.
20. *Daily Mirror*, February 17 1943.
21. *Daily Sketch*, November 25 1943.
22. *Daily Sketch*, January 24 1943.
23. *Daily Telegraph*, January 3 1944.
24. *Daily Sketch*, November 20 1943.
25. *Spectator*, November 26 1943.
26. British Movietone newsreel November 29 1943.
27. *Daily Mail*, November 29 1943.
28. *National Review*, April 1944.
29. *Fortnightly Review*, August 1942.
30. *Listener*, March 18 1943.
31. *The Times*, January 10 1943.
32. *National Review*, January 1944.
33. *The Times*, May 21 1943.
34. *Daily Express*, December 29 1943.
35. *Listener*, December 23 1943.
36. *Daily Telegraph*, May 21 1943.
37. *Spectator*, February 4 1943.
38. Quoted in Dudley Saward, *'Bomber' Harris*, London 1984, p 215.
39. *Spectator*, April 2 1943.
40. BBC R/34/261.
41. PRO AIR 2/7852. Letter from Portal October 26 1943.
42. PRO AIR 2/7852. Letter from Harris October 25 1943.
43. PRO AIR 2/7852. Letter from Air Council December 15 1943.
44. PRO AIR 2/7852. Letter from Harris December 23 1943.
45. *The Times*, May 24 1943.
46. *New Statesman*, April 17 1943.
47. *The Times*, June 25 1943.
48. *National Review*, January 1944.
49. PRO AIR 20/4330. Letter to Sinclair March 17 1943.
50. *Daily Telegraph*, February 10 1944.
51. Ibid.
52. *Daily Telegraph*, February 14 1944.
53. Ibid, February 17 1944.
54. Ibid, February 16 1944.
55. *Sunday Dispatch*, March 14 1943.
56. *New Statesman*, February 12 1944.

Chapter Six

1. *Daily Sketch*, March 15 1945.
2. British Universal newsreel March 22 1945, British Paramount newsreel March 22 1945, British Movietone newsreel March 22 1945.

3. Quoted in Middlebrook, *Berlin*, p 331.
4. *Daily Mirror*, April 12 1944.
5. *Daily Telegraph*, April 12 1944.
6. *Daily Telegraph*, May 22 1944.
7. *Daily Mirror*, May 5 1944.
8. *Daily Telegraph*, May 5 1944.
9. *Daily Sketch*, May 5 1944.
10. *Daily Mail*, April 24 1944.
11. J.M. Spaight, *Bombing Vindicated*, London 1944, p 110.
12. Ibid, p 14.
13. See Bibliography for details.
14. Duke of Bedford, *Wholesale Bombing*, Glasgow 1944, pp 5-6.
15. Ibid, p 6.
16. *Times Literary Supplement*, March 4 1944.
17. Ibid, June 17 1944.
18. Details taken from 'D-Day in a Stirling' in Bowman, pp 109-116.
19. *Daily Mirror*, June 16 1944.
20. Ibid, July 1 1944.
21. *Daily Telegraph*, July 1 1944.
22. *Daily Mirror*, June 20 1944.
23. PRO AIR 20/2955 July 14 1944.
24. Quoted in Webster and Frankland, Vol III, p 93.
25. Quoted in Saward, p 319.
26. Harris, p 233.
27. Information drawn from Middlebrook and Everitt, p 644.
28. *Daily Mail*, September 14 1944.
29. *Daily Sketch*, July 27 1944.
30. *Daily Telegraph*, November 6 1944.
31. *Daily Sketch*, August 14 1944.
32. Ibid, January 16 1945.
33. Ibid, February 22 1945.
34. *Daily Mirror*, February 27 1945.
35. British Universal newsreel February 22 1945.
36. British Movietone newsreel March 12 1945.
37. *Daily Sketch*, August 12 1944.
38. *Daily Mirror*, October 4 1944.
39. *Daily Express*, October 4 1944.
40. *Daily Mirror*, February 23 1945.
41. *Daily Sketch*, March 22 1945.
42. PRO AIR 20/4330 January 29 1945.
43. All quotes taken from David Irving, *The Destruction of Dresden*, London 1963, pp 142-3.
44. Quoted in Hastings, pp 343-4.
45. Ibid, p 343.
46. *Daily Express*, February 15 1945.
47. *Daily Sketch*, February 14 1945.
48. *Daily Telegraph*, February 15 1945.

49. Ibid.
50. *Daily Mail*, March 5 1945.
51. British Movietone newsreel February 22 1945.
52. *Daily Express*, February 17 1945.
53. Flight Lieutenant Herbert, *L for Lucy*, London 1945, p 48.

Chapter Seven

1. *The Times*, May 22 1992.
2. *Sunday Telegraph*, May 31 1992.
3. James Fyfe, *The Great Ingratitude: Bomber Command in World War II*, Wigtown 1993.
4. *Sunday Times*, May 31 1992.
5. *Spectator*, April 25 1992.
6. *Daily Telegraph*, June 1 1992.
7. *Sunday Telegraph*, May 31 1992.
8. *Daily Mail*, June 1 1992.
9. Ibid.
10. *Spectator*, February 8 1945.
11. *The Times*, February 13 1995.
12. *Daily Mail*, February 14 1995.
13. *The Times*, May 25 1995.
14. Ibid, May 6 1996.
15. *Daily Telegraph*, May 15 1945.
16. Ibid, May 16 1945.
17. Ibid, May 17 1945.
18. Harris, p 268.
19. *Daily Mirror*, January 1 1946.
20. *Daily Mirror*, January 2 1946.
21. Saward, pp 326-8.
22. *Times Literary Supplement*, February 8 1947.
23. *Spectator*, January 17 1947.
24. *Times Literary Supplement*, October 20 1961.
25. *Spectator*, October 13 1961.
26. Frankland, p 115.
27. Ibid, p 116.
28. Ibid, p 116.
29. Ibid, p 119.
30. Martin Caidin, *The Night Hamburg Died*, New York 1960, pp 149-50.
31. *Times Literary Supplement*, May 24 1963.
32. Ibid, June 7 1963.
33. *New Statesman*, May 3 1963.
34. *Daily Mail*, September 11 1970.
35. *New Statesman*, September 11 1970.
36. *Times Literary Supplement*, September 11 1970.
37. *The Times*, September 19 1970.
38. *Daily Mail*, January 24 1970.

39.   Alexander McKee, *Dresden 1945: The Devil's Tinderbox*, London 1982, p xv.
40.   Ibid, p 103.
41.   Ibid, p 308.
42.   Ibid, p 116.
43.   Ibid, p 122.
44.   Ibid, p 315.
45.   Ibid.
46.   *The Times*, April 7 1984.
47.   *Daily Mirror*, April 7 1984.
48.   *The Times*, May 25 1984.
49.   *Daily Express*, April 13 1984.
50.   Ibid, April 18 1984.
51.   *Daily Express*, April 18 1984.
52.   Ibid.
53.   A.G. Goulding, *Uncommon Valour: A Personal Viewpoint of Bomber Command*, Taunton 1985, pp 174-81.
54.   *Sunday Times*, June 24 1984.
55.   *Guardian*, August 10 1989.
56.   Ibid.
57.   Ibid.
58.   Ibid.
59.   *Financial Times*, September 6 1989.

Conclusion

1.   Details taken from Overy, p 194.
2.   Ibid, p 195.
3.   Ibid.
4.   Details taken from Overy, pp 195-200.
5.   Quoted in Overy, p 201.

Bibliographical Notes

This essay makes no claim to be comprehensive. It offers a few words on the books and sources I found most useful. It is divided into three parts: an annotated section on published works on the campaign itself; a bibliographical list of other works consulted; an annotated section on works and sources on the propaganda material and other information put before the British people during the war and since. Most of the material was consulted at the British Library (St Pancras and Colindale), the Imperial War Museum Library and Senate House Library, University of London. Material consulted elsewhere is identified by collection.

Part One

The amount of published material on the British strategic air campaign against Germany is impressive. There are hundreds of books covering all sorts of angles and aspects, ranging from straightforward histories, through technical works on the aeroplanes themselves, to works of fiction. In navigating this impressive array of works the reader and student will probably find Jonathan Falconer's *RAF Bomber Command in Fact, Film and Fiction* (Thrupp 1996) invaluable. Falconer's work is well structured allowing the reader to find quickly the area of interest.

In writing the history of the campaign the works I found most useful are the following. Of primary interest and significance is the Official History itself, *The Strategic Air Offensive Against Germany, 1939-1945* (4 Vols, London 1961). The volumes sometimes seem a little repetitive as similar material is quoted in the narrative and analysis chapters, but it does provide a comprehensive and persuasive overview of the campaign. However, as noted, Official History should not be associated with bland or non-controversial in this case. The reader should also bear in mind that the volumes were written to prove a definite thesis.

The development and writing of the Official History was a saga in itself. Noble Frankland has recounted the saga in his *History at War* (London 1998).

Other important works were used in the piecing together of the campaign itself. Martin Middlebrook's and Chris Everitt's *Bomber Command War Diaries: An Operational Reference Book, 1939-1945* (Harmondsworth 1985). This is an indispensable reference work for it lists every raid carried out by the Command during the war. Each chapter is prefaced with a short, helpful, annotation of the period covered. Most of the statistics on numbers of aircraft involved in each raid, tonnage of bombs dropped, percentage and numbers of lost are taken from this work. Also covering the entire campaign is Max Hastings' *Bomber Command* (London 1979). Hastings book is comprehensive and well written. He argued that Bomber Command did not achieve results commensurate with the amount of time and money spent on it. Denis Richards' *The Hardest Victory: RAF Bomber Command in the Second World War* (London 1994) is another good read, but it does tend to put the best possible gloss on the subject. A similar approach fills his biography of Portal, *Portal of Hungerford* (London 1978). John Terraine's *The*

Right of the Line: The RAF in the Second World War (London 1985) is a robust, but not uncritical defence, of the RAF's right to claim pride of place among the armed services during the Second World War. He uses the same forthright style seen in his works on the Great War. No student of the campaign can afford to ignore Sir Arthur Harris's memoirs, *Bomber Command* (London 1947). He ignored certain aspects of his campaign, such as the controversy with Portal, but it is a largely frank, though obviously biased, account. In 1995 his *Despatch on War Operations, 23 February 1942 to 8 May 1945* (London 1995) was published. Sebastian Cox's introduction is helpful for pointing out where Harris overstated his case and where it is a good guide to the effect of bombing. Of added interest is Horst Boorg's comments, giving a German perspective on the campaign. Sebastian Cox produced an equally useful annotation to *The Strategic Air War against Germany, 1939-1945; report of the British Bombing Survey Unit* (London 1997). Like Harris's despatch this document was also suppressed by the government and was held back for nearly fifty years. Dudley Saward's biography, *'Bomber' Harris* (London 1984) is a straightforward, rather colourless account of Harris's life, which defends him from criticism. Charles Messenger's *'Bomber' Harris and the Strategic Bombing Offensive, 1939-1945* (London 1984) is a more balanced account, but does not add much. In fact Harris seems to be crying out for a full-blooded treatment.

For the stories of individual airmen and their place in the campaign the reader has a number of good works to chose from. Richard Overy's *Bomber Command 1939-1945: Reaping the Whirlwind* (London 1996), published in conjunction with the Bomber Command Association, is a handsome book, it lays out the campaign clearly, is well stocked with quotes and well illustrated. The vast bulk of the statistics quoted in the conclusion are taken from Overy. Martin Middlebrook's works have also gathered together the stories of hundreds of airmen, and indeed Germans who fought back and sought shelter from the bombs: *The Nuremberg Raid* (Harmondsworth 1973); *The Battle of Hamburg: Allied Bomber Forces Against a German City in 1943* (Harmondsworth 1980); *The Peenemunde Raid* (Harmondsworth 1982) and *The Berlin Raids: RAF Bomber Command Winter 1943-44* (Harmondsworth 1988). I also found Len Deighton's *Bomber* London 1970) invaluable. This brilliant piece of literature was thoroughly researched and much of my work on the details of planning procedures and the experience of a raid itself were inspired by Deighton's novel.

During the war the Air Ministry produced two accounts of the conflict: *Bomber Command: The Air Ministry Account of Bomber Command's Offensive Against the Axis, September 1939-July 1941* (London 1941) and *Bomber Command Continues: The Air Ministry Account of the Rising Offensive Against Germany, July 1941-June 1942* (London 1942). Both accounts are more interesting for what the Air Ministry wanted the people to know than for any great insights into the campaign itself. However, they are not the complete whitewashes one might suspect.

For technical details of the aircraft I relied on Bill Gunston's *Combat Aircraft of World War Two* (London 1978).

The three major debates engaged by the Official History, Richards, Terraine, Hastings and Saward are the development and intention of the area bombing campaign, the success of the battle of Berlin and the Portal-Harris dispute of 1944-45.

Denis Richards categorically denied that the area attack was a euphemism for killing civilians. For Richards the area attack was one aimed at morale, and morale was to be eroded by causing maximum disruption to German urban and industrial life. He wrote in the *Hardest Victory*: 'it was no part of this policy deliberately to slaughter civilians' (p 86). Max Hastings has taken the opposite view. He argued in *Bomber Command* that civilians were the main targets and there was no great morale debate in Downing Street or the Air Ministry (pp 106-7). The role and intentions of Portal in the evolution of the area attack have also been debated. Richards, in his biography of Portal, as well as in *The Hardest Victory*, defended Portal from the charge of devising a policy aimed at targeting German civilians (*Portal of Hungerford* pp 165-8). John Terraine took the opposite position in *The Right of the Line*. 'Whatever phrases it may be dressed up in, [the area attack] really means only one thing: putting the fear of death into individuals. On a collective scale, it means threatening a massacre' (p 261).

Judgements on the battle of Berlin have differed too. Dudley Saward, unsurprisingly, took Harris's part and claimed that it was a major contribution to the defeat of Germany (*Bomber Harris*, p 221). Denis Richards avoided condemning the battle as a defeat and stressed the effects of the erosion and diversion of German war industries caused by the raids (*Hardest Victory*, pp 219-20). But the Official History and Hastings concluded otherwise (Official History Vol II p 206; *Bomber Command*, p 268). Martin Middlebrook judged: 'The Luftwaffe hurt Bomber Command more than Bomber Command hurt Berlin' (*Berlin Raids*, p 325).

The Portal-Harris debate during the winter of 1944-45 proved a sticky subject for Webster and Frankland. During the writing of the Official History the government, the Air Ministry and Churchill were anxious about the publication of memos and correspondence relating to this clash in particular. Harold Macmillan, the Prime Minister, allowed the inclusion of the documents only once he had received legal advice (Frankland, *History at War*, pp 110-113). The disagreement over strategy during the winter – whether Bomber Command should have pursued an oil/transport campaign or the area offensive – 'was of fundamental importance' according to Webster and Frankland (Official History, Vol III p 77). But Webster and Frankland conceded that it would have been very difficult for Portal to sack Harris even when it became clear that Harris was loath to give up the area attack. Max Hastings was hampered by no such doubts. Portal's attempts to come to a working agenda with Harris were 'a formal letter of surrender'. Which 'greatly diminishes his stature as a director of war', for 'when Harris made clear his continuing commitment to the area offensive despite the reservations of the Chief of Air Staff, he should have been sacked' (*Bomber Command*, p 335, p 350). Saward argued that Harris was right for 'the indications are that... Germany would have collapsed under bombing alone, which was what Harris had always believed to be a certainty (*Bomber Harris*, p 253). He believed that both Harris and Portal could have been right: 'the combination of executing the Oil Plan and maintaining a powerful area bombing offensive against Germany cities... is what caused the rapid collapse of Germany' (p 275). According to Saward, Portal did not show a lack of resolution, courage or intelligence when he avoided sacking Harris (p 276). Richards made a similar point in the *Hardest Victory*, believing that the Official History had overstated the significance of the disagreement (pp 262-7).

The British bombing war has lost none of its controversy. It is a subject still very much alive and opinions are clearly still very much divided as to its morality, nature and efficacy.

Part Two: other works consulted

Official Histories

Richards D. & Saunders H St G. *Royal Air Force 1939-1945*, 3 Vols London 1953-4.

Unofficial Histories and General Titles

Allen H.R. *The Legacy of Lord Trenchard*, London 1972.

Bomber Harris Trust, *A Battle for Truth: Canadian Aircrews sue the CBC over Death by Moonlight: Bomber Command*, Ontario 1994.

Coombes L.F.E. *The Lion has Wings, the race to prepare the RAF for World War II, 1935-1940*, Shrewsbury 1997

Frankland N. *The Bombing Offensive Against Germany: Outlines and Perspectives*, London 1965.

Goulding A.G. *Uncommon Valour*, Braunton 1985.

Granatstein J.L. and Neary P. *The Good Fight: Canadians and World War II*, Toronto 1995.

Grey C.C. *Bombers*, London 1941.

Hawkins D. *War Report: D-Day to V.E. Day*, London 1946.

Macmillan N. *The RAF in the World War*, 4 Vols London 1942, 1944, 1945.

Michie A. *Everyman to His Post*, London 1943.

Michie A. *Their Finest Hour*, London 1940.

Olsson C. *From Hell to Breakfast*, London 1942.

Raymond R. & Langdon D. *Slipstream: A Royal Air Force Anthology*, London 1946.

Revie A. *The Lost Command*, London 1971.

Rothenstein W. & Cecil Lord D. *Men of the RAF*, London 1942.

Rumpf H. (translated from the German by Edward Fitzgerald). *The Bombing of Germany*, London 1975.

Saundby R. *Air Bombardment*, London 1961.

Webb E. and Duncan J. *Blitz over Britain*, Tunbridge Wells 1990.

Wells H.G. *The Shape of Things to Come*, London 1933.

Wells H.G. *The War in the Air*, London 1908.

Weiner M. *English culture and the decline of the industrial spirit, 1850-1980*, Cambridge 1981.

Weisbord M. and Mohr M. *The Valour and the Horror*, Toronto 1991.

Willmott N. and Pimlott J. *Strategy and Tactics of War*, London 1979.

A Wing Commander. *Bomber's Battle*, London 1943.

Group and Squadron Histories

Bowyer M.J.F. *2 Group*, Shepperton 1974.

Lawrence W.J. *No 5 Bomber Group*, London 1951.

Brickhill P. *The Dam Busters*, London 1951.

Goss C. *It's Suicide, But It's Fun*, Bristol 1995.

Lambermont P. *Lorraine Squadron*, London 1956.

Thorne A. *Lancaster at War 4: Pathfinder Squadron*, Shepperton 1990.

Wooldridge J. *Low Attack*, London 1944.

Bombing Campaigns and Individual Raids

Barker R. *The Thousand Plan*, London 1965.

Caidin H. *The Night Hamburg Died*, New York 1960.

Campbell J. *The Bombing of Nuremberg*, London 1973.

Irving D. *The Destruction of Dresden*, London 1963.

McKee A. *Dresden 1945: The Devil's Tinderbox*, London 1982.

Biographies, Autobiographies and Memoirs

Bomber Barons, London 1983.

Bennett D.C.T. *Pathfinder*, London 1958.

Braddon R. *Cheshire V.C.*, London 1954

Brown A.J. *Ground Staff*, London 1943.

Charlwood D. *No Moon Tonight*, Melbourne 1956.

Cheshire L. *Bomber Pilot*, London 1943.

Done T.E. *All Our Mates*, Melbourne 1995.

Gibson G. *Enemy Coast Ahead*, London 1946.

Frankland N. *History at War*, London 1998.

Herbert Fl Lt. *'G' for Genevieve*, London 1944.

Herbert Fl Lt. *'L' for Lucy*, London 1945.

Jaspar R. *George Bell – Bishop of Chichester*, London 1967.

Kay C. *The Restless Sky*, London 1964.

Lawrence T.E. *The Mint*, Harmondsworth 1978 edition.

Mahaddie T.G. *Hamish: The Story of a Pathfinder*, London 1989.

Mahan A. *The Influence of Sea Power upon History, 1660-1783*, New York 1890.

Mahan A. *The Influence of Sea Power upon the French Revolution*, New York 1892.

Morris R. & Dobinson C. *Guy Gibson*, Harmondsworth 1994.

Northrop J. *Joe: the autobiography of a Trenchard Brat*, London 1993.

Raymond R.S. *A Yank in Bomber Command*, Newton Abbot 1977.

Roy J. *The Happy Valley*, London 1952.

Roy J. *Return from Hell*, London 1954.

Smith A. *Halifax Crew*, London 1983.

Tedder A. *With Prejudice: The War Memoirs of Marshal of the Royal Air Force Lord Tedder GCB*, London 1966.

Fiction

Bates H.E. *The Greatest People in the World*, London 1942.

Bates H.E. *How Sleep the Brave*, London 1943.

Bates H.E. *The Stories of Flying Officer X*, London 1952.

Buchanan W. *Pathfinder Squadron*, London 1972.

Campbell J. *Maximum Effort*, London 1957.

Deighton L. *Bomber*, London 1970.

Graves C. *Thin Blue Line*, London c.1942.

Graves C. *The Avengers*, London c.1942.

Graves C. *Seven Pilots*, London c.1943.

Lewis C. *The Pathfinders*, London 1943.

Shute N. *Pastoral*, London 1944.

Smith F. *633 Squadron*, London 1956.

Tripp M. *Faith is a Windsock*, London 1952.

Watson J. *Johnny Kinsman*, London 1955.

Westerman P.E. *Combined Operations*, London c.1944.

Ethics

Garrett S. *Ethics and Airpower in World War Two: The British Bombing of German Cities*, New York 1993.

Part Three

In searching for information on the presentation of the bombing war to the British people a range of sources and archives were consulted. The following divisions occasionally overlap, but it is hoped that the structure will be of most assistance. All of the material listed here has been used in the text.

Published material

Brittain V. *Seeds of Chaos*, London 1944. One of Brittain's many pieces written for the Bombing Restriction Committee.

Duke of Bedford. *Wholesale Bombing*, Glasgow 1944. Another pamphlet on the restriction of bombing. Not as well argued or well balanced as the Brittain pieces.

Over to You: New Broadcasts by the RAF, London 1943. A collection of stories chosen from over 900 broadcasts given by RAF crew and ground staff between March 1942 and May 1943.

Spaight J.M. *Bombing Vindicated*, London 1944. A chief apologist for Bomber Command, arguing that bombing was strictly speaking a defensive policy. He was widely regarded as a commentator on bombing affairs and contributed articles on the campaign to the *Spectator*.

Veale S.E. *Warfare in the Air: The RAF at War since the Battle of Britain*, London 1942, revised edition 1943. A general history of the RAF, pointing out the achievements of Bomber Command.

Home Front and Propaganda

Aldgate A. and Richards J. *Britain Can Take It: British Cinema in the Second World War*, Oxford 1986.

Balfour M. *Propaganda in War, 1939-1945*, London 1979.

Bialer U. 'The Shadow of the Bomber: The Fear of Air Bombardment and British Politics 1932-39', *Proceedings of the Royal Historical Society*, London 1980.

Buckman K. 'The Royal Air Force Film Production Unit, 1941-45', *Historical Journal of Film, Radio and Television*, Vol 17, No 2, 1997.

Calder A. *The People's War*, London 1973.

Coultas C. *Images for Battle: British Film and the Second World War, 1939-1945*, London 1989.

Ross A, *Colours of War*, London 1983.

Short K.R.M. *The Lion Has Wings, screening the propaganda of British air power. From RAF (1935) to The Lion Has Wings (1939)*, Trowbridge 1998.

Short K.R.M. 'RAF Bomber Command's *Target for Tonight* (1941)', *Historical Journal of Film, Radio and Television*, Vol 17, No 2, 1997.

Thurlow R. *Fascism in Britain, a History 1918-1985*, London 1987.

Watt H. *Don't Look at the Camera*, London 1974.

Public Records Office

The following files all deal with Bomber Command and Air Ministry publicity and propaganda and contain much interesting material on how the presentation of the campaign was dealt with at the highest levels. Memos and papers from Harris, Ludlow-Hewitt, Peck (Assistant Chief of Air Staff), Peirse, Portal, the Air Ministry Publicity Department and the Bomber Command Daily Bulletins can be consulted in these files.

AIR 20 2955; AIR 20 4229; AIR 20 4330; AIR 2/7852; AIR 14/85; AIR 14/226; AIR 14/1951.

Hansard Parliamentary Debates

Vol 121 January 27 1942, p 480; Vol 125 February 11 1943, p 1080; Vol 130 February 9 1944, pp 738-46; Vol 378 February 25 1942, pp 316-7; Vol 379 April 29 1942, pp 922-3; Vol 380 June 16 1942, p 1378; Vol 387 March 11, pp 887-962; Vol 395 December 1 1943, p 338; Vol 397 March 2 1944, p 1602; Vol 408 March 6 1945, pp 1901-3.

BBC Written Archives Centre, Caversham Park

R34/261 Bombs and Bombing file, 941, 1942.
R46/8/1 Air Operations File 1, 1942-1943; LR/2094 Report on *Cutting the Skipper*, September 28 1943.
R28/10/2 News, Air Ministry File 2B, 1940-1942. Papers on reporting of Air Ministry communiqués.
R28/10/3 News File 3, 1942-1946. Similar material to above.
R34/856/1 RAF Liaison File, 1941-1942.
R34/857 RAF Programme, 1939-1948. Script references.

Imperial War Museum

The Art Department's files contain material on the commissioning of works for the War Artists Scheme:
GP/55/1 (A) Correspondence file, Eric Kennington.
GP/55/3 (1) and (2) Correspondence file, Paul Nash.
GP/55/74 Correspondence file, Dame Laura Knight.

Drama

Rattigan T. *Flare Path*, London 1942. A successful West End production, which became the basis of the film *The Way to the Stars*.

Films

The British Film Institute Library holds publicity material and press cuttings on the following movies:
The Lion Has Wings. 1939. See also Ware J., *The Lion Has Wings*, London 1940.
Target for Tonight. 1941.
Biter Bit. 1942.
One of Our Aircraft is Missing. 1942. See also *One of Our Aircraft is Missing*, London 1942.
The Way to the Stars. 1945.
Journey Together. 1946.
Appointment in London. 1953.
The Dam Busters. 1954.
633 Squadron. 1964.
Mosquito Squadron. 1969.

Television and Radio

As with the above, the BFI Library can be consulted for material relating to the following programmes:

The Pathfinders. Toledo Film Organisation/Thames TV. 13 1hr episodes, 1972-3.

The World at War. Pt 12. *Whirlwind: Bombing Germany. September 1939-April 1944.* ITV January 24 1974.

Dresden: Forgotten Anniversary? Channel 4. February 13 1985.

Bomber Harris. BBC TV. September 3 1989.

The Valour and the Horror. Death by Moonlight: Bomber Command. CBC & NFBC. Channel 4 August 7 1994.

Bomber. R4. February 18 1995.

Bomber Command: Reaping the Whirlwind. Channel 4 September 10 1996.

Newsreels

The best way to access material on newsreels is via the British Universities Film and Video Council, 77 Wells Street, London, W1P 3RE.

Aircraft Production: Gaumont, December 11 1939, May 7 1942.

General: Movietone December 5 1940.

Bombing (general): Universal, February 22 1945.

Bombing (cities)

Berlin: Gaumont, November 29 1943; Movietone, November 29 1943; Paramount, March 8 1943, November 29 1943; Universal, November 29 1943.

Bremen: Universal, August 20 1942.

Cologne: Gaumont, August 6 1942; Movietone, June 8 1942, March 12 1945, March 22 1945; Paramount, June 9 1942; Universal, June 8 1942.

Dams: Movietone, May 24 1943.

Dresden: Gaumont, February 22 1945; Movietone, February 22 1945; Paramount, February 22 1945.

Hamburg: Gaumont, August 12 1943; Movietone, August 12 1943; Paramount, August 12 1943; Universal, August 12 1943.

Harris: Movietone, August 13 1942, November 11 1943, May 8 1947, May 13 1954, February 23 1956.

Sound Recordings

Daylight over Lubeck, July 16 1942. Recorded for National Savings Movement. CP 1293.

Raid on Cologne, June 1 1942. Recorded for National Savings Movement. CP 1290.

RAF over Essen, c August 1943. OEA 10027-1. HMV RAF II.

Dimbleby over Berlin, January 1 1943. National Savings Movement from BBC recording. CP 1313.

Cutting the Skipper, September 4 1943. 12RM15264/5 BBC acetate.

[All of the above recordings are available on *Bomber Command: Recordings from the Second World War. A Documentary of the Time.* PAST CD 7829.]

Newspapers

Daily Express: September 5, September 30, December 19 1939; March 20, March 21, April 13, May 2, May 13, May 15, May 17, May 21, May 29, June 10, June 14, June 22, July 3, July 6, July 18, July 20, August 27, August 28, September 10, September 23, September 25, September 26, October 25, October 26, October 28, November 12, November 18, November 20, Dec

19 1940; January 3, June 30, July 7, July 8, July 15, July 23, July 24, August 11, September 9, November 10, December 29 1941; February 20, March 5, April 25, June 1, October 19, October 27 1942; March 8, May 18, June 23, June 24, June 26, July 29, August 4, August 19, August 25, November 20, November 24, December 4, December 29 1943; April 11, April 24, May 23, June 16, October 4, October 18, November 14 1944; April 13, April 18 1984; June 1, June 3 1992.

Daily Herald: May 20, November 17 1955.

Daily Mail: December 20 1939; February 23, May 17, May 20, May 28, June 8, June 13, July 3, July 18, September 4, September 10, September 25, October 16, October 23, October 29, December 18 1940; September 9, November 10, December 2 1941; June 1 1942; November 29 1943; April 24, September 14, September 20 1944; March 5, March 15 1945; November 18 1955; September 11 1970; January 24 1974; June 1, June 4 1992; February 13 1995.

Daily Mirror: May 17, May 18, June 3, July 1, July 18, August 27, August 28, August 30, September 12, September 14, September 25, October 18, October 19, November 18, December 16 1940; February 28, March 12, March 13, March 14, April 1, May 2, May 6, May 17, June 30, July 1, July 11, July 15, July 24, July 25, August 7, August 16, August 18, September 9, October 14 1941; February 13, February 14, February 16, March 5, March 30, April 18, April 20, April 25, June 1, June 2, June 3, October 19, October 25, November 30, December 7 1942; January 29, March 3, May 15, May 18, May 19, May 25, June 23, July 26, August 14, August 18, August 19, August 25, November 20, November 26, December 4 1943; January 4, February 17, March 24, April 1, April 6, April 12, April 13, April 24, May 5, June 16, June 20, July 1, October 4, November 14 1944; February 15, February 23, February 27 1945; January 1, January 2 1946; April 7 1984; June 1 1992; February 14 1995.

Daily Sketch: May 17, May 18, September 25, September 27, October 1, October 4, October 5, October 7 1940; March 16, May 19, July 24, September 9, October 15, November 10 1941; January 9, February 14, April 25, April 28, April 30, June 1, June 4, October 24 1942; May 19, May 31, June 24, July 29, August 4, August 25, November 20, November 24, November 25, December 4 1943; January 22, February 17, April 1, May 5, July 25, July 27, August 12, August 14, September 14, November 14 1944; January 16, February 14, February 22, March 15, March 16, March 22, March 24 1945; May 19 1955.

Daily Telegraph: May 20, August 21, August 23, August 26, August 27, September 26 1940; February 12, March 14, March 25, April 10, April 14, April 16, April 19, April 22, May 1, July 11, October 14, November 4, November 5, November 7 1941; February 4, February 12, February 26, March 5, April 27, June 1, June 3, June 27, July 23, August 3, August 27 1942; May 21, June 1, August 25, October 11, December 4, December 18 1943; January 3, February 1, February 10, February 14, February 16, February 17, April 1, April 12, May 5, May 22, July 1, July 25, July 26, July 27, September 13, October 4, October 26, November 6 1944, February 4, February 15, February 16, February 21, May 14, May 15, May 16, May 17, May 19 1945; November 21 1955.

Evening News: May 19 1955; November 15 1955.

Evening Standard: May 19 1955; May 21 1955.

Financial Times: September 6 1989.

Guardian: August 10, September 4 1989.

News Chronicle: May 2 1941; June 2 1942; May 19 1955.

New York Times: January 22 1940; October 18 1941; November 2 1942; November 17 1945; March 4 1946.

Sun: June 1 1992.

Sunday Despatch: May 18, August 3, October 5 1941; March 14 1943.

Sunday Express: May 22 1955.

Sunday Telegraph: May 31, June 1 1992; February 14 1995.

Sunday Times: April 17 1983; June 24 1984; May 31, June 7, June 14 1992; January 10 1993; February 12 1995.

The Times: September 5, October 24 1939; January 9, February 16, March 2, August 19, August 20, August 22, August 29, September 2, October 3, October 8 1940; February 6, March 26, April 19, April 28, July 24, August 5, August 16, October 7, October 14, November 5, November 13 1941; February 28, March 31, April 20, April 30, May 11, June 1, June 3, June 6, June 11, July 29, August 13, September 14, November 19 1942; February 1, February 25, March 27, March 29, May 18, May 19, May 21, May 24, May 25, June 25, July 1, August 9, September 22, October 12 1943; January 10, January 31, February 10, February 23, February 24, February 25, July 3, October 17 1944; February 15, May 17 1945; March 13 1946; June 9 1947; February 16 1953; September 19 1970; April 7 1984; February 13, February 14 1985; May 22, May 25, May 29, May 30, June 1, June 2 1992; February 13, February 14, November 6 1995; May 6, September 10 1996.

Journals

Documentary News Letter: January 1940; August 1941.

Fortnightly Review: June, July 1941; August 1942.

Hollywood Reporter: June 22 1955.

Kinematograph Weekly: July 24 1941.

Listener: November 5 1942; March 18 1943; December 23 1943; November 30 1944; October 5 1961; April 6 1978; October 4 1979; August 31; September 7 1989.

Monthly Film Bulletin: November 1939; August 1941; March 1953; June 1955.

Motion Picture Herald: November 18 1939; April 11 1942; June 25 1955; June 14 1956.

National Review: December 1942; January, April 1944.

New Statesman: November 23 1940; April 17 1943; February 12 1944; October 6 1961; May 3 1963; September 11 1970; August 6 1982.

Nineteenth Century and After: March 1939; June 1941.

Radio Times: September 2 1989; February 18 1995.

Spectator: July 18, August 1, September 12, September 19, September 26, October 3, October 24 1941; May 1, July 17, July 31, August 7 1942; January 22, March 12, March 19, April 2, May 21, July 23, September 3, November 12, November 26 1943; February 4, March 31, April 28 1944; January 17 1947; October 13 1961; June 14 1963; September 12 1970; September 29 1979; July 28 1984; April 25, May 30 1992; February 8, February 11, February 18 1995.

Times Higher Education Supplement: July 25 1997.

The Times Literary Supplement: October 11 1941; March 4, June 17 1944; February 8, March 8, March 15, March 29 1947; October 20 1961; May 24, June 7 1963; September 25 1970.

Today's Cinema: October 3 1945; February 9 1953; November 3 1954; April 18, November 16 1955.

Variety: February 25 1953.

Index